A relationship beset with extraordinary acrimony, the US and Iran rarely see eye-to-eye – and then only to avoid war or nuclear catastrophe. What is at the core of this troubled rivalry that has stymied policymakers and scholars alike? Using a carefully selected collection of White House, CIA, State Department, and other records, *Worlds Apart* provides a reliable, evidence-based approach to this question: starting from the 1979 revolution and hostage crisis, through the Iran–Iraq War and the spread of radical Islam, to 9/11 and the nuclear impasse, to the 2009 Green Movement and the Obama and Trump presidencies. The records which form the heart of the book offer a rare unfiltered view into the perspectives and experiences of the American and Iranian governments over forty years. Providing timelines, glossaries, discussion questions, and a guide on reading declassified documents, Byrne and Byrne explore this complicated relationship accessibly and innovatively in this unique documentary history.

Malcolm Byrne is an award-winning author and editor of several books on US–Iran relations. Since 1997, he has run the nongovernmental National Security Archive's multinational Iran documentation project, based at the George Washington University, and has made numerous trips to the Islamic Republic.

Kian Byrne coordinates the Middle East documentation project at the History and Public Policy Program of the Woodrow Wilson International Center for Scholars where he also co-edits and contributes to the program's blog on new archival findings, *Sources & Methods*. He has researched and traveled through much of the region, including Iran.

WORLDS APART

A Documentary History of
US–Iranian Relations, 1978–2018

Malcolm Byrne

National Security Archive at
George Washington University

Kian Byrne

Woodrow Wilson International Center for
Scholars, Washington, DC

CAMBRIDGE
UNIVERSITY PRESS

CAMBRIDGE
UNIVERSITY PRESS

University Printing House, Cambridge CB2 8BS, United Kingdom

One Liberty Plaza, 20th Floor, New York, NY 10006, USA

477 Williamstown Road, Port Melbourne, VIC 3207, Australia

314–321, 3rd Floor, Plot 3, Splendor Forum, Jasola District Centre, New Delhi – 110025, India

103 Penang Road, #05–06/07, Visioncrest Commercial, Singapore 238467

Cambridge University Press is part of the University of Cambridge.

It furthers the University's mission by disseminating knowledge in the pursuit of education, learning, and research at the highest international levels of excellence.

www.cambridge.org
Information on this title: www.cambridge.org/9781108838528
DOI: 10.1017/9781108975148

First published 2022

A catalogue record for this publication is available from the British Library.

ISBN 978-1-108-83852-8 Hardback
ISBN 978-1-108-97154-6 Paperback

For Leila and Ellie

Contents

Figures

Preface

This volume is primarily intended as a documentary introduction to US policy toward the Islamic Republic of Iran (IRI). As such, it is not a standard scholarly monograph. If anything, it turns that concept inside out. Instead of prioritizing the views and interpretations of an outside observer, accompanied by footnotes to documentary evidence, the historical records themselves take center stage, supported by descriptive materials to provide context.

Why make documents the focus? Over the decades since the creation of the Islamic Republic, hundreds of books and innumerable articles have been written (in English alone) about the country and its relations with the outside world, particularly the United States. Many are invaluable and deeply insightful. Yet, after more than forty years, the US–Iran rivalry still confounds policymakers and experts alike. Few serious observers are confident enough to make broad predictions about where the IRI is heading. Their task is complicated by spotty information, restricted interactions between the two countries, political sensitivities on both sides, and, often, personal preconceptions. The result is frequent disagreement – not just between Americans and Iranians but within the USA – about basic facts as well as a tendency toward polemics.

How is an interested reader not already steeped in the subject supposed to find their way through this thicket? There is no simple answer, but this volume proceeds from the idea, almost as old as the study of history itself, that an excellent place to start is to explore what the key actors – in this case, mainly American policy practitioners – were thinking. What were the issues they grappled with? What were their goals? What factors influenced their choices? How well did they understand what was happening in Iran? What were the ramifications of US policies?

Primary documents such as the ones featured here are essential for gaining a first-hand look at the evolution of US policy toward the IRI. Thankfully, as the 1979 revolution has faded in memory, parts of the available US historical record have expanded. Although government archival budgets are chronically inadequate and declassification systems can be infuriating, researchers now have access to a growing amount of material on the internal workings of most recent presidential administrations. These include memoranda to and from the president, notes of White House meetings, transcripts of conversations with foreign leaders, diplomatic correspondence about secret negotiations, Central Intelligence Agency (CIA) intelligence reports, Pentagon battlefield analyses, and international nuclear inspection reports. This compilation draws precisely on these kinds of once-inaccessible materials.

A principal reason for focusing on the American side of the relationship is the lack of equivalent official records from Iran or other countries. The IRI archives on internal government decision-making during the post-revolutionary period are effectively off-limits to foreigners. Access to other national repositories is highly uneven. British official sources, for example, include many useful materials, including some that reflect on the US–Iran relationship, but tend to be more open for earlier years (the 1953 coup being an extreme exception). On the other hand, quite a bit of valuable material can be found in public sources in Iran, notably its news media, which often print interviews with former officials about historical milestones like the Iran–Iraq War. Another useful source is memoirs of former leaders and senior government representatives, including the likes of Akbar Hashemi Rafsanjani, Ali Montazeri, and Ali Akbar Salehi. With the help of Persian-speaking experts, we have identified and included a number of these items to provide a counterpoint to – or reality check on – the American perspective at key junctures.

The contents of this book derived mainly from research at the US National Archives and Records Administration and its associated presidential libraries. Many are the product of Freedom of Information Act (FOIA) or Mandatory Declassification Review (MDR) requests filed either by the authors or other researchers over the years with the State Department, CIA, Pentagon, and elsewhere. Additional items were located in agency electronic reading rooms (the releases themselves often the result of FOIAs). Other sources mined include Congress, the federal courts, international organizations such as the United Nations and International Atomic Energy Agency (IAEA), and nongovernmental archives. We also combed through both of our organizations' foreign archival holdings acquired over time – Iraqi, Russian, Azeri in addition to Iranian and British – and while they contain fascinating records the physical limits of the current publication forced us to prioritize sources that revealed high-level American thinking. Readers are encouraged to visit our respective websites for more in-depth research.

The aim of this particular collection is to give readers a grounding in how US policy toward Iran developed during and after the Iranian revolution, which peaked in early 1979. The records we have chosen are the product of our own work collecting documents on Iran as well as our own perspectives on the history. We have tried to reveal as many of the complexities of the issues as we could and provide a fair representation of the range of viewpoints that have existed about the scope of American interests, the nature of the Iranian challenge, and the preferred direction of US policy.

There are some obvious limitations to a compendium like this. First of all, it is impossible to go into great depth on the full range of issues covered here while keeping the page count reasonable. To stay within our allotted length, moreover, we have been obliged to reproduce extracts in many cases. Another inevitable hurdle is that while the American historical record is quite excellent for earlier periods, the closer one gets to the present the less is publicly available. Subjects like Iran, nuclear weapons, terrorism, and intelligence operations are highly sensitive and usually do not get declassified for decades. However, enough can be gleaned to allow for important insights up to and including the Obama presidency.

The book is divided into five main chapters that deal roughly with one decade apiece, except for the first chapter, which takes on the crucial period 1977–1981. Each chapter opens with a succinct essay that sets the stage historically and politically. Every document is preceded by a "headnote" that describes its context and significance. An epilogue and conclusion wrap up the main text, but a variety of accompanying features give additional background and guidance. These include a mini-seminar on how to read a government document; a chronology of events; and glossaries of names and organizations. Questions at the end of each chapter and a select bibliography will help those interested in further discussion and sources.

Acknowledgements

This book is the culmination of years of documentary research on Iran, over the course of which we have benefited from contributions too numerous to count.

To begin with, we would like to thank members of the team who helped carry the load with their research and other skills: Sina Azodi, Alexander Chang, and Cheyn Shah. Sina was key to identifying, tracking down, and translating Persian-language sources, while Alexander and Cheyn contributed to general editing as well as to composing the glossaries, chronology, and reviewing other parts of the book. Clara Kaul provided expert copy-editing on the index.

While many of the documents in the collection came from our own research and FOIA requests over the years, several friends and colleagues graciously donated, or pointed us to, materials that deepened the pool. Alexandra Evans provided unstintingly from her research at the Reagan Library. Mark Gasiorowski has been a virtual lending library of documentation and expert advice over the years. Kambiz Fattahi has shared numerous records over time. Tom Blanton and Svetlana Savranskaya made available remarkable White House memcons uncovered during their research at presidential libraries.

Other scholars gave us invaluable suggestions for where to find materials on Iran, areas on which to focus our research, thematic suggestions, and other contributions. They include: Arash Azizi, Alan Eyre, Timothy Nunan, Siavush Randjbar-Daemi, Mahsa Rouhi. We are only sorry we could not fit more of their ideas into the manuscript.

We especially thank everyone who read some or all of our early drafts: Gregory Brew, Charles Kraus, Christian Emery, Farideh Farhi, Mark Gasiorowski, and Bruce Riedel. Bill Burr, Leah Richardson, and Mark Yoffe had helpful comments on "How to Read a Declassified Document." Lisa Thompson provided invaluable support on the index and Rinat Bikineyev helped to design the jacket. Of course, any errors or shortcomings are our own.

Over time, we gained tremendously from the insights of policy practitioners and experts in the field whose interviews and participation in critical oral history conferences with both our institutions – the National Security Archive and the Woodrow Wilson International Center for Scholars – going back to the early 2000s helped shape our understanding of the complex relationship between the United States and Iran. These individuals – from the United States, Iran, the United Kingdom, Russia, and elsewhere – drew on decades of experience as diplomats, politicians, soldiers, and intelligence officials and provided us and our colleagues with riveting perspectives that have frequently found their way into this book. We would like to thank our main partners in this multiyear exploration: John Tirman, Huss Banai, Jim Blight, and janet Lang.

Our own institutions – the National Security Archive and the Wilson Center – have given us a welcome base and financial stability (especially in the time of COVID) to accomplish this project. At the Archive, Tom Blanton, Sue Bechtel, Bill Burr, John Prados, Svetlana Savranskaya, and Fellow-for-Life Jim Hershberg have regularly provided support to the US–Iran Relations Project, while many talented research assistants and interns have contributed to the project over more than a quarter century. At the Wilson Center, Christian Ostermann, Charles Kraus, Pieter Biersteker, and Erin Scrimger provided both substantive and moral support for this project.

In recent years, a number of philanthropies, chiefly the Arca Foundation, the Brenn Foundation, and the Carnegie Corporation of New York, have generously supported our research on the USA and Iran. We are also grateful to John Tirman of MIT's Center for International Studies for his generosity.

We also express our appreciation to the dedicated archivists from the National Archives and Records Administration and its associated presidential libraries – of Jimmy Carter, Ronald Reagan, George H.W. Bush, William J. Clinton, and George W. Bush – along with the often overlooked FOIA and declassification officers at federal agencies who make it possible for all of us to begin to understand our recent history. A special shout-out to Brittany Parris at the Carter Library for her help with innumerable requests.

Many of the people named so far have come from the American side, but a project like this also relies heavily on the Iranian perspective, even if that is not reflected in the share of Iranian records in the Contents list. We gratefully recognize the many Iranian scholars who, often under difficult conditions, have pushed the field of modern Iranian history forward, and specifically the subject of US–Iran relations. We have personally benefited from the generosity of many of these experts since we first began engaging with scholarly counterparts in the Islamic Republic in the late 1990s.

At Cambridge University Press, we have greatly appreciated the interest and support of Cecelia Cancellaro and Natasha Whelan, the improvements of copy editor Ken Moxham, the design ideas of the graphic artists and typesetters, the cover design by Andrew Ward, and contributions from Catherine Smith, Victoria Phillips, Rachel Blaifeder, and others.

From Malcolm: As always, this is for Leila who makes it easy to forget how much I rely on her. *From Kian:* I'm thankful to all my friends and family for their love and support – especially Ellie, for everything she means to me.

How to Read a Declassified Document

For historians of diplomatic history or US foreign policy, archival documents are indispensable. Like an archeological relic, each has a story to tell. Historical records give clues to the thinking of the people who made policy and who carried it out. They shed light on presidential decision-making, interactions with foreign governments, intelligence collection, and the activities of diplomats and the military around the globe. Their immediacy and unfiltered information are what make them such valuable building blocks of history.

But how do you know what exactly you're reading? How can you tell if a document is important, if it made an impact, or if anyone even read it? If it is objective? Truthful? Genuine? Where does it fit in the larger stream of events? Ultimately, documents are only as reliable as the men and women who write them, so readers need to approach with care.

Here we offer some helpful guidelines to aid readers in how to evaluate a government document – or, for that matter, any book or article one might read about the subject. The list starts with a document's metadata – its surface features – which are immediately visible and critical for knowing the who, what, and when about the item. The rest of the questions involve deeper inspection, a search for contexts, and reading between the lines for meaning, purpose, and significance. That in turn requires some knowledge about the subject at hand, who the main players were, what else was taking place at the time, and ideally something about the policy process. This can all be a challenge, no doubt, but it is at the heart of what a historian does – attempt to understand and explain events and thinking from an earlier time.

Questions to ask yourself:

What kind of document is it? There are many different kinds of documents. The cataloguing system at the National Security Archive identifies 390 distinct types. The point is to know whether what you're examining is supposed to be a factual record like a transcript, an advocacy piece, a private communication, a public statement, or something else. Every type has an intended purpose that can help you assess its value for your immediate purposes.

When was it written? This is important for placing the document in the context of other events happening at the time, whether in a person's life, in the course of a policy debate, or on a global scale. Was it written in response to an internal memo, prior to an important UN vote, immediately after a terrorist attack? Nothing happens in a vacuum.

Who is the author? What do you know about them? Do they have a track record of objectivity or, conversely, political or personal partiality? If s/he is not a familiar figure, it may be worth exploring their background to understand something about their perspective or motivations.

Is the document signed? Initialed? Marked "Received"? If not, these are indications it is a draft and not a finished version or an official record, which affects the conclusions we can draw about how it turned out and its potential impact. (It could still be of value for understanding how certain people viewed an issue or how policy thinking evolved, for example.)

Was the document reviewed or approved by others? State Department memos and cables are typically drafted and reviewed by several people who are named at the end of the document. These reflect the position of a particular department, whereas items written by an individual often contain personal opinions. Similarly, major intelligence products like National Intelligence Estimates are signed off on by most or all of the agencies that make up the intelligence community; so they are useful for identifying issue areas of broad consensus but not where one would find out-of-the-box analyses or controversial views.

Who is the intended recipient? Who the audience is inevitably influences how a person presents their case, including their level of candor. A message to a foreign official will be far more formal and guarded than an email to a close colleague. So will a diplomatic cable with a long list of recipients, as opposed to one marked "Eyes Only" or "Personal."

Was it originally classified? A Top Secret memo is more likely to include information the government considers sensitive or to reflect an official's thinking than an unclassified press release aimed at swaying public opinion. Beyond the standard classification levels, codewords and dissemination controls – for example, GAMMA indicating communications intelligence, or NOFORN not to be shared with foreigners – further define limits on distribution.

Are there additional markings made by others? Did anyone add remarks that can serve as a clue as to who read the document or how it was received? Jimmy Carter routinely wrote in the margins of his aides' memos, providing relatively unguarded commentary of a sort that is prized by historians.

Is the document meant to inform or persuade? This could be the author's expressed objective or a hidden aim; either should influence how you assess her/his arguments.

Is the author writing for history? Memoirs, interviews, and published articles can be invaluable but call for abundant caution because of the temptation for an author to put herself in a positive light; contemporaneous, unpublished documents are subject to the same phenomenon.

Is there less there than it seems? There is a tendency when researching government documents to treat them with more reverence than they might deserve. Ordinary people wrote most of these materials and their work may be respected without its significance being overblown simply because it is highly classified or located in a restricted file.

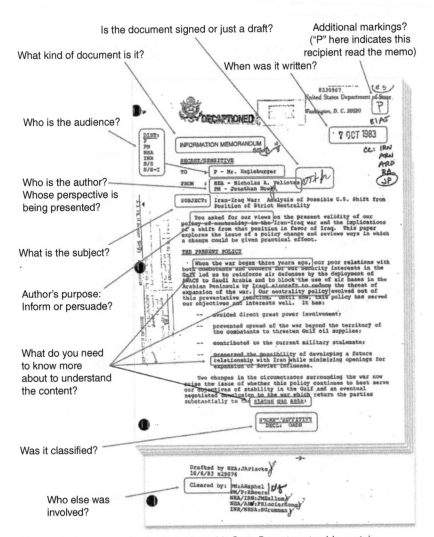

Like any text, government records such as this State Department cable contain clues to understanding the authors' intent as well as the broader context of the document.

Chronology

1977

January 20 – Jimmy Carter is inaugurated president of the United States.

December 31 – In Tehran, Carter toasts the Shah's "great leadership."

1978

January 8 – The government-backed *Ettela'at* publishes an inflammatory article against Ayatollah Ruhollah Khomeini, sparking a cycle of protests and suppression that builds throughout the year.

November 2 – After months of rising turmoil in Iran, the Carter administration's high-level Special Coordinating Committee (SCC) meets for the first time on the crisis.

December 29 – The Shah appoints Shapour Bakhtiar prime minister.

1979

January 16 – The Shah leaves Tehran for Cairo, Egypt.

February 1 – Khomeini returns to Iran.

February 5 – Khomeini appoints Mehdi Bazargan to head the Provisional Government.

February 14 – Members of the leftist group Fedayeen attack the US Embassy in Tehran.

April 1 – The Islamic Republic is declared following a national referendum.

October 22 – The Shah arrives in New York for medical examinations.

November 1 – National Security Advisor Zbigniew Brzezinski meets with Bazargan in Algiers.

November 4 – The US Embassy in Tehran is overrun, marking the beginning of the 444-day Iranian hostage crisis.

November 6 – The Bazargan government resigns and the Revolutionary Council takes over.

November 14 – Carter freezes Iranian assets.

December 3 – A new constitution including the concept of *velayat-e faqih* is approved. Khomeini is named Supreme Leader shortly afterwards.

December 25 – The Soviet Union invades Afghanistan.

1980

January 23 – Carter delivers the State of the Union address announcing the USA will use military force, if necessary, to defend its interests in the Persian Gulf.

April 7 – The US severs diplomatic ties with Iran.

April 25 – Operation Eagle Claw, an attempt to rescue the hostages, ends in disaster. Secretary of State Cyrus Vance resigns over the rescue decision.

July 27 – The Shah dies in Cairo.

September 22 – Iraq invades Iran, marking the beginning of the eight-year Iran–Iraq War.

1981

January 20 – Ronald Reagan is inaugurated president. Iran releases the hostages on the same day.

June 28 – A bombing at the Islamic Republican Party headquarters kills Secretary General of the IRP Mohammad Beheshti and seventy-two other officials. It is one of several violent attacks on Islamic Republic officials that summer.

October 2 – Ali Khamenei is elected president of Iran.

1982

May 24 – Iran liberates Khorramshahr from Iraqi forces, setting the stage for a counter-invasion.

June – Following the Israeli invasion of Lebanon, Iran dispatches more than 1,000 Revolutionary Guards personnel to the country, where they play a part in the formation of Hezbollah.

1983

April 18 – A suicide bombing targets the US Embassy in Beirut.

October 23 – A truck bomb explodes at the US Marine barracks in Beirut.

1984

January 23 – The Reagan administration places Iran on a list of governments supporting terrorism.

1985

June 3 – CIA officer William Buckley dies in captivity in Lebanon.

August 14 – Israel ships the first tranche of TOW antitank missiles to Iran as part of the Reagan-approved arms-for-hostages deals.

1986

May 25–28 – Former National Security Advisor Robert McFarlane leads a delegation to Tehran for secret talks as part of the arms-for-hostages deals.

November 3 – The Lebanese news magazine *Ash-Shiraa* exposes the secret Reagan arms deals.

1988

July 3 – The USS *Vincennes* shoots down an Iranian passenger plane after mistaking it for an Iranian fighter jet.

August 20 – The Iran–Iraq War enters a UN-brokered ceasefire.

1989

January 20 – George H.W. Bush is inaugurated president.

February 14 – Khomeini issues a fatwa calling for the death of British author Salman Rushdie.

March 28 – Khomeini rescinds the designation of Hossein Ali Montazeri as his successor.

June 3 – Khomeini dies. Ali Khamenei becomes Supreme Leader the following day.

August 3 – Akbar Hashemi Rafsanjani is elected president of Iran.

1990

August 2 – Iraq invades Kuwait.

1991

December 4 – The last American hostage in Lebanon is freed with Iranian assistance.

1993

January 20 – William J. Clinton is inaugurated president.

1995

May 6 – Clinton imposes comprehensive economic sanctions on Iran.

1996

June 25 – A truck bomb targets US Air Force personnel in Khobar, Saudi Arabia.

August 4 – Clinton signs the Iran and Libya Sanctions Act (ILSA) into law.

1997

April 10 – A German court finds the Iranian government responsible for killing Kurdish leaders at the Mykonos Restaurant in Berlin in 1992.

May 23 – Mohammad Khatami is elected president of Iran.

July 8 – The USA designates the Mujahedin-e Khalq as a terrorist organization.

1998

January 7 – Khatami on CNN calls for a dialogue among civilizations.

1999

June – Clinton sends a letter to Khatami via the Omani foreign minister.

2000

March 17 – Secretary of State Madeleine Albright acknowledges US involvement in the 1953 Iranian coup.

2001

January 20 – George W. Bush is inaugurated president.

September 11 – Terrorist attacks by al-Qaeda take place in the USA. Khamenei and Khatami condemn the events.

2002

January 29 – Bush labels Iran a member of the "Axis of Evil" in his State of the Union address.

2005

June 24 – Mahmoud Ahmadinejad is elected president of Iran.

2007

October 25 – The US imposes the most sweeping unilateral sanctions on Iranian entities since 1979.

November – A National Intelligence Estimate concludes that Iran halted its nuclear weapons program in 2003.

2008

July 19 – Under Secretary of State William Burns joins a P5+1 session that includes Iranian lead negotiator Saeed Jalili.

2009

January 20 – Barack Obama is inaugurated president.

March 20 – Obama sends a videotaped *Nowruz* greeting to the people of Iran. Khamenei responds the next day.

June 12 – Ahmadinejad is declared the winner in a widely disputed presidential election, sparking the formation of the Green Movement.

October 21 – Iran initially agrees to a UN-sponsored nuclear fuel swap deal.

2010

May 17 – Iran, Brazil, and Turkey sign the Tehran Declaration.

June 9 – UN Security Council Resolution 1929 further increases sanctions on Iran.

2011

February 14 – Protests break out in Iran in response to the Arab Spring.

December 6 – The State Department launches "Virtual Embassy Tehran."

2013

March 1–3 – High-level American and Iranian negotiators meet as part of the secret back channel facilitated by Oman.

June 15 – Hassan Rouhani is elected president of Iran.

November 24 – The intermediate Joint Plan of Action nuclear accord is signed.

2015

July 14 – The P5+1 and Iran sign the Joint Comprehensive Plan of Action (JCPOA).

2017

January 20 – Donald Trump is inaugurated president.

2018

May 8 – Trump announces the United States' withdrawal from the JCPOA.

Introduction: A Measure of Context

We sat on opposite sides of a long table, too weighted down by history to
enjoy the view or the moment.

William J. Burns, *The Back Channel*, p. 363

The focus of this volume is the period 1978–2018, the months leading up to
the Iranian revolution and the years that followed. But history, of course,
does not unfold in neat, self-contained units. Everything that happens has
antecedents that are often murky and require context in order to be properly
understood. (This is the purpose of the "headnotes" accompanying each
document.) It is not possible in this confined space to do justice to the
complexities involved in this story. For rich detail and expert analysis, we
refer readers to the relevant sources in the Select Bibliography, starting with
Abbas Amanat's history of Iran. Our aim here is simply to note a few points
of background information that are worth keeping in mind as you put
yourself in the shoes of decision-makers over the years who had the hard
task of devising effective approaches toward the Islamic Republic.

One of the keys to developing a successful policy and understanding
Iranian attitudes and character is to be aware of the country's remarkable
history and the impact of that bygone greatness on the worldview of its
people. Persia, as it was known to the West for centuries, established the
world's first empire more than 2,500 years ago. The Achaemenid empire's
most illustrious ruler, Cyrus the Great, was renowned not only for his
military conquests, from the Eastern Mediterranean to Central Asia, but
for his reputation for wisdom, justice, and tolerance. The high point of
ancient Persian civilization came during the Sassanid period from the early
third century CE to the mid-seventh century. Advances and innovations in
government, the arts and architecture, science and technology, medicine,
education, and other areas, not to mention the rise of one of the world's
oldest religions, Zoroastrianism, were among the many achievements of pre-
Islamic Iran and are still sources of great pride to Iranians today.

The advent of Islam is another key to grasping the complexity of modern
Iran. Iranians are mostly Shiites but the sect makes up only 10–15 percent of
all Muslims, while the Sunnis constitute 85–90 percent of the Islamic world.
The differences between the two sects originated with a dispute over who were

the rightful heirs to the Prophet Muhammad. Shiites believe the mantle should have followed bloodlines, passing to Ali, Muhammad's cousin and son-in-law. (The term Shiite is short for Shi'at Ali, or followers of Ali.) The killing of not only Ali but later his two sons, Hassan and especially Hussein, has elevated the concepts of fighting injustice and seeking martyrdom to sacred levels. The impact can be seen in the virulence of revolutionary antipathy toward the Shah and the readiness for self-sacrifice during the Iran–Iraq War.

Iranian Shiites further differentiate themselves by their belief in the existence of twelve divinely ordained imams, descendants of Muhammad, who are owed unquestioning obedience. They hold that the Twelfth Imam disappeared but will return to usher in the final judgment. Ayatollah Ruhollah Khomeini introduced a radically new innovation under Shiism called *velayat-e faqih* that allowed for a cleric, in the absence of the final imam, to assume all temporal power in the Islamic Republic. The position of Supreme Leader remains the final arbiter of Iranian official policy.

Iranian worldviews were shaped yet again in the nineteenth and early twentieth centuries under the rule of the Qajar dynasty. A succession of mostly weak and corrupt rulers and disastrous conflicts led to significant losses of territory and attempts by feckless monarchs to compensate by granting heavily lopsided commercial concessions favoring outside powers, notably the UK and Russia. A growing sense of humiliation and anger sparked an extraordinary revolution in 1905 that united merchants, intellectuals, and mullahs, and produced a new constitution as well as a parliament. This was a rare positive development, however, during a period that mainly instilled, or intensified, a deeply rooted Iranian suspicion of outside powers, resistance to external interference in the country's sovereign affairs, and resentment toward foreign exploitation of the country's resources. These attitudes are all easily recognizable today.

It is in this context that the earliest sustained contacts between the USA and Iran occurred during the first half of the nineteenth century. Formal diplomatic relations were soon established, but the main interactions involved American missionaries who by and large left positive impressions by building hospitals and schools and generally showing a sensitivity to local customs. Two prominent Americans, Howard Baskerville, a missionary and teacher, and Morgan Shuster, who had been invited by the government to modernize the country's financial systems, backed the 1905–11 Constitutional Revolution. Other notable American advisors and educators played constructive roles through the first half of the twentieth century.

After these initial, low-level interactions, World War II brought Iran squarely onto America's radar. Bordering the Soviet Union to the south, it became a key transportation route for the Red Army, bypassing the Eastern front. When Moscow reneged on a pledge to withdraw from the country after the war, President Harry Truman reacted vocally and, even though the actions of Iranian political figures were the real difference, the United States was hailed for defending the sovereignty of a smaller state. In short, Americans enjoyed a highly positive reputation in Iran at least through mid-century.

After the war, US strategists, alarmed at the possible spread of Soviet-led Communism, determined that Iran was "vital to the security of the United States."[1] The designation reflected Washington's assessment that its interests were worldwide, effectively claiming for American leaders the right to intervene anywhere they deemed necessary – a premise that did not sit well in many locales. When a popular politician named Mohammad Mosaddeq became premier of Iran in 1951, he nationalized the country's petroleum industry, which – under yet another concession – had been under UK control for fifty years. Mosaddeq claimed, as many other Iranians felt, that the terms of the oil deals struck with Britain were not only unfair but demeaned Iran and undermined its sovereignty.

In 1953, US and British intelligence combined with local Iranian actors to overthrow Mosaddeq, forever changing Iranian politics. A number of basic facts about the coup are still being debated, but the ouster had several repercussions worth noting. It reinstated to power an ally, Shah Mohammad Reza Pahlavi, who would be a stout defender of American interests for the next quarter century, an outcome that led US officials to see it as a major success. But the American role had been a poorly kept secret, and as the Shah became increasingly autocratic this fact prompted growing popular resentment based on the belief that the prospects for democracy in the country had been dealt a major blow.

While it is risky to make assumptions based on a single historical variable, even as momentous as a coup, there is no doubt that steadfast US backing of Mohammad Reza Shah for the next twenty-five years had an enormous impact. To be sure, there were nuances to the relationship. For example, until President Richard Nixon in 1969, American leaders felt little enthusiasm for the monarch because of his hesitancy to enact meaningful reforms. But those concerns paled next to Cold War fears of Communism. More specifically, the urgency of devising an exit strategy from the Vietnam War (which ultimately involved proxies like Iran taking on the primary burden of regional defense) made him indispensable for American interests. Therefore, even when Iranian troops opened fire on crowds and the government became openly dependent on the repressive SAVAK secret police, US presidents mainly offered gestures of support. When the Shah finally did launch reforms, they were coincidentally followed by surges in oil revenues, which created a rosy picture of the country. As a State Department Iran expert put it: "Iran was a success for American policy and we didn't want to know" about its "weaknesses."[2]

By the time the luckless Jimmy Carter entered the White House in January 1977 on a promise to hold dictators accountable, it was too late to avoid revolution, especially after he reversed course and wound up becoming closer to the Shah. Khomeini, who had emerged as public enemy number one for the monarchy in 1963 and was expelled from the country the following year, homed in on offenses that evoked old historical sensitivities: American hegemony and interference in Iran's affairs, kowtowing by the Shah to a foreign power,[3] and contamination of Islamic values by Western culture. Those views have continued to animate the Islamic Republic's behavior to this day even though they have failed demonstrably to improve the situation.

Readers of this volume will have a close-up view of developments from the height of the revolution, over frequent ups and downs, to the (temporary) resolution of one of the thorniest problems in the bilateral relationship. The portion of the record reproduced here provides direct, unfiltered evidence about what happened, how officials reacted, where they stumbled or succeeded, and how the two governments somehow managed to return essentially to where they began over forty years ago. The documents offer fascinating insights into the challenges of dealing with deeply hostile states and raise fundamental questions about how to move forward – questions policymakers themselves continue to struggle with.

Notes

1. Report to the National Security Council by the Executive Secretariat, "The Position of the United States with Respect to Iran," Top Secret, July 21, 1949.
2. Henry Precht, in "Interview with Charles Naas," Association for Diplomatic Studies and Training Foreign Affairs Oral History Project, Library of Congress, initial interview date October 8, 1988.
3. Khomeini was especially galled by the regime's signing of a so-called Status of Forces Agreement in 1964 granting US soldiers legal and other privileges not available to local citizens; he said that it "reduced the Iranian people to a level lower than that of an American dog." The memory remained so raw that it was explicitly mentioned in the preamble to the Islamic Republic's 1979 constitution. (Bager Moin, *Khomeini: Life of the Ayatollah* [New York: Thomas Dunne Books, 2000], p. 123; see generally, Kenneth Pollack, *The Persian Puzzle: The Conflict between Iran and America* [New York: Random House, 2004], pp. 93–100.)

1

Blindsided: Confronting the Revolution and the Hostage Crisis, 1977–1981

Introduction

The inauguration of Jimmy Carter as president of the United States in January 1977 seemed, initially, to mark a turning point in US–Iran relations. Under Richard Nixon and Henry Kissinger, the United States had looked to authoritarian leaders to serve as bulwarks against the spread of Communism, often turning a blind eye toward local human rights abuses in the name of the Cold War. As a conspicuous beneficiary of this policy, Mohammad Reza Pahlavi greeted Carter's election with trepidation, fearing the new president would pressure the Shah on civil liberties and stop the flow of American weaponry which he so prized.

Jolted by the realities of international politics, Carter ended up making few major adjustments toward Iran, however. The Shah took nominal steps to respond to critics, such as easing restrictions on the press, promising to end torture by SAVAK, and reshuffling unpopular prime ministers. For his part, the president backed away from some of his campaign pledges – such as cutting military-related sales, including approving the provision of state-of-the-art AWACS reconnaissance aircraft to Iran. Although they were unaware of it at the time, the administration's reneging on campaign promises to challenge the Shah meaningfully on human rights grounds would deeply disappoint the Iranian opposition and vastly complicate attempts to establish good relations with the Shah's successors.

When signs of serious domestic unrest surfaced in Iran in 1978, the consensus among experts was that the Shah could easily handle them, as he had in the past. As always, the main focus of American concern was the potential threat to American interests in Iran emanating from the Soviet Union, either directly or by way of the Tudeh Party, although in reality Moscow's support for its Communist allies in Iran was lukewarm.[1] A CIA report that summer insisted the Shah was likely to rule well into the 1980s [Document 1]. But as US policymakers turned to other priorities – the Strategic Arms Limitation Talks (SALT II) with the Soviet Union and the Camp David peace process among them – the situation in Iran deteriorated.[2]

The year 1978 got underway with Carter raising a New Year's Eve toast to the "great leadership of the Shah" and referring to Iran as an "island of stability in one of the more troubled areas of the world." Days later, a newspaper article, clearly with government approval, attacked the regime's harshest critic, the exiled Shiite cleric Ayatollah Ruhollah Khomeini. It sparked indignation among his followers who took to the streets in the holy city of Qom. Local police fired into the crowd, leaving many casualties. The episode led to a cycle of protests and violent crackdowns that lasted through the year, as revolutionary fervor swiftly built up. The Shah's attempts at amelioration failed and it became obvious he was running out of answers.

Meanwhile, some American intelligence experts persisted in downplaying the threat. In August 1978, the same month when hundreds died in an arson attack at a cinema and a pipe bomb was thrown into the US consulate in Esfahan, a CIA report determined Iran was "not in a revolutionary or even pre-revolutionary situation." Shah supporters dismissed the protesters as leftist troublemakers.

Some Iran specialists in the US government voiced concerns at the time [Document 2], but their messages made no impact at the White House. On September 8, now known in Iran as Black Friday, nearly 100 protesters were killed at Jaleh Square in Tehran. Carter limited his response to calling the Shah to reassure him that the United States remained behind him. Preoccupied by the historic Camp David talks, the president's advisors fell back on outdated assumptions about the stability of the monarchy.

Only when US Ambassador to Iran William Sullivan, a staunch defender of the Shah, suddenly changed his tune in early November [Document 4] and suggested that the monarch might not survive the turmoil did the White House finally grasp the scope of the crisis. Looking back at the unfolding of events a year later, National Security Council (NSC) Iran expert Gary Sick was struck by the lack of senior level attention to events until late in the day: "The most astonishing thing is that we had no [high-level] meetings at all on the subject until the crisis assumed overwhelming proportions in early November." Moreover, "it was only after the ... Khomeini takeover on February 11 that principals began to engage themselves formally and regularly in decision-making."[3]

The scramble to reassess policy brought out profound disagreements among Carter's top advisors. National Security Advisor Zbigniew Brzezinski tenaciously argued the USA should show full support for the Shah, by any means necessary [Documents 5 & 10]. He warned against Soviet exploitation of the crisis and the high political and diplomatic costs of abandoning an important ally. Secretary of State Cyrus Vance felt the Shah could no longer lead as he had in the past, but hoped that the USA could salvage the situation by pushing him to engage with the opposition and possibly establish a civilian government of national unity. In the end, Carter opted to let the Shah handle matters himself. In a private remark that may sound naïve or even self-deluding given America's history with Iran, he told an advisor: "I cannot tell another head of state what to do."[4]

A chronic problem for the president and his inner circle was their general ignorance about the political forces in Iran, particularly the mullahs. This was partly a byproduct of years of extraordinary acquiescence to the Shah's insistence on limiting US contacts with opposition elements. The NSC's Gary Sick called the knowledge gap "abysmal" and placed the USA "light years" behind the British, who had a deeper involvement in the country. A few weeks before the enormously popular Ayatollah Khomeini returned from exile as the country's de facto leader in early 1979, the director of the CIA had to explain to a cabinet meeting what an ayatollah was.[5]

Despite Khomeini's prominence, Carter, persuaded by Brzezinski to overrule Vance and Sullivan, decided not to open an early direct channel to him in order not to appear to undermine the Shah. By early January 1979, when the president and most of his advisors finally agreed the Shah should go [Document 5], the country was in near chaos and he was no longer the main driver of events. Only Brzezinski among Carter's top aides urged continuing to prop him up.

The question was what would happen next. The Shah had just appointed a moderate nationalist named Shapour Bakhtiar prime minister, but his support base was thin, which underlined the importance of the military as a potential stabilizing force. The president sent a special envoy, General Robert Huyser, to assess their loyalties and readiness to act if called upon. Although he was in Iran for only a month, Carter came to trust his reporting of events over Sullivan's. In the chaotic atmosphere of the capital, Huyser's presence soon touched off rumors that he was there to foment a coup.

Typically, both Khomeini's and the Shah's supporters feared they were the target – but in this case each had grounds to be nervous. Sullivan was reporting that some of the generals wanted to move against the Shah if he failed to act decisively, while for the Americans a coup option to keep Khomeini or the Communist Tudeh out of power was very much on the table. (Vance split with Brzezinski and Defense Secretary Harold Brown on this but still believed military action might be needed to stave off "disorder, bloodshed, and violence.") Ultimately, they could not reach a consensus before new intelligence showed conditions were no longer favorable.[6]

Mohammad Reza Pahlavi departed Iran for "vacation" on January 16. Two weeks later, Khomeini arrived to a tumultuous welcome that bespoke both his own unique standing and the power of political Islam. Belatedly, the White House reached out to him [Document 6] while simultaneously trying to build a relationship with the new Provisional Government. Repeated attempts to connect with religious circles went nowhere, especially after Khomeini banned any contact, although embassy officials still managed to interact with certain clerics. These meetings helped establish the depths of the pent-up distrust that existed among the revolutionaries for the Shah's former patrons [Document 8], particularly Carter whom they seemed to revile.

Throughout 1979, despite the evident shakiness of the Provisional Government, American officials commonly assumed a clerical regime could not succeed for long.[7] Khomeini's popularity and resilience would consequently continue to surprise as he rallied networks of mullahs and mosques to consolidate his position in a still frenzied and uncertain political environment. He established the Islamic Revolutionary Guard Corps (IRGC) to defend against internal threats ranging from leftist attacks to ethnic uprisings at the nation's peripheries, while other new entities such as the komiteh, or Revolutionary Committees, sprang up, working outside Provisional Government structures to enforce religious edicts that were becoming more pervasive.

The world's first Islamic Republic came into being on April 1 after a recorded 98 percent vote of national approval [Document 7]. By year's end a new constitution enshrined the concept of velayat-e faqih, or absolute rule by a "religious jurist" [Document 11]. Khomeini developed the notion while in exile. It envisioned empowering a chosen individual to act on behalf of the Hidden Imam, at the core of Shia belief, until his promised return to Earth. Khomeini's aim was to invest political power in the ulama, or clergy, instead of the state, and was controversial even for some senior Shiite clerics. These developments were as clear a signal as there could be that a sense of divine purpose and revolutionary resolve would animate true believers in Iran's new era.

As radicalization spread through 1979, so did anti-US opinion. Religious leaders lashed out at the United States for interference – treating administration policies, congressional actions, and news media criticisms of repressive revolutionary methods as originating from the same source. In May, the Javits Resolution in the US Senate condemning the persecution of Jews, opposed by the State Department because it would disrupt diplomacy, incited large demonstrations outside the embassy. Meanwhile, the moderate prime minister of the Provisional Government, Mehdi Bazargan, who favored limited ties to Washington, was attacked as an American puppet. In October, general anger turned to outrage when the United States admitted the Shah for medical treatment, rejecting Tehran's demands to return him to Iran [Document 8]. Shortly afterwards, a photo of Bazargan and Brzezinski shaking hands at a meeting in Algiers went public. As both countries would become prone to doing, Iranians misread a series of random events as proof of malicious intent.

In this case, the consequences were enormous. As rumors mounted of an impending 1953-style coup after the Shah's admittance to the USA, a group made up mostly of students took events into their own hands and on November 4, 1979, seized the US Embassy and all of its staff [Document 9], an extraordinary act that would severely damage US–Iran relations.

American shock at this flagrant violation of international law quickly hardened into enmity as Khomeini not only failed to end the takeover but instead embraced it. At such a raw moment, neither side was disposed to consider the other's reasons [Document 10]. Feelings of humiliation and threat, respectively, deepened after a US rescue attempt the following year ended in a fiery disaster in the Iranian desert leaving several American servicemen dead [Documents 13 & 14].

In December 1979, the Soviet Union invaded Afghanistan, precipitating a new global crisis [Document 12]. In another notable misinterpretation, Western observers took the development as confirmation of their worst fears about international Communist aggression. But as Russian archival records would show, the invasion was chiefly a reaction by Moscow to their own unfounded fear that the United States planned to make up for the geostrategic loss of Iran by seizing control of neighboring Afghanistan.[8]

The move turned out to be a strategic blunder, dragging the Soviets into a failed war that weakened the political foundations of the USSR itself. Its immediate consequence, in combination with the Iranian revolution and hostage crisis, was to draw the United States into formally identifying its own interests with the independence of the region. In his State of the Union address in January 1980, Carter enunciated a new doctrine: "Let our position be absolutely clear: An attempt by any outside force to gain control of the Persian Gulf region will be regarded as an assault on the vital interests of the United States of America, and such an assault will be repelled by any means necessary, including military force."[9]

Beyond its international implications, the hostage crisis had huge domestic consequences in both Iran and the United States. It marked the end of the road for political moderates in Iran as hardliners strengthened their hold on power – even as the episode seriously tarnished the Islamic Republic's international standing. In the USA, national embarrassment at the hands of a regime few Americans understood contributed to Carter's re-election defeat and embedded in American political discourse a level of resentment against Tehran that so far has proved impossible to overcome.

Document 1. Central Intelligence Agency, Intelligence Report, "Iran in the 1980s," SECRET, August 1977

For almost twenty-five years, the Shah of Iran has ruled with only occasional outbursts of restiveness among the population. Through the 1970s his position seems to be strengthening as oil money flows in and some economic reforms are put in place. But not far beneath the surface, virtually every stratum of society is manifesting discontent. Even as evidence mounts, the tendency in Washington is to wave it off, confident in the Shah's ability to weather the dissatisfaction as he has before. Moreover, the Nixon White House's tendency of giving the Shah special treatment because of his value as a Cold War ally fosters complacency in US strategists who usually assume the worst when it comes to threats in vital regions.

Some of the rosy assumptions that have grown up around the Shah shine through in this preface to a lengthy CIA country study half a year into the Carter presidency. Assessing what the next ten years likely have in store for Iran, the authors predict that not much will change from the general status quo since the 1953 coup removed the monarch's most potent political antagonist, Prime Minister Mohammad Mosaddeq. Unfortunately, three out of four of the "basic assumptions" made at the start of the document will prove to be dead wrong. Only the statement that oil will continue to dominate the economy holds up. The Shah will be driven into exile in less than a year-and-a-half, forced out by just the kind of "radical change" the authors say will not materialize, and in the first year of the 1980s Iran will in fact find itself at war. Jimmy Carter is later disparaged for "losing" a crucial ally in the Middle East, in part by badly miscalculating the state of affairs inside the country; this and similar official forecasts show that he was hardly alone in misreading events in Iran.

PREFACE

In the last 10 years, that is to say since the accession to the throne of the Pahlavi dynasty, Iran has been affording the spectacle of a burst of activity which will go down in history. The Army, courts, and public finances have been completely re-organized. A powerful drive is developing agriculture and industry. The Ministry of Public Education is increasing the number of schools, supervising the restoration of all monuments and infusing new life into the fine arts. Hygiene and urbanization have transformed many cities. The building of railways and of many highways is hastening the fulfillment of these impressive developments.

This passage, written in 1938 by Henri Masse could almost without change be repeated today but when Masse wrote, he could not have foreseen that within three years Iran would be invaded and occupied by Britain and the USSR, that the Shah who had produced that "burst of activity" would be in exile where he would die, and that it would be 30 years before his words would again be pertinent.

So, prophecy is precarious and prediction is only slightly less so. Even the more modest estimate can maintain a validity only by generalizations that are all things to all men. This paper attempts, for the most part, to be conservative. It makes these basic assumptions:

- The Shah will be an active participant in Iranian life well into the 1980s.
- There will be no radical change in Iranian political behavior in the near future.
- Iran will not become involved in a war that would absorb all of its energies and resources. Oil will continue to dominate the Iranian economy.

The Shah *could* die suddenly or be assassinated; a combination of political personalities and forces *might* reduce the Shah to a figurehead; Iran *could* become involved in a war with one of its neighbors or in a more general outbreak of hostilities. None of these is predictable at present, but the occurrence of any one of them would require substantial reevaluation of the country's status in the future.

The Shah's plans call for almost simultaneous development in nearly every field. This strains every level of the Iranian society and economic structure, but the Shah has adopted the forced-draft approach to make sure that Iran is set inexorably on the path to a modern industrial state while he is still around to oversee the process. Because the programs are so interrelated, a serious failure in one could affect the others. All programs, of course, are dependent on a continuing flow of income from oil revenues; declining oil sales have recently forced a cutback in some programs, and a sharp decline could affect everything else. Iran's increasing population provides the potential for the manpower it will need in the next 15 years, but at the same time this manpower must be trained, straining the educational system, and the larger population must be fed, putting pressure on agricultural production. In turn, innovations designed to increase agricultural production are, in many respects, unproven, and involve the government bureaucracy in the process to a greater extent than ever before. Finally, the whole process depends – and for the foreseeable future will continue to depend – on the Shah. His control of the decisionmaking apparatus is so complete that he is literally irreplaceable at this point. A successor to the Shah, although committed to the same programs, would have to establish his right to govern, a process that might take years. The Shah seems to hope that he can institutionalize his programs so that they will have a life of their own after he is no longer in charge. This is unlikely to be the case.

We are, then, looking at evolution not revolution and are identifying trends to be watched, not results that can be productive. Most of the significant decisions, actions, and attitudes that will influence the next decade are already in operation, and this will be identifiable in the pages that follow. Background data will permit the reader to see the bases for the author's conclusions, to draw his own conclusions if he chooses, and serve as a reference to those areas of politics, economics, and society which will create the Iran of the 1980s. Research for this paper was concluded in July 1977. [...]

[*Source: Central Intelligence Agency Freedom of Information Act release*]

Document 2. American Embassy Tehran, Airgram, Charles Naas for the State Department, "Uncertain Political Mood: Religious Development, Tougher Royal Line on Demonstrations," SECRET, August 1, 1978

By August 1978, the unrest in Iran is gaining significant momentum and some of the key figures and themes that will come to define the revolution are beginning to surface in US analyses of events. Carter's ill-fated "island of stability" toast to the Shah in Tehran on December 31, 1977, is almost immediately followed by the publication of a diatribe against Ayatollah Ruhollah Khomeini in the newspaper Ettela'at, *sparking a series of protests and violent police crackdowns.*

This document, sent out over the signature of the chargé d'affaires at the US Embassy in Tehran and reporting information from well-placed local sources, shows that officials on the ground are well aware of the political impact of religious forces in the country – earlier than critics would later assume: Khomeini, the author writes, "retains an almost mystic respect" among parts of the population, and the cable describes in some detail the politics playing out within religious circles, including the reluctance of some senior clerics to disagree too broadly with Khomeini in public. The cable also points to two major concerns that will prove critical in the coming months. The first is the high level of corruption running rampant in key sectors of society, especially among the royal family and its circle. The second, not fully appreciated in Washington at the time, is the poor state of the Shah's health [see Document 8].

Overall, the conclusion is that US overreliance on the Shah to handle the crisis is becoming a liability as the usual attempts to mollify the masses (firing and shuffling cabinet members, replacing the head of SAVAK) fail and faith in the monarch reaches an all-time low. As one Iranian informant explains it, "it does not matter how one arranges the garbage cans."

....

[...]

Hedayat Eslaminia, who has been discussing the religious situation with Embassy Political Officers for the past few months, opened a July 25 meeting with Political Officer Stempel in somewhat low spirits. The religious situation has "come apart." Eslaminia learned from General Fardoust and SAVAK Chief Moghaddam that the Shah was most distressed that Ayatollah Shariatmadari did not publicly oppose Ayatollah Khomeini's call for a subdued, "politicized" celebration of 12th Imam's birthday July 21. Eslaminia says Shariatmadari and his supporters have increased their dislike for Khomeini until it borders on hate because pro-Khomeini groups are blackmailing Shariatmadari supporters by threatening to shut down or burn their shops in the Bazaar.

With respect to Ayatollah Shariatmadari, Eslaminia said recent events have increased Shariatmadari's concern for his own position. Khomeini retains an almost mystic respect of mass of illiterate population and Shariatmadari feels he cannot differ to a significant degree with Khomeini in public. [Comment: We are not sure just how independent Shariatmadari actually is.] Eslaminia noted that all senior Ayatollahs in Iran are beginning to jockey for personal position. This could create a situation in which moderate religious figures would have trouble maintaining centrist policy in the face of challenges from more reactionary groups.

In the wake of disturbances in Iran July 21–22, Shah met on July 22 with his aide, General Fardoust and SAVAK Chief Moghaddam to discuss future policy towards demonstrators. Eslaminia, who is close to both Fardoust and Moghaddam, said the Shah was depressed with the outcome of the religious demonstrations and after a somewhat mercurial session in which Moghaddam was heavily criticized, the Shah directed that demonstrations would henceforth be broken up by military force and the army was authorized to fire on demonstrators. In response to a question, Eslaminia said he had been working for three days to reverse or moderate this decision, but the Shah and his principal advisors were now convinced that compromise with religious leaders may not be possible. Eslaminia believes this is an extreme position which will hopefully change, but it is clear that the throne is taking a much tougher line against dissidents in the wake of Shariatmadari's inability or unwillingness to oppose Khomeini publicly. For example, Shah is now against letting Mullah Falsafie speak publicly because it is feared he might ignite a sizable riot.

In passing, Eslaminia noted that Fardoust and Moghaddam, who are good friends of his, expressed some concern at the Shah's health. Political Officer mentioned rumors were prevalent in Tehran that something had happened. Eslaminia quickly replied that Shah was physically all right as of July 22 but somewhat "down" mentally. According to Eslaminia, medical blood tests

had been ordered to determine if there was any physical problem.
Later in conversation, Eslaminia noted that the U.S. and others
should keep an eye on the Shah and if something were wrong, they
should urge him to convene the Regency Council and prepare Iran
for change, not just depart Iran abruptly as his father had done.
When Political Officer expressed thought that this might be
premature, Eslaminia merely smiled sadly and noted it pays to
think ahead (absence of Shah from visible public eye has given
rise to number of rumors. Eslaminia is concerned because those
nearest Shah whom he knows well are concerned. This situation
has arisen as a result of the Shah's current vacation during
which he has made few public appearances. The Embassy has no
evidence to indicate there is anything wrong, but the rumors are
beginning to take on a life of their own.)

When asked how religious leaders viewed the recent ministerial
changes Eslaminia sighed and said "it does not matter how one
arranges the garbage cans." The Prime Minister and the Cabinet are
doing virtually nothing about religious/political challenges
and persist in the view that this is the Shah's and SAVAK's
problem. Only the Shah himself and the Court Minister are
concerned and time is passing. A bad situation is developing
because Tudeh (communist) and radical groups are lining up behind
Khomeini very quietly. They plan to let the Khomeini faction
discreetly back candidates to parliament [sic] who will, after
they are elected, reveal true colors and ban [sic] together to
"wage war" against the present system. Eslaminia believes this
tactic may well work because the GOI is currently in political
disarray – the resurgence party is confused and the Prime Minister
is not moving with sufficient speed to consolidate his forces.
   [...]
Eslaminia sees an even bigger problem with corruption.
A number of key Bazaar merchants, including all major leaders,
wrote a public letter recently to the Minister of Finance asking
for an investigation of certain deals favoring the wealthy
importers. Eslaminia ticked off three: A) Ali Rezaie imported
two million tons of iron at 20 rials per kilo without paying
customs tax and is selling it at 36 rials per kilo. Small iron
shops have no or little profit margin and are being driven to the
wall while Rezaie is reaping immense profits. B) Fabric maker
Yassini, a close confident [sic] of Princess Ashraf, has imported
two million meters of cloth without paying requisite customs

duties. He is selling it at virtually double what he payed [*sic*] for it. C) Textile maker Lajevardi has also imported cheap textiles and sold them at a higher price.

In addition, a number of importers of vehicle spares with known ties to Princess Ashraf have raised their prices to retailers without any apparent justification, thus squeezing profits of this group. The result, says Eslaminia, is the beginnings of a major new wave of dislike for the royal family as well as the government, raising the question of corruption as a major political issue. Eslaminia said he thought the Shah had better take a hand before small merchants and some manufacturers become convinced their interests lie with the opposition. [*Comment*: While the problem of corruption has been a consistent Eslaminia concern in past, Embassy has heard from a number of sources that financial wheelings and dealings keyed to royal family and friends are beginning to affect a sizable number of people and merchants are getting both smarter and bolder about raising these questions in the public arena.]

[*Comment*: This conversation being reported by airgram because it emphasizes several themes which we have heard often elsewhere during the past month relating to confusion in the Iranian political system: A) concern for health of Shah; B) increasing difficulties in getting the regime and religious leaders on compatible tracks; and C) growing concern with corruption and problems of GOI political disorganization.]

The actual situation is not, of course, as bad as tableau being painted by pessimists. There is much uncertainty and anxiety in political circles which has increased both suspicions and manic-depressive tendencies of Iranian political figures. Iranian politics are undoubtedly going through a "summer of discontent." New alliances may or may not emerge. Observers should not, however, jump to conclusion that country is going to hell in a hand basket. Situation seems to be one of trying to manage long overdue political growing pains under somewhat less than optimum conditions.

Naas

[*Source*: Documents from the US Espionage Den, *vol. 25: 50–53.*]

Document 3. White House, Memorandum of Telephone Conversation, Zbigniew Brzezinski with the Shah, SECRET, November 3, 1978

This extraordinary conversation between National Security Advisor Zbigniew Brzezinski and the Shah takes place as revolutionary momentum escalates rapidly in late 1978. The US government repeatedly expresses public backing for the Shah, even after events like the Jaleh Square massacre ("Black Friday") in early September when security forces opened fire on protesters, killing more than 100. But the monarch is obviously despondent, as Brzezinski reports to the president in a memo after the phone call: "The Shah sounded very depressed, and indicated that the situation is 'very bad' and appears to be deteriorating further. His tone sounded very grim and he was not forthcoming."[10]

The awkward conversation, lasting just six minutes, captures the confusion of the moment in Iran as well as Washington's general lack of information and indecisiveness. Brzezinski affirms that the United States supports the Shah "without any reservation whatsoever" and is careful to convey that Carter does not want to push any particular course of action, but he cannot resist an appeal not to go soft: "Concessions alone," he warns, "are likely to produce an even more explosive situation." The distracted Shah seems to focus on the remark, asking Brzezinski to repeat it. His next question, whether Ambassador William Sullivan has been briefed, prompts a comment in the margin, presumably by Brzezinski, that hints at a growing gulf between the White House and Sullivan. Carter's initial appears at the top of the transcript, indicating he read it.

....

```
Participants:     The Shah of Iran
                  Zbigniew Brzezinski
Date and time:    Friday, November 3, 1978
                  9:05-9:11 A. M.
```

ZB: Your Majesty.

SHAH: Hello, how are you?

ZB: Very well. How are you?

SHAH: Well, busy.

ZB: I can well imagine. I am very pleased and privileged to have the opportunity of talking to you. The President asked me to call and tell you that he is currently campaigning around the United States because we have our elections next week, and this is why he is not calling personally. But he will be up at Camp David later on Sunday, and if it was useful he would certainly be delighted if a conversation between you and him were to take place.

SHAH: I will be always very glad to talk to him. I don't know if we can do it over the phone.

ZB: In the meantime, he asked me to tell you that our ambassador is instructed to convey the following message to you.

SHAH: I will see him tomorrow.

ZB: The message essentially makes three points: first, the US supports you without any reservation whatsoever, completely and fully, in the present crisis.

SHAH: Thank you.

ZB: You have our complete support without any reservation whatsoever. Secondly, we will support whatever decisions you take regarding either the form or the composition of the government that you should decide upon.

SHAH: Yes.

ZB: We are not, and I repeat not, encouraging any particular solution.

SHAH: Yes.

ZB: And I hope that is very clear, and the ambassador has been instructed to make it very clear, that we are not advising or encouraging you to go in any particular direction. We will support whatever decision you take and whatever steps you feel are necessary to maintain your authority and order and the reestablishment of effective leadership and decisive action that may be needed.

SHAH: Well, thank you very much. Obviously I am very touched by this, but it is a very peculiar situation.

ZB: In what sense?

SHAH: That extreme measures if at all possible should be avoided.

[*Handwritten comment in the margin referring to the previous line: "I think he was hinting that this is what we have been telling him."*]

ZB: Well, you, in effect, it seems to me, have the problem of combining some gestures which would be appealing in a general sense with a need for some specific actions which would demonstrate effective authority.

SHAH: Yes.

ZB: It is a critical situation in a sense, and concessions alone are likely to produce an even more explosive situation.

SHAH: Would you repeat that please?

ZB: What?

SHAH: The last sentence.

ZB: Concessions alone are likely to produce an even more explosive situation. It is very hard for us to judge from here what your domestic needs are. You will be interested to know that there is more and more public support for you – newspaper editorials, which, as you know sometimes have been critical in the past, are now almost uniformly supportive of you, and it is an interesting shift and a recognition of the very important role you have been playing in modernizing your country and stabilizing the area.

SHAH: Is your ambassador briefed?

[Handwritten comment in the margin referring to the previous line: "A rather revealing question!"]

ZB: I sent him a message yesterday to this effect, and I shall call him after we have concluded our conversation. As I said, it is very hard for us to have a good feel here in Washington what the best course for you to take would be, but we are prepared to support you – whether you choose a coalition government, military government, whichever combines the more effective basis for stability and progress and once order and authority have been reestablished dealing with stabilization and coping with corruption.

SHAH: Thank you very much for calling. I will obviously study this and ... [*Ellipsis in original.*]

ZB: what is your assessment of the situation currently?

SHAH: Very bad.

ZB: Is it deteriorating?

SHAH: It seems to.

ZB: Well, if there is anything you feel that we could do, I wish you would let us know.

SHAH: I will. I will see your ambassador tomorrow.

ZB: All right.

SHAH: Thank you for calling anyway.

ZB: Your Majesty, it was good to talk to you. The President feels himself to be your personal friend, and we want to do whatever we can.

SHAH: Thank you. Please transmit my best wishes to the President.

ZB: Thank you.

SHAH: Goodbye.

ZB: Goodbye.

[Source: Jimmy Carter Library and Museum, Records of the Office of the National Security Advisor, Zbigniew Brzezinski Material – Country Files (NSA 6), Iran, 9/78-11/16/79, Box 29, Folder: Iran, 11/78]

Document 4. American Embassy Tehran, Cable, William Sullivan for the Secretary of State, "Thinking the Unthinkable," SECRET, November 9, 1978

Less than a week after Brzezinski's dispiriting conversation with the Shah [Document 3], Ambassador Sullivan rocks the White House with this now-famous cable introducing the possibility of life without Mohammad Reza Pahlavi. Sullivan characterizes the analysis as a "useful" thought exercise, saying "it is probably healthy to examine some options which we have never before considered relevant." The language of the cable is somewhat casual, suggesting Sullivan has no idea how it will be received.

According to the ambassador's memoir, the key changes to the situation that have altered his perspective are the "vitality of the religious side" of Iranian society and the dwindling of the Shah's support to essentially the military – and even their backing has become tenuous at best. Sullivan, who took a two-month vacation in the summer, returning in August, now believes that even if the military is able to take control of the economy and put down the social unrest, it will necessitate an "accommodation" with the religious sector that will see the majority of senior officers leaving the country. Sullivan does envision a cooler relationship with Iran, but one that could still benefit the USA and would certainly be better than "inchoate revolution."

Even though the self-described "Pollyannish" assessment is not wholly negative or meant as a prediction, Carter and Brzezinski are exasperated at what they see as a significant undermining of the administration's position. Secretary of State Vance has to intercede personally to convince Carter not to fire the ambassador. The ripple effects continue through the end of the year as the White House struggles to re-evaluate its strategy. Sullivan recalls later that his team at the embassy "drifted through the remainder of November and into December with no guidance from the Department of State or from Washington in general."[11]

....

1. With the incidence of Shi'i holy day Id-e-Ghorban on Saturday, November 11, and with its normal Thursday–Friday weekend, Iran has entered on a long three-day holiday. Current indications are that it will be quiet, but we shall have to test its temper as the days pass. Sunday, November 12, will be a critical day, because only then will we see whether the military government will be successful in getting this country back to productive work.

2. In the meantime, it might be useful to engage in some fundamental examinations of the situation in Iran and the future of U.S.-Iran relations. In doing this, it is probably healthy to examine some options which we have never before considered relevant.

3. For foreigners, the general cliché about Iran has been that its society rested on two pillars – the monarchy and the Shi'a religion. For the past fifteen years, the religious pillar has been very much subordinated and the tilt has been decidedly towards the monarchy. It is not necessary in this message to describe the way in which the religious pillar has been enhanced in the past ten months. However, it may be necessary to examine very closely the changes which have taken place in the monarchic pillar.

4. First, the authority of the Shah has considerably shrunk. His support among the general public has become almost invisible these days. Portraits of the imperial family, which formerly adorned every shop window, have nearly totally disappeared. Whether [sic] the views of the silent majority, the only tangible evidence of Iranian support for the monarchy comes from the armed forces. It has therefore become commonplace to refer to the monarchy as the "Shah - supported by the military."

5. However, even within that relationship, events of recent days may have produced a subtle change. It may be more correct at this time to speak of the monarchy pillar as being constituted essentially of the military - which (currently) supports the Shah. In consequence, the two elements that need our examination are the military and the religious.

6. At the moment, these two elements are ostensibly in confrontation. The religious have called for the equivalent of *Satyagraha* - passive resistance with strikes in strategic areas of the economy. The oil production facilities, Iran Air and the telecommunications system seem to be the prime targets of their attention. If the military can get these areas of the economy back in full production peaceably, they will probably be able to prevail over the religious, but the relationship between the two pillars will be tinged with tension, and the probability of terrorism, sabotage and xenophobia (see Tehran [embassy cable] 10706).

7. On the other hand, if the military fail to restore production and to break the tide of passive resistance, they will reach the point of making a fateful decision - either to enforce production by a bloodbath or to reach an accommodation with the religious. Since the latter are dominated by Ayatollah Khomeini, it must be assumed that a precondition for an accommodation would be the acceptance of his insistence that the Shah must leave and the monarchy be dis-established in favor of an Islamic Republic.

8. It is rather difficult to imagine a man like Prime Minister General Azhari willingly plunging his country into a blood bath. It is equally difficult to imagine him, or most military officers of his vintage, inciting the Shah to abdicate.

However, if the Shah and the military both shy away from the bloodbath, it may eventuate that both the Shah and the more senior military would abdicate, leaving the armed forces under the leadership of younger officers who would be prepared to reach an accommodation with the religious.

9. If such a turn of events should transpire, it would be important for the U.S. to have done a careful evaluation of its consequences for our position and that of our allies with respect to Iran. The following considerations are relevant:

(A) Both the Iranian Armed Forces and the Khomeini Muslims are strongly anticommunist and anti-Soviet. We say this despite reports of alleged communist infiltration of Khomeini's circle of advisors.

(B) The younger military officers have a genuine pro-West orientation. All Air Force, most Army, and many Navy officers have been trained in the U.S. Those Navy not trained in U.S. have been trained in U.K. and Italy.

(C) Despite religious complaints that the West is "stealing" Iranian oil, logic of Iran's economic ties with West would have to assert itself in any realistic appraisal of Iran's economic survival.

(D) Iranian military ought to be able to preserve its integrity and not RPT [repeat] not evaporate. Religious would find it useful for military to remain intact, because they have no RPT [repeat] no Islamic instruments for maintaining law and order or the integrity and defense of the nation.

(E) As consequence of any military–mullah accommodation, Khomeini could be expected return to Iran in triumph and hold a Gandhi-like position in the political constellation. He has said that, at such time, he would reveal the name of his candidate for political leadership. However, it would presumably have to be someone acceptable to the military rather than a Nasser–Qadhafi type that might be the Ayatollah's preferred candidate.

(F) If, as result of foregoing considerations, non-communist, moderate political figures like Bazargan and Minatchi should emerge in positions of responsibility, they would call for elections to a constituent assembly to draw up a constitution for an Islamic Republic of Iran. If elections are held in any atmosphere other than one of frenzy, such assembly ought to contain a strong percent of non-communists, non-Islamic-fanatics, and pro-western moderates who would have considerable influence in developing a responsible constitutional document.

(G) While it is difficult to predict the sort of government which might emerge from subsequent general elections, there would be reasons to hope that it would maintain Iran's general international orientation except that it would cease its ties with Israel and associate itself with the Arabs, probably closer to the Rejectionist Front than to Saudi Arabia. It would probably be a Kuwait writ large in its general orientation.

(H) Although U.S. involvement would be less intimate than with the Shah, it could be an essentially satisfactory one, particularly if the military preserves both its integrity and its status as one of the "pillars" of the nation. There would presumably be fewer Americans here and they would have a reduced status. But they could probably stay if they chose.

10. All this rather Pollyannish scenario could come about only if every step along the way turned out well. Any single misstep anywhere could destroy it and lead to unpredictable consequences. Therefore, it should not RPT [repeat] not be interpreted as this Embassy's prediction of future events.

11. Our current posture of trusting that the Shah, together with the military, will be able to face down the Khomeini threat is obviously the only safe course to pursue at this juncture. However, if it should fail and if the Shah should abdicate, we need to think the unthinkable at this time in order to give our thoughts some precision should the unthinkable contingency arise.

Sullivan

[*Source: National Archives and Records Administration; Access to Archival Databases; Central Foreign Policy Files; Department of State Records; Record Group 59; Electronic Telegrams, 1978.*]

Document 5. White House, Memorandum for the Record, "Informal NSC Meeting, 12:00–1:15 PM, Wednesday, January 3, 1979, The Cabinet Room," TOP SECRET, January 3, 1979

As the New Year begins, the Carter administration finds itself at a critical moment of decision on whether the Shah should stay or go. The White House has faced huge pressure from Republicans, notably long-time backers of the Shah like Henry Kissinger and David Rockefeller, to solidify US support for him. This top-level, uncensored memcon offers an unusually clear picture of who supports which approach within the administration.

Secretary of State Cyrus Vance and CIA Director Stansfield Turner make the argument for removing the Shah. Their belief is that reinforcing the Shah's decision to leave the country would give newly appointed Prime Minister Shapour Bakhtiar a greater chance of success. However, as Vice President Walter Mondale points out, this would come at a significant political cost. On the other side is Brzezinski, who strongly advocates backing the Shah to the hilt. To Brzezinski, the implications of abandoning the Shah would have far-reaching consequences for the United States, including encouraging the Soviet Union to expand its influence in the region and elsewhere.

The group agrees to send a special envoy, General Robert Huyser, who has personal experience in Iran, to work with the Iranian military, determine their outlook, and recommend courses of action. Carter comes to trust his reporting over Sullivan's. Huyser's month in-country becomes grist for rumors of a coup. Khomeini believes the US goal is to keep him out of power while the Shah's supporters conclude the opposite – that Carter wants to use the military to prepare the ground for Khomeini's return. Khomeini's suspicions are closer to the mark, according to Pentagon records, as Brzezinski and Defense Secretary Brown lead the argument for Iran's generals to take military action to prevent either a Khomeini or Communist Tudeh government. But as often happened, the president and his advisors after long discussions could not reach consensus and events took their course. Interestingly, much of the debate was over practical questions like the reliability of Iranian commanders and troops, and the unpredictability of events, rather than the ethics of mounting a coup.[12]

The question of whether Carter abandoned the Shah or did what he could to preserve American interests is one of the many issues analysts and critics of US policy continue to quarrel over.

....

1. Iran. The President asked those present whether in their view we should ask the Shah to step aside. ZB indicated he was

against this on the assumption that the question is whether we ask and not whether it is desirable that he step aside. Turner indicated the Shah has to leave. Vance suggested we support steps the Shah has taken, including his decision to leave the country, since it would give Bakhtiar more of a chance to succeed. The President said we could assume it is the Shah's decision. ZB argued that we should not delude ourselves that the above would not be interpreted by the Iranians as a recommendation that the Shah step aside. We have to take into account the likely consequences of this for our friends in Iran. Seeming U.S. disengagement could plunge the country into anarchy or even civil war. Vance argued that the military cannot govern. The President indicated that parliament could be a source of stability. A genuinely non-aligned Iran need not be viewed as a U.S. setback.

(In the meantime it was agreed that, if needed, Annenberg would provide a haven for the Shah's family and the Shah himself.)

The Vice President felt that we should encourage the Shah to leave without appearing to have said so. The President stated that the central issue is whether the Shah's early departure is favorable to the U.S. Turner said he was not sure the Shah wants to leave. Duncan suggested that General Huyser should go immediately to reassure the Iranian military of continuing U.S.-Iran military arrangements. ZB argued that if the Shah has to leave we should compensate for this by clearcut commitments to Iran so that, if worse comes to worst and violence is used, the Iranian military will feel confident of U.S. military support.

It was decided that a cable will be sent to the Shah indicating that in line with his decision to leave the country when Bakhtiar is confirmed, the U.S. is prepared to offer him hospitality for the duration of his stay here.

It was also agreed that General Huyser will leave for Iran immeidately [sic], with a message for the Iranian military that the U.S. supports them completely, no matter what transient political circumstances may arise, and we urge the Iranian military leaders not to leave the country.

On other matters: (1) It was decided not to deploy the F-15 squadron to ~~Iran~~ Saudi Arabia until after the Bakhtiar government has been established. When such deployment takes place, both Israel and Egypt ought to be informed. (2) The President approved removal of some of our sensitive equipment and personnel from two U.S. facilities.[13] (3) Precautionary measures regarding sensitive U.S. military equipment were also discussed.

2. Nicaragua. It was agreed that the U.S. will back a plebiscite under close OAS supervision but not direct control. Registration and voting should be combined, despite Somoza's objections. The U.S. will support the FOA position on the other three contentious issues, including the actual wording of the plebiscite.

At the end of the meeting, ZB commented that we should not lose sight of the fact that every U.S. action with respect to Iran seems to indicate disengagement – civilian evacuation, removal of personnel and equipment, indirect encouragement to the Shah to leave. This is bound to have political ramifications.

Secretary Duncan is to submit wording for the Huyser instructions by c.o.b. today. It was agreed that the instructions should be particularly strong and positive.

Secretary Vance to send telegram to Sullivan for the Shah.

[*Source: Jimmy Carter Library; NSC Institution Files, 1977–81; Container 56; NSC-015A – Iran, 1/3/79*]

Document 6. American Embassy Paris, Cable, Christian A. Chapman for the Secretary of State, "Message to USG from Khomeini," SECRET, January 27, 1979

On January 16, 1979, the ailing Shah leaves Iran, never to go home again. On February 1, Ayatollah Ruhollah Khomeini makes his triumphant return after more than fifteen years in exile, stepping into de facto leadership of the country. Even as it becomes clear that the USA will have to deal with him if it wants to build a relationship with the new Iran, Carter balks at reaching out directly, a decision Ambassador Sullivan tells Secretary Vance is a "gross and perhaps irretrievable mistake."[14] Carter opts instead to use the French government as an intermediary. The message below is Khomeini's first direct communication to the US government.

Future Foreign Minister Ibrahim Yazdi acts as emissary and interpreter of Khomeini's meaning. His counterpart is Warren Zimmermann, political counselor at the American Embassy in Paris. Khomeini's first major point is to call for Prime Minister Bakhtiar's ouster. He intends to establish his own government and there is no room for the Shah's appointees. Khomeini, through Yazdi, declares that he has no "particular animosity with the Americans" and that the new Islamic Republic is "nothing but a humanitarian one." This contrasts sharply with the anti-American rhetoric Khomeini is already known for (for example, calling Carter "the vilest man on earth"[15]), but it does seem to imply that at this early stage he has not written off the possibility of working with Washington – assuming the Americans acknowledge his new role as Iran's leader and don't interfere in Iranian affairs.

The message is an interesting snapshot of the turbulence and ambiguity of the political scene, and Khomeini is still an enigmatic figure to the White House. It is plain that he already wields substantial power, even before setting foot in the country, but his exact role in the new state is unknown, likely even to the Ayatollah himself. It is little wonder the US struggles to create a coherent policy toward Iran with so many question marks.

....

1. (S – Entire text)
2. Yazdi gave Zimmermann at 1015AM Paris time January 27 a personal message from Khomeini to the USG. It is the first first-person message from Khomeini passed in the Yazdi-Zimmermann channel. Zimmermann had proposed a meeting with Yazdi on the basis of Reftel [referenced telegram] (We report Yazdi's reaction to Reftel in Septel [separate telegram]); while Zimmermann was driving out to meeting place, Yazdi went to see Khomeini; when Zimmermann arrived, Yazdi gave him the message. Yazdi had apparently taken it down verbatim in Farsi from Khomeini; he translated it while reading it to Zimmermann. Khomeini message is quoted below; interpolations in – [sic] are Yazdi's responses to Zimmermann's requests for clarification.
3. Begin text of Khomeini message. The activities and works of Bakhtiar and the present leaders of the Army are not only harmful for Iranians but also are very harmful for the

American government, and especially for the future of the
Americans (Yazdi: That means the Americans in Iran), those
activities may force me to issue new orders in Iran. It is
advisable that you recommend to the Army (Yazdi: The Army as
a whole, not just the leadership; we draw a distinction
between the two) not to follow Bakhtiar and to cease these
activities. The continuation of these activities by
Bakhtiar and the Army leadership may bring a great disaster.
If Bakhtiar and the present Army leadership stop
intervening in the affairs (Yazdi: Of Iranians); we will
quiet down the people, and this will not create any harm for
the Americans. These kinds of activities and behavior
(Yazdi: By Bakhtiar and the Army leadership) will not bring
calm or stability to the region. The nation will listen to me
and, through my command and implementation of my plan,
stability will come. When I announce the provisional
government, you will see that many of the points which are
vague will disappear (Yazdi: Khomeini means areas which are
fuzzy to the USG) and you will see that we are not repeat not
in any particular animosity with the Americans, and you will
see that the Islamic Republic, which is based on Islamic
philosophy and laws, is nothing but a humanitarian one which
will benefit the cause of peace and tranquility for all
mankind. Closing down the airports and preventing me from
going back to Iran will disturb further the stability, not
only failing to stabilize the situation but even
destabilizing it further. I have been asked by forces
following me to give them permission to go and open the
airports for my return (Yazdi: By force). However, I have not
given such permission. Also, armed forces from within the
military, as well as non-military armed forces (Yazdi: For
example, militias and underground armed forces all of them
within the Islamic movement), including the tribes, have
requested permission to act and end the present situation
(Yazdi: That is, to force Bakhtiar and the military leaders
out of power). However, I have not given them the
permission yet, I prefer that the problem be solved in peace
and without violence or bloodshed and that the destiny of the
country be given to the nation to decide. End text of
Khomeini message.

4. Zimmermann requested further clarifications. What did
   Khomeini mean by the "activities and works" of Bakhtiar and
   the Army leadership? Yazdi said that they had closed down the
   airports for three days and nights. Yesterday they opened
   fire on the people; at least 16 were killed in Tehran, and in
   Sanandash [phonetic] in Kurdistan, police forces and troops
   have attacked civilians and burned down many houses and
   shops. Also yesterday at least a dozen daily press
   journalists were arrested. These, said Yazdi, are examples
   of the "activities and works" referred to.

5. Zimmermann asked about the distinction between the Army
   leadership and the Army as a whole. Yazdi said that the
   present Army leadership is associated with the Shah and
   responsible for many of the massacres, while the rest of the
   Army is different and is even sympathetic to the
   Islamic movement.

6. Zimmermann asked about the reference to the appointment of
   the "provisional government"; what vague points would be
   cleared up? Yazdi said that, when Khomeini announced the
   members of the provisional government, "You will know what
   kind of people you are dealing with and can talk to them in an
   official capacity." Yazdi went on: "If Khomeini announces
   that Engineer Bazargan is head of the government, you can
   talk to him officially and Bazargan would make clear what is
   vague to you. You have in mind that communists or some others
   will take over the country. When the government is
   announced, you will see that none of this is correct. You
   will see that the provisional government is capable of
   bringing stability."

7. Yazdi then said that the closing down of the airports
   represented a very sensitive situation. Millions of people
   have come to Tehran to welcome the Ayatollah, since Bakhtiar
   has said in the past that the Ayatollah can come to Iran
   anytime he wishes and since there are problems inside which
   could be solved only if he goes back, preventing his return
   to Iran has created a "very explosive situation; we may have
   a problem in controlling the temper of the millions who have
   poured into Tehran."

8. Zimmermann asked Yazdi about Khomeini's travel plans. Yazdi
   said that the three-day airport closure ends Saturday at

midnight, and Khomeini had planned to depart Paris at 1100PM
Paris time Saturday night. However, the Iranian authorities
have refused landing permission Sunday morning for the Air
France charter flight; apparently they want to extend the
closing down of the airports. "We will therefore suspend our
plan. I don't know yet what the Ayatollah will decide. If the
government says that the airports are closed for another
three days we will wait for another three days." [*Comment:*
Zimmermann was struck by the contrast between Yazdi's
relatively relaxed tone here and the more ominous tone of the
Khomeini message.]

9. Yazdi then volunteered that Khomeini's people are in
contact with Bakhtiar and the Army leadership. Bakhtiar
sent a letter with his envoy to Paris; the Ayatollah did not
accept the envoy but did receive the letter. It does not
contain anything new, asking only that the Ayatollah delay
his return to Iran. Zimmermann asked: How long a delay? Yazdi
said the delay was unspecified.

10. Yazdi then went on that "our people" have to solve the
problem in the present crisis and have suggested a formula
to Bakhtiar. This formula is that Bakhtiar either come to
Paris or be present at airport when Khomeini returns and
submit his resignation to Khomeini. Khomeini will then
agree to re-appoint him as a member of the provisional
government immediately. "This, we believe, will be of
benefit to all parties involved and will also give a chance to
Bakhtiar to gain back his popularity and political dignity
and bring also the unity necessary for the future stability
of Iran. We think that this is a tremendous concession that
our people in Iran have made." Yazdi added that Bazargan and
Beheshti have been involved in the negotiations and are
Khomeini's authorized representatives to conduct
the negotiations.

11. Before Yazdi gave the Khomeini message to Zimmermann,
Zimmermann gave Yazdi a text of President Carter's press
conference statement January 26 that political change
should be conducted in an orderly fashion and in accordance
with the Iranian constitution. Yazdi asked if we could
confirm that 200,000 barrels of oil were being shipped to
Iran. Zimmermann confirmed it, then noted that President

Carter had made clear that the shipment was intended to ensure energy supplies for the Iranian people.

Chapman

[*Source: Jimmy Carter Library; RAC Project: NLC-16-25-4-59-9.*]

Document 7. Islamic Republic of Iran, Speech, "Khomeini Address to Nation," UNCLASSIFIED, April 1, 1979

Just weeks after his return to Iran, Khomeini shepherds in the establishment of the world's first Islamic republic. While factionalism and chaos will help define this early period, Khomeini is already very much the face of the revolution.

But what is his vision for the country he now leads? This speech to the nation gives some insight into his plans, which will evolve and coalesce in the coming months. He refers to the recent referendum that has brought closer to fulfillment "God's promise" to "make the weak among the people triumph over the arrogant." He insists that "only an Islamic republic can fulfill all the objectives of the Iranian nation" and that "the commands of the Islamic republic override all others." Ultimately, it is the Islamists who will prevail, but only after a period of significant internal conflict.

Another point that comes through clearly is Khomeini's well-known "nei-ther East, nor West" philosophy. He bemoans the continuing influence of the Western powers in particular and declares that "everything that exists in Iran today must be changed." The depiction of Iran as a victim of oppressive foreign influence – built up over many decades – will remain an enduring part of the leadership's narrative for the next forty-plus years. For Khomeini, the solution is an Islamic state where "the mighty cannot oppress the weak or exploit the weak and the poor."

In the name of God, the Compassionate, the Merciful: the Almighty has promised, with his grace and his [word indistinct], to make the weak among the people triumph over the arrogant, and [words indistinct] to make them leaders.

The fulfillment of the Almighty God's promise is close. I hope that we will witness the triumph of those deemed weak over the arrogant, as they have done so far. So far, all that the nation has indicated has been in the direction of obeying Islam and its commands. We should make Islam known to the world, as it really is, and so that attention is drawn to it. What Muslims offer is something precious, but this should be made known.

I thank all the Iranian people for their participation in the referendum and for having cast their decisive vote, which should be regarded as nearly 100 percent in favor of an Islamic republic. The Iranian people had already given their favorable vote. We did not see any need for a referendum, but it was decided to hold a referendum in order to end certain voiced excuses and ramblings. Now, those who were making excuses have realized that the situation is not as they imagined, and that the nation is with Islam, with the spirituality of Islam. The nation wants the teachings of the blessed Koran to be implemented in Iran. Praise be to God that all sections of the Iranian people throughout the country cast their vote, with enthusiasm and eagerness, with love and dedication, in favor of an Islamic republic and nothing else. Only an Islamic republic can fulfill all the objectives of the Iranian nation. The commands of the Islamic republic override all others.

We say that those who make claims about democracy practise democracy in one form in the West, and another in the East. In the East, the people are facing a monumental dictatorship; the same applies to the West. We say to those who say they respect human rights and to human rights organizations that, over a period of 50 years – while the usurping Pahlavi rule and that of his son imposed themselves upon the nation and robbed the nation of everything it had through killings – our young people languished in jails, many of our young people's legs were sawn off in jail, many of them were still in jail until recently, many of them were suffering under torture until recently, many of them lost all they possessed to the executioners of the former shah.

All through this period, we did not see the supporters of human rights protesting. We saw the U.S. President on the side of the miserable shah, the former oppressive shah. We saw him supporting the former shah, supporting an executioner who threw all our possessions to the winds. But the advocates of human rights did not say anything to the U.S. President. [Illegible].

Only those with piety enjoy social distinction. Those with the spirit of humanity enjoy social distinction. Social distinction is not governed by wealth and material possessions. All such privileges must be eliminated, and everybody made equal. Every group's rights will be granted to them (?All ethnic groups) are equal. Religious minorities' rights will be observed and respected. All other groups with different ideologies are all part of the same nation, adherents of the same religion. I hope that the seditionists who go to various parts of the country and incite the people to engage in fratricide will themselves come to their senses. We are all brothers, they should not do such things in these regions. We are all brothers. The Sunnis are our brothers. We should not act as superior to others. We all have equal rights. And the law that is going to be approved by the nation protects the rights of all strata [words indistinct].

I congratulate the nation on this Islamic festival, on their Islamic republic. But we must all observe the Islamic commands. Our bazaar must be an Islamic bazaar. [Words indistinct] our government, and all future governments, must be governed by Islamic principles. Government offices must be run on the basis of Islamic principles. [Words indistinct] a satanic state should be converted into a state believing in God's commands. We are not afraid of what might be said about us in the West. [Words indistinct] we should act on the basis of justice. We shall in time make them understand what democracy means. The Western style of democracy is corrupt, and the Eastern style of democracy is equally corrupt. Only Islamic democracy is correct. Given the opportunity, we shall prove to both East and West that what we have is not the democracy they have – neither that in which big capitalists are favored nor that which supports superpowers and in which all the people are subjected to a monumental repression. There is no repression in Islam; there is freedom in Islam for all sections, for men and women, black and white, for everybody.

The people should fear themselves, not the government. They should fear themselves doing anything wrong. The rule of justice prevents wrongdoing, punishes wrongdoing. We should fear ourselves so that we do not do what is wrong. An Islamist government does not do wrong. There is no longer any SAVAK, or any of its tortures. Nobody can bully our police, bully our nation. No government can bully the nation. It should be the nation's servant; even if the prime minister acts unjustly, he should be brought to task. And if his crime is proved in court, he should be punished. There is no such thing in Islam as one law for the prime minister and another for someone else. [Words indistinct] Islam honors the humanity of a man [words indistinct].

At any rate, I call upon the whole nation to transform itself; transform the attitudes they have under the satanic regime into Islamic attitudes. In Iran today, we have many needy people, many injured people, many people who have lost all their possessions in the course of recent events. The wealthy should help them. The government should bear in mind their plight. It should build homes for them; it should provide them with a proper living; it should provide government employees with a proper living. I told a group of industrialists who had come to see me a few days ago to go and try to put things right yourselves, to get together and invest capital jointly to build houses for the workers and to provide them with welfare. I told them if you don't do that they might, God forbid, rebel one day, and if they do, we will no longer be able to stop them. God willing, I promise the workers and other employees and the weak classes that Iran will provide you with jobs, Islam will provide you with prosperity, Islam will build your homes.

Islam is more concerned about the needy than others. I wish success for all Muslims on this festive day, the day of victory for our nation. I hope Islamic nations will unite and cut off the hands of satans from the countries.

[*Source: Tehran Domestic Service in Persian, translated in Foreign Broadcast Information Service, Daily Report, Middle East & North Africa, April 2, 1979.*]

Document 8. American Embassy Tehran, Telegram, L. Bruce Laingen for the Secretary of State, "Shah's Desire to Reside in the US," SECRET, July 28, 1979

Since the collapse of the Shah's regime, the Carter administration has tried almost desperately to develop ties with Iran's new leaders. Their hope is to recreate something of the old strategic relationship with one of the United States' most important regional allies in the battle against Communism. Numerous cables recovered from the embassy when it was overtaken in November 1979 show repeated attempts by diplomats to assure wary Iranian officials that Washington is ready to accept the existence of the Islamic Republic and cooperate – this remains a core requirement of Iranian officials.

Here, Chargé d'Affaires Bruce Laingen gives an excellent review of where the relationship with the Provisional Government of Iran (PGOI) stands, sprinkled with perhaps some wishful thinking. But the main thrust of this cable relates to the circumstances of the Shah, who still figures in the saga, even though he is no longer in the country. Carter continues to face political heat at home for his supposedly poor handling of the monarch. Now, Mohammad Reza is facing the need for cancer treatment and his highly placed friends are pressing hard for his admittance into the US.

The White House and State Department are keenly aware that this could pose a threat to American personnel in Tehran. Already, in February, leftists occupied the embassy grounds. Responding to an unusual, direct request from the secretary of state for his "personal and private evaluation" of the situation, Laingen warns that if the Shah enters the USA within the next two to three months it would be "seriously prejudicial to our interests and to the security of Americans in Iran." Although he adds that things could change, the risks are clear. In late October, Carter makes the fateful decision to admit the Shah. Within days, the embassy is overrun, ushering in the darkest period in US–Iran relations.

....

1. Your message asks for my personal and private evaluation of the effect, on the safety of Americans in Iran and on our relations with the government of Iran, of the Shah being allowed to establish residence in the United States.

2. A judgment on that issue must inevitably be (and remain) speculative, clouded by the enormous uncertainties of the current Iranian scene – where there has been almost no progress to date toward resolution of the ultimate power structure. Subject to that reservation, I conclude that for the Shah to take up residence in the U.S. in the immediate future, by which I mean the next 2–3 months, would continue as before to be seriously prejudicial to our interests and to

the security of Americans in Iran. On the other hand, I believe that this situation could begin to change within that time period to make the risks manageable by late fall. Even that judgment, I must confess, is inevitably speculative and presupposes a good deal of good fortune for all concerned. My rationale follows.

3. I believe the next 2-3 months present the wrong time period for two basic reasons: first, the high degree of frustration (and thus the potential for a search for scapegoats) in the current Iranian political scene and, second, the still sensitive nature of our bilateral relationship.

4. Iran today remains politically adrift, its "government" under Bazargan still subject to the whims and ultimate control of the Ayatollah and his entourage at Qom. Day-to-day decision making is diffused, exercised more often than not by revolutionary groups and individuals scattered in and out of the formal administrative apparatus of government. There is growing popular frustration over the fact that the revolution has not changed things very much in Iran; indeed for many segments of the population, conditions are worse than they were before.

5. In this atmosphere, we remain the convenient scapegoat, to the point where Khomeini this past week targeted us as somehow behind the burning of harvests in the fields in certain parts of Iran. For us now to give refuge to the Shah would almost certainly trigger demonstrations against our embassy. With luck, they may stop at that, without a physical assault of the kind we experienced last February. But there could be no assurance of that, since Iran's regular military police forces remain largely demoralized and cannot yet be relied on to apply the force that might be needed to prevent violence against us. Indeed the government here has yet to find the strength or means to replace with a uniformed force the irregular guerilla force assigned by Khomeini to "guard" our compound since last February. The possibility of individual or group terrorist action against our chancery and personnel would of course also be greater were the Shah to come to the U.S. now, though that is a possibility that already exists.

6. Nor is our bilateral relationship yet of the mutual confidence
   and substance easily to weather a gesture of this kind toward
   the Shah. I think we are making progress in removing at least
   some of what has been a deeply felt suspicion among
   revolutionary Iranians that we have not yet accepted the new
   realities in Iran and that we are conniving with the Shah,
   Zionism, or with Savakis to undermine the revolution. But it is
   slow going, and we doubt very much that our credentials have
   been enhanced much at all as yet with Khomeini. Granting asylum
   to the Shah now would negate much that we have achieved to date,
   and I would not exclude a repeat in some fashion, dictated by
   Khomeini, of a knee-jerk type of policy action against us as
   demonstrated at the time of the [Sen.] Javits resolution.
7. What I am saying is that we need some added cushion on both
   fronts - on the internal Iranian scene and in our bilateral
   relations - before we accept whatever risks there may be for
   our interests in doing what I believe we eventually should
   do - allow the Shah refuge in the U.S.
8. The next 2-3 months are crucial and possibly hopeful in both
   respects. Internally, Bazargan is making a new and stronger
   effort to get Khomeini to transfer to his provisional
   government some of the authority now exercised by the
   revolutionary and [sic] courts and by the loose hierarchy of
   revolutionary committees that stretch to the street level.
   Growing problems with the Kurds and the Arab minority in
   Kuzistan seem to be reminding at least some of the
   revolutionary elements that steps must be taken to restore the
   status of the military in terms of both authority and material
   [sic] . But the real key to strengthened governmental
   authority and control lies in the successful carrying out of
   the electoral process (a kind of constituent assembly is to be
   elected August 3) which is supposed to result in a
   constitutionally endowed government in power by autumn.
9. It is of utmost importance, in my view, that we not inject
   ourselves in that process by any premature gesture toward
   the Shah, with all the suspicions about our attitudes and
   about USG interferance [sic] that this could arouse and the
   the [sic] opportunity it could provide for those
   revolutionary hotheads who would probably like nothing
   better than a chance to frustrate the political timetable
   and take a crack at us at the same time.

10. Similarly, I believe it important that we not burden our still thin bilateral relationship with the revolutionary leadership here until it has gained added substance and depth. Again there is promise. Despite continued problems on many issues between us, we have sensed in recent weeks a growing appreciation, at least within the Bazargan government, of the importance of a better U.S. relationship. Last week's congressional approval (in the DOD [Department of Defense] supplemental) of funds to purchase the four Spruance destroyers originally destined for Iran has given us and the Iranians the fleixibility [sic] to begin allowing the Iranians access to more urgently needed spares for their air force and other military forces. This will help remove lingering suspicions in the Bazargan government that we have had ulterior political motives in holding back on such shipments.

11. Assuming that this more hopeful trend in our bilaterial [sic] relationship continues and deepens, and assuming also that the constitutional timetable here results in a somewhat stronger government in place by autumn, with enhanced authority over Iran's security forces, the risks in a gesture on our part toward the Shah could be much more manageable. I would therefore hope that we could delay any final decision until we see how things develop over the next 60-90 days. It would help measurably, in my view, if during that same time period we were able to name an ambassador, an act that in itself will be seen as a vote of confidence in the new realities in Iran.

12. The judgment described above would of course differ if the Shah were publicly to renounce his claim and that of his heirs to the throne before coming to the U.S. Such action on his part would substantially lessen the risks to our interests. (I confess, however, to finding it hard to imagine his taking such action in the short term future). On the other hand, I do not see that a public statement by the Shah simply foreswearing political activities of any sort would have much impact. It would scarcely be credible here.

Laingen

[Source: Department of State declassification release.]

Document 9. Muslim Students Following the Line of the Imam, "Communiqué No. 1," UNCLASSIFIED, November 4, 1979

It is almost impossible to overstate the significance of the Iran hostage crisis as a defining moment in US–Iran relations. For many Americans, the crisis is their first introduction to Iran, and the images of weapons-brandishing Iranians parading blindfolded American citizens before the world that appear on the evening news every day for months engender a deepening feeling of national humiliation.

The crisis explodes on November 4, 1979, when a large group of mostly students from universities around Tehran overruns the American Embassy grounds in the center of the capital and begins to round up diplomats and other staff who are caught by surprise. The architects of the takeover call themselves "Muslim Students Following the Line of the Imam" – the Imam being an honorific for Ayatollah Khomeini. They are true believers in the revolution, and their anger against the "world-devouring America" and Israel, among others, is apparent in their first communiqué below. According to their spokeswoman, Massoumeh Ebtekar, they are particularly motivated by the legacy of the 1953 coup, which removed Prime Minister Mohammad Mosaddeq with the support of US and British intelligence. Their fear following the Shah's admittance to the United States reportedly for medical treatment is that Washington is plotting a new coup against the Islamic Republic.

The hostage saga has monumental implications for Iran's domestic politics and international standing. The evidence suggests that Khomeini was not involved in the planning or decision to storm the embassy. But after the students take the initiative, he quickly lends his support and eventually uses the event to consolidate his own position and further marginalize moderate political elements. The crisis will also prove the final straw for the Provisional Government and forces Prime Minister Mehdi Bazargan, a moderate voice and advocate for cooperation with the USA, to step down days later with his entire cabinet. The window for a positive relationship between the United States and Iran has now shut for the foreseeable future.

Ebtekar, who lived for several years as a child outside Philadelphia and speaks in American-accented English, is derisively called the Iranian Tokyo Rose by some American officials. Over time, she and several of her colleagues appear to rethink the advisability of the embassy seizure, but many still insist it was justified at the time. (A State Department analysis while the crisis was still going on noted that for some Iranians the act was "the result of 35 years of pent-up moral outrage" and not an issue of international law.)[16] *Ebtekar eventually becomes a vice president in the reform-oriented Khatami government.*

....

In the Name of God, the Merciful, the Compassionate.

Communiqué No. 1

It is incumbent upon students (secondary school, university and theology) to forcefully expand their attacks against America and Israel, so that America will be forced to return the criminal, deposed shah.

[Excerpt from the Imam's message on the occasion of the thirteenth of Aban.]

The Islamic Revolution of Iran represents a new achievement in the ongoing struggle between the peoples and the oppressive superpowers. It has kindled flames of hope in the hearts of the enchained nations and has set an example and created a legend of self-reliance and ideological steadfastness for a nation contending with imperialism. This was in reality a conquest over the curse of blindness that the superpowers had imposed so that even the intellectuals of the oppressed world could not conceive of any other freedom than under the benediction of another superpower.

Iran's revolution has undermined the political, economic and strategic hegemony of America in the region.

The world-devouring America which has exploited the vital resources of the nations for years, is now indulging in new, spiteful attempts to regain and secure its interests. These include the candidacy of Egypt as a new gendarme for the region, recruitment of military stooges in South Korea or the likes of the criminal Saad Haddad in South Lebanon, the heavy assaults and attacks of Israel and numerous plots against the Iranian Revolution within and outside of the country.

We Muslim students, followers of Imam Khomeini, have occupied the espionage embassy of America in protest against the ploys of the imperialists and the Zionists. We announce our protest to the world; a protest against America for granting asylum and employing the criminal shah while it has its hands in the blood of tens of thousands of women and men in this country.

We protest against America for creating a malignant atmosphere of biased and monopolized propaganda, and for supporting and recruiting counterrevolutionary agents against the Islamic Revolution of Iran; for its inhumane instigation and plotting in various regions of the country and its infiltration of the executive branches of the government.

And, finally, for its undermining and destructive role in the face of the struggle of the peoples for freedom from the chains of imperialism, wherein thousands of revolutionary and faithful humans have been slaughtered.

Muslim Students Following the Line of the Imam

[*Source: Massoumeh Ebtekar,* Takeover in Tehran: The Inside Story of the 1979 US Embassy Capture, *as told to Fred A. Reed (Vancouver, TalonBooks, 2000), pp. 69–70.*]

Document 10. White House, Memorandum, Zbigniew Brzezinski for President Carter, "Black Room Report," TOP SECRET, November 20, 1979

The revolutionaries in 1979 consider it a given that the United States will stop at nothing to regain control over what used to be a pillar of its Middle East policy. They see the comings-and-goings of American diplomats from the embassy under the previous regime, their interactions with the Bazargan government, and finally the taking in of the Shah for medical treatment as clear evidence of their intention to do just that. While there is no sign that the USA ever decided to carry out a much-feared coup, Washington certainly considered the possibility.

In this uncensored memo, Zbigniew Brzezinski gives President Carter a rundown of what can candidly be called bare-knuckles options for retaliation against Iran for the embassy seizure. The "Black Room" was one name given to the deputy-level interagency group responsible for formulating proposals for covert action during the Carter administration. The president's initials and handwritten comments confirm he read it. The document warns darkly about the prospect of Iran's disintegration, civil war, and Soviet intervention and proposes a range of alternatives from working with local tribes and exile groups to set up a new government to "direct overt US intervention." He declares bluntly that "We are never going to be able to work with the Khomeini regime. We might as well recognize that fact."

In the end, Carter does not approve any of these courses of action, and in fact never manages to create a cohesive strategy for dealing with the Iranian revolution. But he considered these ideas to be serious options. This and similar once-classified records underscore the point that while both governments have frequently exaggerated the threats against them, with regrettable consequences, they also have occasionally had reasonable grounds for suspecting the worst.

....

Black Room Report

We have been examining the situation in Iran from the standpoint of influencing the course of political developments. These developments are likely to include one of the following:

- a hostile Islamic state or hostile leftist state – either supported by the USSR.
- disintegration of Iran with possible Soviet intervention in the north.

To influence events, there are several approaches which could be followed. Each involves an increasing level of U.S. commitment:

1. Contingency Planning. Let nature take its course and be prepared to weigh in at the appropriate moment by virtue of indirect contact with dissidents.
2. Destabilization. Propaganda and black operations intended to discredit Khomeini and breed dissent among him and his followers.
3. Contact Opposition. Direct U.S. contact with potential alternative leaders indicating support for their efforts. Expanded contacts with tribal elements, initially aimed at better intelligence collection.
4. Encourage/Organize Alternative. On political side, aim at a government-in-exile or creation of a political cadre which could move in quickly. On the tribal side, provide arms, support and coordinating mechanism for regional movements.

Several basic policy questions must be answered in considering our approach:

1. Are we prepared to accept a commitment to destabilize the situation in Iran and try to replace the present leadership? [*Note: In the left margin, Carter writes, "not yet."*]
   - It could be a protracted effort, and success is by no measure assured.
   - The commitment will tend to grow over time and to become increasingly visible.
   - This could weld the left and religious extremists together on a common anti-American theme.

   But
   - Friendly opposition forces are unlikely to act effectively without a clear signal from us.
   - Continuation of Khomeini's rule is likely to destroy the moderate elements in the political spectrum, leaving the left as the only credible alternative to religious fanaticism when Khomeini inevitably falls or passes from the scene.

2. If we make such a decision, what is our strategy? Should we focus our efforts on the regime in Tehran and attempt to replace the central government?
   - Tends to preserve territorial integrity and unity
   - Minimizes risks of Soviet (or Iraqi) dismemberment.

   But
   - Khomeini is strongest in Tehran - controls the streets.
   - Our assets are very limited there.

3. Alternatively, should we <u>focus</u> our efforts on the periphery to build up an alternative government?
   - Tribal opposition is real and could undermine Khomeini authority.
   - The oilfields are the possible prize. We would maximize our chances of holding the oil in the event of complete collapse or Soviet intervention.

   But
   - The risk of civil war and complete disintegration is serious.
   - The danger of Soviet intervention in the north is increased. This is likely to be a partition option.

What <u>assets</u> do we have?

- Egypt should be willing to cooperate with us for broadcasts and possibly other operational assistance. Iraq may be willing to work with us in certain areas. Saudis and Gulf states possible allies.
- Some key figures inside Iran may be willing to cooperate (Admiral Madani, Governor of the oil region, Ayatollah Shariat-Madari).
- We have good contact with some of the tribes, and this could be expanded.
- Exile groups are begging for a signal from us. There are some good people (Amini, Bakhtiar), outside Iran that can have an impact there, but they would need a lot of help to become a significant factor.
- Ultimately, direct overt U.S. intervention could be required. <u>The extent of our commitment should be no greater than our willingness to play it out to the end.</u> This is particularly important the more we involve the Saudis and Egyptians.
- The Iranian military at present belongs to no one. Although our capability to swing it to our support is limited, neutralizing it is a realistic objective.

Our liabilities

- Khomeini is viewed as a saint by much of the Iranian population and the embodiment of the national will. Opposing him directly may only strengthen his appeal. He is ruthless and thrives on confrontation.
- Khomeini controls Tehran and the streets. It is hard to visualize any leader or organization taking him on his own turf.
- There is no obvious alternative leader. Most have been tainted by association with the Shah. This is particularly true of the exiled military.

Three alternative assessments:

1. The only way to find out how much strength Khomeini really has is to test it. That means we have to take some action, e.g. mounting a propaganda/disinformation effort, probing weak spots in the military and political structure, and increasing our level of contacts with tribal elements and

exiles. We are never going to be able to work with the Khomeini regime. We might as well recognize that fact and begin a systematic effort to build an alternative infrastructure. Letting nature take its course in fact means abandoning the field to the left as the only viable alternative. The longer Khomeini remains in power, the more tempting it will be for the moderates to move to the left or be crushed. A center coalition will emerge only if we encourage and support it.

2. Although we do not like Khomeini, we lack the assets to bring him down. By opposing him directly, we play into his hands and strengthen his appeal. Khomeini is his own worst enemy. Left to his own devices, he will destroy himself. We should prepare for that event and use our covert assets to urge it along. But we should not get ourselves committed to his overthrow. We will probably not be able to bring it off, and the commitment is open-ended. The Iranian revolution was a true expression of deep-seated national will, and the anti-Americanism we are seeing is a true expression of national outrage at U.S. actions over the past 26 years. To support the overthrow of Khomeini will be seen in Iran as an attempted replay of 1953 and the return of the Shah. Such a move opposes the fundamental trend of events and will foreclose any future cooperation.

3. We are not in control of events, and we must prepare for the worst. The oil fields are what count in the final analysis. We should focus our attention on the south and prepare to hold it no matter what. That is where our best assets are located, and we should play from strength.

Our Choices:

Actions

- Destabilize the current situation – this can be done without showing the American hand and could contribute to undermining Khomeini and the emergence of more moderate leadership but equally could hasten the advent of a more radical leftist regime.
- Increase contacts with dissidents. To be more effective to our current contacts, this would have to involve some financial support. Our hand would begin to show.
- Support for tribal elements.

Strategy

- Focus on developments in Tehran.
- Focus on tribal support with emphasis on securing a base in the oil producing region in the south.

> [Note: President Carter handwrites:]
>> *Be extremely cautious about U.S. action for now, but assess options within CIA. Let them give me analysis of all potential Anti-Khomeini elements.*
>> *J*

> [*Source: Jimmy Carter Library, Zbigniew Brzezinski Collection, Box 38, Serial Xs – Sensitive, 3/79-12/79.*]

Document 11. Islamic Republic of Iran, Constitution of the Islamic Republic, UNCLASSIFIED, approved by plebiscite December 3, 1979

After the founding of the Islamic Republic in spring 1979, the next step of forging a constitution begins. The process itself contributes to shaping the new system. Initially, more moderate officials within the Provisional Government produce a draft modeled extensively on the document created during the Constitutional Revolution of 1905–1911, the last great popular political movement in the country.[17] *But some of Khomeini's fundamentalist advisors, notably Ayatollah Mohammad Beheshti, persuade him of the need to recast it extensively.*

An Assembly of Experts, which will remain a significant institution in the IRI, is formed to draft a new version. The Assembly is dominated by the Islamic Republican Party. The final document is a first-of-its-kind in that it enshrines the controversial concept of political rule by a supreme religious figure (velayat-e faqih). That notion does not exist in orthodox Shiism, which shuns clerical involvement in politics, but Khomeini has been developing the idea and begins to express it more openly in the months prior to the revolution. Article 5 of the constitution spells out the qualifications of the faqih, which everyone realizes only Khomeini has the stature to fulfill. Other articles define the new ruler's powers, which amount to virtually total control over the government and the military with no checks on his authority. Still others ensure a central role in government for the clergy and establish key institutions like the Guardian Council.

The idea of velayat-e faqih *is not without its critics, not only from the moderate and left secular wings but from the traditional* ulama, *including some of very high rank. In the turbulent atmosphere of fall 1979, however, there is little else to unify them, and they are unable to coalesce around a figure of sufficient standing to challenge Khomeini.*

While the national debate rolls on, events once again intervene to the benefit of the hardliners. When the US Embassy is overrun in early November it effectively transforms Iran's political arena. In the newly radicalized environment, anyone criticizing the takeover or indeed any position promoted by the Khomeinists risks allegations of colluding with the enemy. Although it will take years for the Islamists to assert undisputed control over the country, as a result of these developments they have managed to strengthen the institutional foundations of their rule and demonstrate their political ascendancy.

In the years ahead, hardliners (sometimes labeled "principlists") will regularly invoke tenets of the constitution – ending foreign domination, protecting the weak against the arrogant, forbidding foreign control over a country's natural resources – to justify their uncompromising methods. This helps to explain their zeal and the difficulties faced by more progressive forces trying to push their agendas – opening up to the West, for example – because they are constantly in the position of seeming to oppose the founding principles of the revolution.

....

In the name of God, the compassionate, the merciful.
   [...]

Article 1:

The Government of Iran is an Islamic Republic, endorsed by the Iranian nation by an affirmative vote of 98.2 percent of the majority of eligible voters, in a referendum held on the 10th and 11th of Farvardin, of the year 1358 Hijri Shamsi [solar year], coinciding with 1st and 2d of Jamadi-ol-Avval, of the year 1399 Hijri Qamari [lunar year] based on its ancient belief in the administration of truth and justice of the Koran, following its victorious Islamic Revolution, under the leadership of the high exalted religious authority [*marja-e taqlid*], the Great Ayatollah Imam Khomeini.
   [...]

Article 5:

During the absence of the Glorious Lord of the Age [the missing 12th imam of the Shiite sect], may God grant him relief, he will be represented in the Islamic Republic of Iran as religious leader and imam of the people by an honest, virtuous, well-informed, courageous, efficient administrator and religious jurist, enjoying the confidence of the majority of the people as a leader. Should there be no jurist endowed with such qualifications, enjoying the confidence of the majority of the people, his role will be undertaken by a leader or council of leaders, consisting of religious jurists meeting the requirements mentioned above, according to Principle 107.

[...]

Article 107:

Whenever one of the jurists who fulfills the conditions mentioned in Principle 5 of the law is recognized by a decisive majority of the people for leadership and has been accepted - as is the case with the Great Ayatollah Imam Khomeini's high calling to the leadership of the revolution - then this leader will have charge of governing and all the responsibilities arising from it. Otherwise, experts elected by the people from all those qualified for leadership will be investigated and evaluated. Whenever a candidate who has outstanding characteristics for leadership is found, he will be introduced to the people as a leader. Otherwise, 3 or 5 candidates who fill the conditions for leadership will be appointed members of the Leadership Council and introduced to the people.

[...]

Article 152:

The foreign policy of the Islamic Republic of Iran is founded on the basis of ending any type of domination, safeguarding the complete independence and integrity of the territory, defending the rights of all Muslims, practicing nonalignment with respect to the dominating powers and maintaining mutual peaceful relationships with nonbelligerent nations.

Article 153:

Any type of agreement that allows a foreign power to dominate the natural resources, with the economic, cultural, military and other affairs of the country is forbidden.

Article 154:

The Islamic Republic of Iran considers its goal to be the happiness of human beings in all human societies. It recognizes the independence, freedom and rule of right and justice for all people of the world. Therefore, while practicing complete self-restraint from any kind of influence in the internal affairs of other nations, it will protect the struggles of the weak against the arrogant, in any part of the world.

[...]

[*Source: Kayhan, November 17, 1979, No. 10858, pp. 1–4 translated by Foreign Broadcast Information Service; reproduced in Rouhollah K. Ramazani, "Constitution of the Islamic Republic of Iran," Middle East Journal, Spring, 1980, Vol. 34, No. 2, pp. 181–204.*]

Document 12. White House, Memorandum, Zbigniew Brzezinski for President Carter, "Reflections on Soviet Intervention in Afghanistan," SECRET, December 26, 1979

The year 1979 has been a nightmare for US standing in the world – between the revolutions in Iran and Nicaragua and other developments that give the impression of American influence dramatically on the wane. Perhaps the most ominous of these events is the Soviet Union's invasion of Afghanistan, an act that seems to confirm the West's deep-seated fear of Moscow's aggressive intentions. Only after the collapse of the Soviet Union in the early 1990s when historians gain access to Politburo records does the world discover that in fact the Kremlin was largely acting out of defensive concerns rather than naked ambition. But at the time, the Afghanistan invasion terrifies American strategists in particular who see it as proof of Russia's menacing historical quest for the warm waters of the Persian Gulf.

One day after the Christmas assault, Brzezinski, ever the Cold Warrior, underscores for President Carter in a personal memo the "extremely grave challenge" he sees "both internationally and domestically." One of the main implications of the Soviet move involves Iran – a reminder that the recent revolution has not happened in a geostrategic vacuum and that US policy toward Iran will inevitably take account of all events in the surrounding region.

This will not be the last time Afghanistan comes into play in the US–Iran relationship. Although Brzezinski does not explicitly say so here, the crisis to Iran's east actually creates some common ground between Washington and Tehran. The Soviets, and later the Taliban, represent a mutual enemy for the Islamic Republic and United States to fight together.

··

Memorandum for: The President
From: Zbigniew Brzezinski
Subject: Reflections on Soviet Intervention in
                Afghanistan

I will be sending you separately a proposed agenda for the NSC meeting on Friday, and it will focus on both Afghanistan and Iran. In the meantime, you are receiving today's SCC [Special Coordination Committee] minutes on both subjects. This memorandum is meant merely to provide some stimulus to your thinking on this subject.

As I mentioned to you a week or so ago, we are now facing a regional crisis. Both Iran and Afghanistan are in turmoil, and Pakistan is both unstable internally and extremely apprehensive externally. If the Soviets succeed in Afghanistan, and if Pakistan acquiesces, the age-long dream of Moscow to have direct access to the Indian Ocean will have been fulfilled.

Historically, the British provided the barrier to that drive and Afghanistan was their buffer state. We assumed that role in 1945, but the Iranian crisis has led to the collapse of the balance of power in Southwest Asia, and it could produce Soviet presence right down on the edge of the Arabian and Oman Gulfs.

Accordingly, the Soviet intervention in Afghanistan poses for us an extremely grave challenge, both internationally and domestically. While it could become a Soviet Vietnam, the initial effects of the intervention are likely to be adverse for us for the following domestic and international reasons:

Domestic

A. The Soviet intervention is likely to stimulate calls for more immediate U.S. military action in Iran. Soviet "decisiveness" will be contrasted with our restraint, which will no longer be labeled as prudent but increasingly as timid;

B. At the same time, regional instability may make a resolution of the Iranian problem more difficult for us, and it could bring us into a head to head confrontation with the Soviets;

C. SALT is likely to be damaged, perhaps irreparably, because Soviet military aggressiveness will have been so naked;

D. More generally, our handling of Soviet affairs will be attacked by both the Right and the Left.

International

A. Pakistan, unless we somehow manage to project both confidence and power into the region, is likely to be intimidated, and it could eventually even acquiesce to some form of external Soviet domination.

B. With Iran destabilized, there will be no firm bulwark in Southwest Asia against the Soviet drive to the Indian Ocean;

C. The Chinese will certainly note that Soviet assertiveness in Afghanistan and in Cambodia is not effectively restrained by the United States.

Compensating Factors

There will be, to be sure, some compensating factors:

A. World public opinion may be outraged at the Soviet intervention. Certainly, Moslem countries will be concerned, and we might be in a position to exploit this.

B. There are already 300,000 refugees from Afghanistan in Pakistan and we will be in a position to indict the Soviets for causing massive human suffering. That figure will certainly grow, and Soviet-sponsored actions in Cambodia have already taken their toll as well.

C. There will be greater awareness among our allies for the need to do more for their own defense.

A Soviet Vietnam?

However, we should not be too sanguine about Afghanistan becoming a Soviet Vietnam:

A. The guerrillas are badly organized and poorly led;
B. They have no sanctuary, no organized army, and no central government – all of which North Vietnam had;
C. They have limited foreign support, in contrast to the enormous amount of arms that flowed to the Vietnamese from both the Soviet Union and China;
D. The Soviets are likely to act decisively, unlike the U.S., which pursued in Vietnam a policy of "inoculating" the enemy.

As a consequence, the Soviets might be able to assert themselves effectively, and in world politics nothing succeeds like success, whatever the moral aspects.

What is to be Done?

What follows are some preliminary thoughts, which need to be discussed more fully:

A. It is essential that Afghanistani resistance continues. This means more money as well as arms shipments to the rebels, and some technical advice;
B. To make the above possible we must both reassure Pakistan and encourage it to help the rebels. This will require a review of our policy toward Pakistan, more guarantees to it, more arms aid, and, alas, a decision that our security policy toward Pakistan cannot be dictated by our nonproliferation policy;
C. We should encourage the Chinese to help the rebels also;
D. We should concert with Islamic countries both in a propaganda campaign and in a covert action campaign to help the rebels;
E. We should inform the Soviets that their actions are placing SALT in jeopardy and that will also influence the substance of the [Harold] Brown visit to China, since the Chinese are doubtless going to be most concerned about implications for themselves of such Soviet assertiveness so close to their border. Unless we tell the Soviets directly and very clearly that our relations will suffer, I fear the Soviets will not take our "expressions of concern" very seriously, with the effect that our relations will suffer, without the Soviets ever having been confronted with the need to ask the question whether such local adventurism is worth the long-term damage to the U.S.-Soviet relationship;

F. Finally, we should consider taking Soviet actions in
Afghanistan to the UN as a threat to peace.

[*Source: Jimmy Carter Library, National Security Affairs, Brzezinski Material, Country File, Box 1, Afghanistan: 4–12/79.*]

Document 13. White House, Memorandum, Zbigniew Brzezinski for President Carter, "Getting the Hostages Free," TOP SECRET, April 10, 1980

After the storming of the embassy on November 4, 1979, and despite a number of other pressing issues – including the SALT II negotiations and Egyptian–Israeli peace talks – Carter makes freeing the hostages his top priority. The crisis preoccupies him and dominates US domestic politics. Innumerable policy proposals and tactical ideas cross his desk as part of the desperate attempt to find a resolution. One idea that comes up early on is a rescue attempt.

Ever a proponent of action, Brzezinski leads the push for the rescue operation. The most influential policy driver after the president himself, Brzezinski is often effective in his arguments and, to some critics, cutthroat in his approach. He jealously protects his proximity to Carter, acting as gatekeeper for most of the memo traffic addressed to the president. Here, he once again uses his advantage to make a direct case to Carter, and does so with unusual intensity.

His arguments, characteristically, take in larger strategic considerations and home in on the dire implications of not acting forcefully. Although he does not explicitly acknowledge it, some of the proposals amount to acts of war, such as mining Iran's harbors and bombing economic targets. His preferred course, however, is a rescue operation that he urges Carter not to dismiss, adding, "[t]here may never be a better moment." Carter's initial "C." at the top of the memo indicates he read it, and shortly thereafter he gives his approval.

The rescue operation, codenamed Operation Eagle Claw, turns out to be another disastrous decision for Carter. Blasted later by critics as ill-conceived and likely to fail from the start, the attempt ends in flames, killing eight US servicemen and injuring four others. Some Iranians believe the rescue was actually an overthrow attempt, which aggravates old fears, while Americans become even more embittered by images of Iranian officials appearing to celebrate over the wreckage and charred bodies.

Memorandum for: The President
From: Zbigniew Brzezinski
Subject: Getting the Hostages Free

The steps announced on Monday bought us some time and set a new process in motion. We need to think now about what we will do with the time we have gained and how we manage the coercive process.

Having taken these initial steps, we must be prepared to back them up or else risk a further loss of credibility. Iran does not believe that we will use force. The measures announced Monday have raised some doubts in their mind, but those doubts will soon be put to rest unless followed by additional measures.

Gradual escalation makes sense only if it is part of a strategy which has some promise of freeing the hostages. In my view there are two strategies available to us which could succeed:

1. A graduated application of force designed to persuade the Ayatollah and his followers that the continued holding of the hostages is self-defeating because it endangers Iran's wellbeing.
2. A rescue operation which deprives the Ayatollah of his bargaining leverage and punctures his aura of invincibility.

Both strategies entail significant risks and both are clouded by uncertainties. The following is an effort to examine systematically the risks and prospects.

Graduated Pressure

It is now clear that the diplomatic option is closed. The hostages are going to be held at least until the Majlis [parliament] convenes in June, and the prospects that a new Parliament dominated by the clerics will vote to release them on terms even marginally acceptable to us are very remote. In short, unless something is done to change the nature of the game, we must resign ourselves to the continued imprisonment of the hostages through the summer or even later.

Accordingly, a sharp increase in the pressures on Iran is one way of changing the environment. For example, we could undertake a deliberate program of increasingly severe steps every week or two weeks until the hostages are delivered. We might wish to inform the Iranians in advance of the schedule, or we could simply proceed step by step and let them draw their own conclusions. The following steps represent an illustrative program:

1. Sharply increased surveillance of shipping enroute to and from Iranian ports, combined with some overflights.
2. Declaration of a state of belligerency with Iran, coupled with a screening program of Iranian nationals in this country.
3. Technical interruption of power at a key point, e.g. the refinery complex in Abadan or cities such as Tehran or Qom.
4. Mining of harbors, leaving the Kharg Island facility untouched.
5. Closure of Kharg Island and/or occupation of the Tunbs and Abu Musa at the mouth of the Persian Gulf.
6. Selective air strikes on economic targets.

The objective of undertaking such a program would be to free the hostages before the program had to be carried to its logical conclusion of outright hostilities. However, once embarked, we would have to be prepared to persevere or else be perceived as paper tigers.

There are several difficulties with this strategy in terms of getting the hostages released. First, the deliberate progression of actions, even if fairly rapid in succession, will encourage the Iranians to seek some counterpressure to force us to stop. The recent threat by the militants to kill the hostages in the event of U.S. military action represents the kind of pressure tactics we can expect to encounter.

The second problem is the uncertainty of the political reaction inside Iran. The Ayatollah would attempt to use this program to arouse public opinion and to unite the nation against the common enemy. He might succeed, at least initially, but over time, as it became clear that the Ayatollah was unable to prevent the disruption of the internal economy and as the citizens begin to bear increasingly heavy penalties because of his obstinacy, the mood might begin to shift from defiance of the U.S. to discontent with the irresponsibility of their own leaders.

A third, very serious problem is the danger that our actions will inspire the tribal elements and other opposition forces to rise up against the clerical regime, with a complete breakdown of public order or even civil war. Not only would this situation endanger the hostages, but it would sorely tempt the Soviets to move across the border. The Soviets might cite our military actions as armed intervention, permitting them to invoke the 1921 Treaty. They might also be able to assemble a Tudeh-dominated government in Azerbaijan or even in Tehran in the name of protecting the Islamic Revolution. The Soviets have steadily been building their military capability near the Iranian border, and they have been accumulating political support by their support of Khomeini against the U.S. A small, disciplined group with outside resources can be very effective in conditions of anarchy and political collapse.

Finally, even if we succeed in pressuring Khomeini to strike a deal, we will have a problem in extricating ourselves from the confrontation. In short, though superficially cautious and controlled, it is a high-risk strategy which sets in motion forces that are dangerous and beyond our power to control.

Rescue Operation

The alternative is to force the issue to a resolution by unilaterally seizing the hostages away from the Iranians. From a political point of view, this course of action has enormous appeal. It is quick and almost totally under our control. A sudden strike with the sole objective of rescuing our people would be understood - and perhaps applauded - by regional states and allies alike. It would provide almost no opportunity or excuse for the Soviets to intervene. And it would embarrass the Ayatollah and show him and his regime to be inept.

The difficulties of making a decision turn almost entirely on questions of capability and risk. Can we get in and out before the Iranians can react militarily? Can we get all the hostages? Do we believe that we could act swiftly enough to avoid having many of the hostages executed? Can we avoid losing many of our own military people?

I am struck by the evaluation of some of those closest to the situation. My staff assistant, Gary Sick, who has been living with this issue day and night for the past five months, has personally and privately urged me in the strongest terms to adopt this course of action, and has proposed this memo. He has also informed me that the three best Persian-speaking officers in the Foreign Service have recently gone to Cy with the same recommendation. They all believe that the risks of continued incarceration or of military escalation are far greater than a surprise rescue operation. They are convinced that true surprise is possible and that penetration of the Embassy is a realistic prospect.

I find this argument persuasive. There may never be a better moment to undertake such an operation than the next few weeks. The security at the Embassy must have settled into a routine by now, and the Iranians are almost contemptuous in their certainty that rescue is not a feasible option. Even the U.S. press has totally accepted our explanation that such an operation is impossible. The Iranian military is in nearly total disarray and preoccupied with the Iraqi threat. The chance of maintaining true surprise is good, and with true surprise, our chances of a successful operation grow.

We have no risk-free options. Even the risks of inaction are considerable. No other option offers as many potential benefits or gives us as many opportunities to keep the timing and control in our own hands. We could even build in a little protection for any hostages who might not be freed by "arresting" some of the militants and bringing them back under kidnapping and even murder charges.

In my view, a carefully planned and boldly executed rescue operation represents the only realistic prospect that the hostages – any of them – will be freed in the foreseeable future. Our policy of restraint has won us well-deserved understanding throughout the world, but it has run out. This is the painful conclusion we must now face.

I understand that your preference is not to undertake a rescue except as a reaction to the killing of our hostages. But that is really tantamount to dismissing the rescue option altogether. Please consider the following: the lead time on any rescue operation is a minimum of eight days. If a hostage is killed, there will be an immediate outcry for retaliation; there will be mass hysteria; there will also be a heightened state of alert in Tehran and perhaps even additional killings. I very much doubt that we could afford to wait for days to undertake a rescue operation, and could be thus forced to retaliate, which would then further reduce the element of surprise which is so crucial to a successful rescue.

Post-Rescue

It is essential that we be ready to react to any post-rescue consequences. These would include threats to the lives of any hostages left behind, or to any prisoners taken in the operation, or to any Americans available in Tehran. In addition, we have to consider the need to react to any large-scale failure that could occur, and which could maximize the foregoing complications.

Accordingly, in addition to the rescue operation, we should be prepared to initiate almost immediately large-scale retaliatory strikes against key Iranian facilities. Upon the completion of the rescue operation, the Iranian government should be informed, and we could also make it known publicly, that the U.S. will initiate large-scale retaliatory action if any reprisals follow the rescue. If the rescue operation itself fails, we might want to initiate such retaliation in any case in order to reduce the negative consequences of the aborted undertaking. I believe that the U.S. public will be with us whatever happens.

Procedure

I would recommend that at some point soon you consult with your advisers on the above. If you decide to undertake the rescue, I would suggest that you inform your advisers that you have decided against it. Afterwards, a much smaller group could meet with you to initiate the actual plans and to monitor their execution through completion. I would think that such a small group would be confined to the Vice President, Vance, Brown, Jones, Turner, and myself, as well as perhaps Ham and Jody. At the very last minute, additional advisers could be brought in, but it would be essential to enforce iron discipline and minimum participation (on a need-to-know basis.)

Conclusion

The above recommendation is not easy to make. It is even more difficult for you to consider and accept. However, we have to think beyond the fate of the 50 Americans (and also some Iranians) and consider the deleterious effects of a protracted

stalemate, growing public frustration, and international
humiliation of the United States.

[*Source: Jimmy Carter Library, Zbigniew Brzezinski Collection,*
NSC Accomplishments Iran: 4/80–10/80.]

Document 14. Jimmy Carter, Annotated Diary Entries, UNCLASSIFIED, January 20, 1981

Jimmy Carter's final day in the White House is buffeted by more than the usual emotions for an outgoing president. The Iranian authorities, judging that the hostages are worth more to them as free men and women, finally agree to end the 444-day saga the same day. Remarkably, they delay the release so that it will not become final while Carter is still president, such is the depth of Khomeini's anger. These moving entries from Carter's diary tick off the final hours on January 20 as officials from several countries and more than a dozen banks labor to put the pieces in place. After so many months – and several last-minute hitches – it takes only a few seconds to transfer almost $8 billion to the agreed upon account. More steps will follow under the Algiers Accord signed by US and Iranian officials, albeit in different cities.

Carter, known as a micromanager in normal times, has been on overdrive for more than forty-eight hours straight, forgoing sleep as he pushes for a conclusion. His wife, Rosalynn, finally has to cajole him into getting a haircut and shave before changing into a rented morning suit for the inauguration. Elsewhere in his diary he describes incoming President Ronald Reagan as shockingly out of touch and seemingly uninterested in the details of the process, telling anecdotes on their way to the ceremony that are "remarkably pointless." The differences between the two men are stark.

Carter's understandable wistfulness as he witnesses Reagan's triumphant swearing in comes through in these brief excerpts. He believes that his relentless focus on bringing the hostages home somehow contributed to his electoral loss. But even though he does not have the gratification of making the formal announcement to the nation that the remaining fifty-two Americans are free – that honor falls to the new president – he declares that learning that the planes carrying the group are almost out of Iranian airspace is enough to turn a bleak day into "one of the happiest moments of my life."

January 20 – The final approval from Bank Markazi began coming to the 12 banks by telex at 2:00 a.m. and had to be absolutely clear and accurate.

[...]

2:23 Bill Miller[18] reports, "It looks good!" [In fact, it was garbled, but Bill didn't have the heart to tell me.]

3:05 Miller: "The test number is correct, but we'll have to correct the errors."

I decide: "Tell the banks to use the garbled text."

3:16 Miller: "The money is moving to London." (Cheers.)

3:40 Carswell[19]: "U.S. federal attorneys in Algiers refuse to sign the agreement."

I ask President [Anthony] Solomon of the Fed [Federal Reserve Bank] in New York to instruct the attorneys to sign. One of the attorneys in Algiers says that he is fainting and cannot discuss the situation further. Again I tell Solomon, "Have them sign the agreement." Solomon: "We can sign with some minor amendments."

4:35 Miller: "The money [from private banks] is in." A total of $7.977 billion has to be transferred from us to the Algerians – the last step before the hostages can be released.

4:38 Christopher[20]: "Algeria will not accept any amendments unless they are first approved by Iran." I participate in a conference call and finally convince everyone that the total package is adequate.

5:00 Solomon to his attorneys: "Sign it!"

5:20 Miller: "It only took two seconds to transfer the money."

6:05 From Tehran control tower: "Line up Flight 133" [containing our hostages].

6:35 Christopher: "The bank of England has certified that they hold $7.977 billion the correct amount."

6:47 I place a call to Governor Reagan to give him the good news and am informed that he prefers not to be disturbed.

7:35 Rosalynn [Carter] comes with a razor and a barber. She says, "Jimmy, you have forgotten to shave, and you need a haircut." The barber cuts my hair while I'm on the phone.

7:55 I get the word from Tehran airport, "Flight 133 ready for takeoff!" We all knew that this flight was three airplanes: two 727s and the other to serve as a backup or possible decoy that would carry home the Algerian medical team.

8:28 From Operations Center: "The planes are now at the end of the runway. One Iranian F-4 is active. May be escort."

10:45 Rosalynn: "Jimmy, the Reagans will be here in fifteen minutes. You will have to put on your morning clothes and greet them."

I looked in the mirror as I put on the rental clothes, and wondered if I had aged so much as president or whether I was just exhausted.[21]

I made arrangements for the Secret Service to keep me informed on the way to the inaugural ceremonies. Reagan seemed somewhat disconcerted that no one was in the reviewing stands and there were a large number of ERA [Equal Rights Amendment] banners. He told a series of anecdotes that were remarkably pointless. [...]

I consider him to be affable and a decent man, remarkably old in his attitudes. His life seems to be governed by a few anecdotes and vignettes that he has memorized. He doesn't seem to listen when anybody talks to him. He'll have my support and my sympathy when he's president. It's a tough job and I think he'll have to rely heavily on his advisors and subordinates to make the ultimate policy decisions.

On the inaugural platform, my feelings were of regret that I had lost the election but a sense of relief to be free of the responsibilities for a while. Persistent, though, was my concern that at the last minute the hostages might not be released. I watched the ceremonies as a somewhat detached spectator, without any emotional feelings. I thought the speech was remarkably hackneyed, nothing new and just a collection of campaign material. I was glancing back at the Secret Service agent when the MC said, "Will the president and first lady please come forward." I had an involuntary inclination to stand up with Rosalynn, but I realized he was talking about the Reagans.

As we passed the agent I was informed that all the hostage planes were on the way to the Turkish border. This was one of the happiest moments of my life and colored the entire day – indeed the week – making it enjoyable.

[*Source:* Jimmy Carter, White House Diary *(New York: Picador, paperback, 2011),* pp. 511–513.]

Questions for further discussion

- Why did the Iranian revolution come as such a shock to the West and United States?
- What were the historical roots of the revolution?
- How did the November 1979 seizure of the US Embassy in Tehran come about?
- What were the main effects of the hostage saga on Iranian politics, Iran's global standing, American presidential politics, and the two countries' views of each other?
- How did President Carter's foreign policy change in the wake of events in 1979 – from the revolution to the hostage crisis to the Soviet invasion of Afghanistan?

Notes

1. For example, in July 1980 the Soviet leadership received a request from Tudeh leader Nureddin Kianuri for "pistols, automatic weapons, hand-held anti-tank rocket launchers, and grenades," but KGB chief Yuri Andropov and Central Committee International Department head Boris Ponomarev politely demurred: "we think it possible to study the request of Comrade Kianuri and return to consider it somewhat later." Yuri Andropov and Boris Ponomarev, memorandum, "Concerning the request of Cde. Kianuri, First Secretary of the CC of the People's Party of Iran," July 6, 1980. (Russian State Archive of Contemporary History [RGANI], Fond 89, Opis 32, Reel 1.1000, File 10 of "Guide to the Archives of the Soviet Communist Party and Soviet State Microfilm Collection, 1903–1992," Hoover Institution Archives; see also Wilson Center Digital Archive, Record ID 134568.)
2. US diplomats in Tehran were naturally more attuned to developments, at least to the point of acknowledging how little information they had. As early as 1973, Ambassador Richard Helms complained to his staff: "[Iran] is a black hole. We don't know the society. We have no appreciation for what's going on beyond the Embassy walls." Quoted by State Department official Henry Precht in "Interview with Charles Naas," Association for Diplomatic Studies and Training Foreign Affairs Oral History Project, Library of Congress, initial interview date October 8, 1988.
3. Gary Sick, memorandum to Zbigniew Brzezinski, "Iran Meetings," November 5, 1980.
4. George Ball testimony in "Relations in a Multipolar World," Senate Foreign Relations Committee hearings, November 6, 1991, p. 29.

5. Gary Sick comment at the conference "The Intervention in Afghanistan and the Fall of Détente," hosted by the Norwegian Nobel Institute, Lysebu, Norway, September 17–20, 1995, p. 50; part of the National Security Archive's Carter-Brezhnev Project, https://nsarchive2.gwu.edu/carterbrezhnev/fall_of_detente_intro.html.

6. Cyrus Vance, *Hard Choices: Critical Years in America's Foreign Policy* (New York: Simon & Schuster, 1983), pp. 334–341. The purpose of Huyser's mission is still hotly debated. Most of his daily reports to the Pentagon have been declassified, however, and show that he believed "Option C," a military coup to support a civilian government acceptable to Washington, was a viable option. Vance and Sullivan, among others, opposed Brzezinski and Brown, who sided with Huyser. Fresh intelligence soon indicated that Huyser's assessments were overly optimistic. For a well-documented account, see Edward C. Keefer, *Harold Brown: Offsetting the Soviet Military Challenge, 1977-1981*, Secretaries of Defense Historical Series, Erin R. Mahan, General Editor, Historical Office, Office of the Secretary of Defense (Washington, DC, 2017), pp. 291–297.

7. The mix of reasons included not just an underestimation of popular support for the clergy but a belief that mullahs could not run a complex national government. (This harkened back to the British belief about Iran's incapacity to manage its oil industry.) See, for example, Harold Saunders, Briefing Memorandum for the Secretary, "Policy towards Iran," September 5, 1979; also, Gary Sick, *All Fall Down: America's Tragic Encounter with Iran* (New York: Random House, 1985), p. 138.

8. See Soviet/Russian and American declassified materials and transcript from the Lysebu conference (see note 5 above).

9. "Address by President Carter on the State of the Union before a Joint Session of Congress," *Public Papers of the Presidents of the United States: James E. Carter, Jr: 1980*, Book I, pp. 194–200.

10. Zbigniew Brzezinski, memorandum to the President, "Iran," November 3, 1978.

11. William H. Sullivan, *Mission to Iran* (New York: W.W. Norton, Inc., 1981), pp. 201–204.

12. See note 6 above.

13. The two clandestine TACKSMAN monitoring stations in Iran were the CIA's most important overseas facilities for tracking Soviet missile testing beginning in the 1950s, and the Shah's willingness to accommodate them was a further reason why he was such a valuable Cold War ally.

14. Amembassy Tehran, Cable, William Sullivan for the Secretary, SECRET/EYES ONLY, "USG Policy Guidance," January 10, 1979.

15. Quoted in Sick, *All Fall Down*, p. 145.

16. State Department, Ronald Spiers to Secretary of State Edmund Muskie, "The Hostages and Iranian Domestic Politics," May 8, 1980, in Foreign Relations of the United States, 1977–1980, Volume XI, Part I, *Iran: Hostage Crisis, November 1979-September 1980*, pp. 771–772.

17. The Constitutional Revolution of 1905–1911 was a popular uprising that imposed significant limits on the monarchy through a constitution that among other things provided for the country's first parliament, or Majlis, and required that a government cabinet be formed subject to Majlis approval. (See Abbas Amanat, *Iran: A Modern History* [New Haven: Yale University Press, 2017], ch. 6.) Another useful source on the constitution is Mohsen M. Milani, *The Making of Iran's Islamic Revolution: From Monarchy to Islamic Republic* (Boulder: Westview Press, 2nd ed., 1994), pp. 154–162.

18. William G. Miller was a State Department official who had been in line to take over as ambassador to Iran in 1979.

19. Robert Carswell was deputy secretary of the Treasury and helped put together the financial deal that freed the hostages.

20. Warren Christopher was deputy secretary of state and signed the Algiers Accord ending the hostage crisis. He went on to become Bill Clinton's secretary of state in 1993.

21. Carter's annotation inserted in the published diary (not from 1981).

2

Turmoil in the Gulf: The Iran–Iraq War and the Spread of Radical Islam, 1980–1989

Introduction

The defining event of the 1980s in the Middle East was the Iran–Iraq War. Saddam Hussein's invasion of Khuzestan in September 1980 [Document 15] aimed to control the oil-rich province and weaken a long-standing adversary at a moment of perceived vulnerability. Baghdad's aggressive move alarmed the Carter administration, still in the throes of the hostage saga and worried about residual impacts – on captive Americans, access to oil, and Soviet designs on the region. To the surprise of many, President Ronald Reagan would continue Jimmy Carter's officially neutral stance, although the USA would soon "tilt" toward Iraq after Iran went on the offensive on the battlefield, and tensions would escalate between the two sides to the point of military conflict.

Reagan's inauguration in January 1981 coincided exactly with the release of the remaining fifty-two hostages from Tehran. That this was intentional on Iran's part showed the depth of their resentment. Khomeini and other Iranian leaders, the CIA reported as early as summer 1980, had resolved to "humiliate the US in general and the president [Carter] in particular" for buttressing the Shah and then refusing to turn him over to revolutionary justice.[1]

With the crisis settled, Reagan relegated the troublesome Islamic Republic to the policy margins – at least for the time being. The administration had other priorities, topped by its preoccupation with the Soviet Union. Moreover, few US officials could claim to fathom the nature of radical Islam, much less devise a coherent approach to managing it. To be sure, there was genuine anger within the administration against the mullahs in Tehran and strong pressure from conservatives to retaliate. But military strikes were quickly ruled out and when Reagan authorized a quiet CIA-backed plan to subvert the regime, it quickly fizzled, reinforcing the growing consensus that Khomeini would not be easy to topple.[2]

This last point highlights an irony: Iranian hardliners have been wrong to believe that regime change has been a consistent US policy objective; but they would not have been wrong to assume that Washington's rationales have not always been strictly ethical ones.

In mid-1981, Reagan administration strategists came to a surprising conclusion – that the United States would be better served by reaching out to Iran, if only to keep it out of the Soviet camp [Document 16]. As one option, the Senior Interagency Group, which was responsible for formulating policy proposals, contemplated supplying arms to the IRI at an appropriate point in the future.[3] The Joint Chiefs of Staff and CIA were opposed, but the idea would resurface and gain Reagan's approval during his second term.

In early 1982, Iranian forces gained the advantage on the battlefield and within months pushed Saddam's army out of the country. It was an astonishing achievement for a comparatively poorly armed and trained force whose senior officer corps had been purged for real and perceived disloyalty to the regime and whose American-made arsenal severely lacked for parts and maintenance. At the same time, the country's leadership labored to settle the political scene in the face of attacks by radical leftists and ethnic elements.[4] Internationally, Iran found itself almost entirely isolated as few governments condemned Iraq for its aggression, greatly rankling Iran's leaders.

Evidence of the impending Iranian invasion alarmed US strategists who decided to step in to save Iraq from outright defeat [Document 18]. There was no love lost for Saddam Hussein in Washington but the Islamic Republic was widely seen as the graver threat to American interests. For the rest of the war, the administration took steps – political, diplomatic, commercial, and most significantly military – to bolster Saddam. In July, a senior CIA officer traveled covertly to Baghdad to brief the Iraqis on Iran's order of battle, initiating a significant intelligence-sharing relationship that would later include guidance on targeting Iranian forces.[5] Despite being officially neutral, the USA did not object to other countries sending weapons to Baghdad and in 1983 the State Department instituted Operation Staunch to block world arms shipments to Tehran. (Washington was aware that at least since 1980 Israel had been covertly supplying arms to the Islamic Republic in hopes of extending a relationship begun under the Shah.) Most controversially, senior administration officials tolerated Iraq's use of chemical weapons in violation of international law.[6]

As the war dragged on, another arena of conflict between Islamic forces and the West emerged in Lebanon. In 1982, partially in response to Israel's invasion that summer, Tehran deployed some 1,000 members of the Islamic Revolutionary Guard Corps to the country as part of its perceived sacred duty to spread the revolution. Lebanon has a large Shiite population with close ties between its clerical leaders and Iran's *ulama*. The main long-term outcome of this venture was the formation of the militant group Hezbollah.

Hezbollah and its operational affiliates quickly became a factor in Lebanese and regional politics. In 1983, vehicle bombs destroyed the US Embassy (April) and Marine barracks (October), and later the embassy annex (September 1984). Hundreds of American servicemen and diplomats died. The barracks attack was the largest loss of American lives in a single strike since Iwo Jima. Like the Iran hostage crisis, US officials took the experience personally – especially considering many of the casualties were friends and colleagues – and it would inevitably color their views of Iran since Iran was believed to be behind the incidents.[7]

The following year, Islamic radicals adopted another tactic in earnest – hostage-taking. In coming years, dozens of Westerners disappeared off the streets of Beirut, including Americans. The main driver behind the kidnappings was the idea of setting up a swap for Lebanese members of the Al Dawa movement being held prisoner in Kuwait for an attack on the American and French embassies there in late 1983. Although Al Dawa and Hezbollah militants both had connections to Tehran, they were certainly capable of acting on their own without Iran's specific imprimatur.

Reagan became emotionally caught up in the slow-rolling hostage crisis. Freeing the Americans became an "obsession," aides revealed later. One of many approaches they employed during 1985–1986, at the president's behest, involved US officials and private middlemen making covert deals through Israel (later directly) to sell the Iranians weapons for the war in return for the release of captives from Lebanon [Documents 22–24].

The resulting Iran-Contra affair evolved into the American political scandal of the decade and served as a warning against risky clandestine dealings with the Islamic Republic. Ironically, the amateurishly conceived arms-for-hostages deals succeeded in establishing contacts with relatively senior Iranian government representatives, something that had not been achieved since the Carter period. The channel worked for a time despite the two governments being on opposing sides in the war with Iraq. This showed that it was more than theoretically possible for the two governments to interact despite their abiding differences. Once the scandal broke, however, both sides pulled back and hopes for diplomatic engagement receded.

During the next two years, the United States built up a large military presence in the Gulf, a development that sent shivers through official Washington because of the risk of uncontrolled escalation. These fears became more real in 1987 and 1988 when US warships escorting Kuwaiti oil tankers struck Iranian mines, eventually leading Reagan to order a forceful response [Document 25] in April 1988. Dubbed Operation Praying Mantis, it destroyed a sizable portion of Iran's navy in a single day. Somehow, the two governments managed to prevent tensions from spiraling into a wider conflict.

Worse was about to come, however. Less than three months later, in July, the USS *Vincennes*, a guided missile cruiser patrolling the southern Gulf, mistook a civilian Iranian airliner for a military fighter jet and launched a missile that destroyed the aircraft and tragically took 290 Iranian lives. Iran's leadership condemned it as a deliberate assault and yet another moral outrage – perhaps the worst to date – by the United States. Ultimately, the tragedy had another unexpected consequence. After consulting with his close advisors, Khomeini declared in July 1988 that Iran could not fight both Saddam Hussein and the United States and therefore decided to end the war [Document 26].

The 1980s caused horrific damage to Iran even while the chaos of the period helped the theocratic leadership consolidate its power by invoking existential foreign threats. Over the course of eight years, Iran and the United States hardened their mutual aversion. The Iranians – sometimes accurately, other times in error – accused the USA of variously encouraging Saddam's invasion, refusing to blame Iraq for the war, abetting its resort to chemical weapons, and targeting a civilian airliner. Washington in turn abhorred Iran's human wave tactics and use of child soldiers on the battlefield, its refusal to enter negotiations, its decision to become the aggressor in 1982, and its role (not always clearly established) in terrorist attacks across the region.

In June 1989, Ayatollah Khomeini died, leaving the Islamic Republic in the hands of a far less exalted figure and opening the way for a hotly contested internal reassessment of the country's future. A succession of US presidents would respond, as always, with a mix of wariness and optimism – and the inevitable misreading of signals.

Document 15. Director of Central Intelligence, Alert Memorandum, Stansfield Turner for the National Security Council, "Iran – Iraq," TOP SECRET, September 17, 1980

The 1980s are a period of enormous hardship for Iranians. The first decade of the Islamic Republic is characterized by eight years of horrific warfare and jarring political violence at home. The years of existential struggle also cement Iran's hardliners in their view of the country as isolated from the outside world and in particular convince them of US antagonism and malevolent intent.

The Iran–Iraq War takes most observers by surprise, despite a series of border incidents and other signs in prior months. This high-level memo from CIA Director Stansfield Turner to the president and his top advisors comes just five days before the invasion. Though details are redacted, the source (as confirmed by a former CIA officer present at the debriefing) is an émigré Iranian general named Gholam Ali Oveissi who has just come from Baghdad where he claims to have spoken to Saddam Hussein himself. After the invasion, Tehran quickly charges the USA with complicity, in part because of the virtual silence from Western governments about Saddam's clear act of aggression.

It may be tempting to conclude from this document that Washington could have raised the alarm publicly or possibly prevented the attack, but intelligence experts point out that previous warnings had not proven out, that the source provided few specifics as to the exact time and place, and that the USA had little influence with Saddam. While some prominent figures like Henry Kissinger and even National Security Advisor Zbigniew Brzezinski initially hoped the Iraqi invasion would put pressure on the Iranians to release the hostages, there is no evidence that President Carter knew specifically about, much less approved of, the attack. His priorities, according to the contemporary record, were the hostages' safety, regional stability, and keeping Persian Gulf oil flowing to the West.

....

Alert Memorandum

Memorandum for: National Security Council
Subject: Iran – Iraq

The intensification of border clashes between Iran and Iraq has reached a point where a serious conflict is now a distinct possibility. I believe the most immediate danger – should the hostilities widen – is the possibility of a disruption of Iraq's oil exports. The attached Alert Memorandum outlines this and other potential dangers of a major conflict between the two states.

[Signed]
Stansfield Turner

17 September 1980

Alert Memorandum[8]

Iran-Iraq Conflict

Border clashes between Iran and Iraq have escalated significantly since the beginning of September. Last weekend, Iraq apparently moved significant elements of an armored division to the central border area; Baghdad has occupied territory it claims should be returned under the 1975 Algiers Accord and threatened to seize more. [1 line redacted] suggest that major elements of two Iraqi mechanized divisions either are preparing to leave or have left their garrisons, possibly for the border area.

Both Baghdad and Tehran have been constrained from initiating a major conflict in the past by numerous political and economic factors, including the threat of superpower intervention, the proximity of their oil installations to the border, and the danger that war would exacerbate domestic political unrest. These factors continue to restrain both Iran and Iraq, but Iraq's willingness to seize and hold disputed territory and its military movements represent a qualitative change that increases the danger that clashes will escalate out of control or that either side's perception of the constraints will suddenly change.

If major hostilities between Iran and Iraq should occur, the US hostage crisis could be further complicated. Iran has long accused the United States of encouraging Iraqi aggression, and the militants holding the US hostages have threatened to kill them if Iraq launches a "full-scale" attack. Although Iranian propaganda cannot be accepted at face value, the threat to the hostages probably could be increased especially if Iran suffered a serious defeat.

In the event of major hostilities, Iraq is capable of occupying the Khuzestan oilfields. Iraq's close ties to Iranian dissidents provide the means to set up a puppet government. But, a major Iraqi offensive into Khuzestan would involve Iraq in a costly and protracted struggle with Iran. Iran, for its part, could disrupt Iraqi shipping in the Gulf.

Both Iraq and Iran have much of their oil infrastructure located near the border – two-thirds of Iraq's exports move through vulnerable Persian Gulf facilities – and these facilities would probably be damaged by fighting and sabotage if the conflict lasted more than a few days. Disruption to Iraq's oil exports would result in immediate renewed pressure on world oil prices. A prolonged cutoff of oil exports would have a severe impact on supply availability of crude oil per day, most of which is imported by Western Europe, Japan, and Brazil. The United States obtains only about 1-2 percent of its requirements for imported oil from Iraq. Iran currently exports about 800,000 barrels of crude oil and products per day; none goes to the United States.

An expanded conflict could also have a destabilizing impact on other Middle Eastern states. Iraq would seek to portray the conflict as one between Arabs and Persians in order to gain Arab backing. Iran might appeal, probably unsuccessfully, to Syria for support against their mutual enemy. Tehran would probably step up its appeals to the Shias in Iraq to revolt and might also urge the Shias in Saudi Arabia, Kuwait, Bahrain, and other Gulf countries to attack Iraqi and US interests.

The Soviets have long been concerned that military clashes between Iran and Iraq will damage their ties with both countries. They may also be worried that the United States could use intensification of the conflict to justify intervention in Iran or that Tehran would move to resolve its conflict with the United States in order to better confront Baghdad. Consequently, the Soviets probably consider their interests best served by the prevention of the outbreak of full-scale hostilities.

Should major hostilities occur, the Soviets might offer to act as a mediator and seek to arrange a ceasefire. If this effort fails, the Soviets might attempt to use their arms relationship with the Iraqis to persuade them to desist. The USSR, however, is unlikely to cut off arms. The consequence of limiting Iraqi arms supply would be to force Baghdad to search for alternative Western sources of arms and damage bilateral Soviet-Iraqi relations. If Iraq were to seek to occupy large parts of Iran – such as the oilfields – Soviet efforts to dissuade Baghdad would probably be even stronger, possibly including warnings that Iraqi occupation could lead to Soviet military intervention in Iran to protect the USSR's interests along the southern border.
    [Remainder of document redacted.]

[*Source: Central Intelligence Agency, CREST Database,*
CIA-RDP81B00401R000500050003-2.]

Document 16. White House, Draft National Security Decision Directive, "Policy toward Iran," SECRET, July 13, 1981

When Ronald Reagan takes office in January 1981, the common assumption is that he will hit back hard against Iran for the humiliation of the hostage crisis. Instead, he largely picks up where Carter leaves off, starting with implementation of the Algiers agreement that brings home the hostages. This draft presidential directive, written less than six months into Reagan's presidency, reflects a surprising consensus within the high-level Senior Interagency Group, which is responsible for presenting policy proposals to the president and his top advisors.

The document begins by indicating broad continuity with Carter's policy of ensuring the free flow of Gulf oil, keeping the Soviets at bay, and maintaining stability in the region. Among other assessments, the authors acknowledge America's inadequate intelligence capabilities in Iran. They accept the widely held view [see Document 17] that Iran is on the brink of "total anarchy" or "civil war," and resolve to reach out to groups "in and outside Iran" who "share the US interest" in Iran's "independence and territorial integrity."

Contrary to the Reagan administration's tough public stance, the SIG expresses a readiness to "initiate . . . an informal dialogue with key Iranian leaders," and even to consider, at an appropriate time, allowing allies to ship arms (as, in fact, Israel is currently doing unilaterally) to the Islamic Republic as a way to keep Tehran from turning toward Moscow. The Pentagon and CIA oppose the idea and an eventual presidential directive walks it back somewhat, but it will resurface – along with the notion of encouraging "moderates" within the regime – as a core piece of the Reagan administration's infamous arms-for-hostages deals a few years later.

....

Draft
   National Security Decision Directive

Policy toward Iran

The territorial integrity and sovereignty of an independent, albeit Islamic revolutionary Iran, is essential to our Southwest Asia security strategy which in turn will be bolstered by a strong U.S. global posture towards the Soviet Union. Our policy toward an independent Iran will be directed toward achieving the following objectives:

- ensure uninterrupted flow of Persian Gulf oil to world markets;
- prevent Soviet dominance of Iran;

- seek a stable balance of Arab and Iranian influence in the Gulf region and prevent a dominant role for either;
- discourage the export of the Iranian revolution or Iranian terrorism to other states in the area;
- promote actively Iranian cooperation with Pakistan to resist the Soviet presence in Afghanistan;
- mitigate the extreme anti-westernism of the Iranian revolution;
- encourage, to the limited extent feasible, forces in Iran favoring a more moderate government which would be less injurious to U.S. interests in the region;
- step up U.S. intelligence capabilities in Iran to develop a deeper understanding of the political dynamics of the country with an eye toward improving the U.S. ability to anticipate developments adversely affecting our interests;
- support the interests of U.S. claimants against Iran in a manner consistent with the foregoing objectives;
- allow for the eventual normalization of U.S.-Iranian relations in the future.

Since the current instability in Iran could turn to total anarchy or some form of civil war maximizing opportunities for the extreme left or h[e]ightened Soviet interference through covert means or possibly proxy forces, appropriate U.S. civilian and defense agencies should immediately begin formulating contingency plans for contacting and supporting those in and outside Iran who share the U.S. interest in maintaining Iran's independence and territorial integrity.

U.S. policy toward the present unstable and hostile Iranian regime will be to:

- initiate as soon as possible an informal dialogue with key Iranian leaders through the Swiss or Algerians, as appropriate, setting forth our views on specific issues of bilateral interest. Discussions of this nature could be made more attractive to Iranian leaders by also conveying U.S. intelligence assessments on subjects of particular interest to the Iranians, e.g., Afghanistan, Soviet activities in the Transcaucasus and the Soviet threat to Poland.

[...]

– Accompany the "open door" dialogue described above with
  selected measures designed to thwart anti-American Iranian
  policies and to undercut government officials who threaten
  U.S. interests.

[...]

– permit U.S. governmental representatives to maintain
  informational contact with key Iranian exile groups. The
  exiles should be urged to seek an Iranian solution to Iran's
  problems with the help of those still in Iran. Should any of the
  exile groups develop sufficient unity and strength (including
  support in Iran) to be able to challenge the present regime,
  this policy of keeping our distance will be reviewed.
– continue to ban the direct and indirect transfers of U.S.
  origin arms to both Iran and Iraq for the duration of the war.
  The U.S. will not oppose transfers of non-U.S. origin arms to
  Iran by our European allies and other countries such as China,
  Turkey, Pakistan and Israel since such transfers would
  minimize opportunities for new Soviet involvement in Iran
  through arms aid offers.*

Should over time a more stable Iranian government emerge
indicating interest in normalizing relations with the U.S., our
commercial and arms policies will be to:
  [...]

– Offer to resume direct, overt arms supply to Iran and
  encourage parallel allied and friendly country support as
  political stability materially improves in Iran and as an end
  to the fighting between Iran and Iraq is achieved, in order to:
  o improve the longer-term strategic balance in the Persian
    Gulf by strengthening Iran's ability to resist future
    external threats and contain domestic subversion and
    reduce opportunities for Soviet involvement in Iran as an
    alternative arms supplier;
  o Pave the way for full normalization of U.S. relations with
    Iran when this becomes mutually desirable – provided
    direct resupply of the Iranian military takes place only

---

* [Footnote in the original] DOD and CIA believe that any arms supplies would encourage Iran to
  resist efforts to bring an end to the war and that all arms transfers to Iran should, therefore, be
  actively discouraged.

after an end to the present Iran-Iraq war, any negative
Iraqi or Arab reactions should be manageable. (Care would
have to be taken to explain to the U.S. public how U.S.
interests would be served by a decision to support what
will be seen as the Iranian regime that violated
international Law by seizing and holding our diplomats.)

[*Source: Ronald Reagan Library, NSC: Records, Near East and South Asia Affairs
Directorate, Folder SIG (Senior Interagency Group) on Iran 07/21/1981,
Box 91144.*]

Document 17. White House, Memorandum, Richard V. Allen for President Reagan, "Iran," CONFIDENTIAL, attaching memorandum "Iran: The Advent of Islamic Fascism," August 21, 1981

More than two years after the revolution, Iran is still in a state of political turmoil. The foundations for the Islamic Republic have been put in place, including a constitution and other Islamic institutions, but domestic violence, often by radical leftists and ethnic separatist movements, is taking its toll.

On June 28, 1981, seventy-three Islamic Republican Party members are killed in a bombing at party headquarters, including Chief Justice Ayatollah Mohammed Beheshti, at the time the second most powerful figure in Iran. (The day before, future Supreme Leader Ali Khamenei was wounded in another attack.) Two months later, the leftist radical group Mujahedin-e Khalq, responsible for the massive "Haft-e Tir" (named for the date on the Iranian calendar) bombing, explodes another device at the prime minister's office, killing both the prime minister and the president of Iran. Far from breaking the new republic, however, the attacks solidify in the minds of regime hardliners the justification for adopting extreme measures in defense of the revolution.

This memo shows the National Security Council staff's view of the situation on the ground. Many within the Carter and Reagan administrations are convinced that the new government cannot survive the chaos of the period. Most American observers are equally dismissive of Khomeini's vision for the country, which the author of the attached memo refers to as "a philosophical construct, not a system of government." Khomeini himself is deemed "increasingly irrelevant." Despite these assessments of the poor odds for Iran, and its "2500 years experience with mismanagement, corruption and tyranny," the

*consensus among US experts is that none of the myriad opposition groups
seeking Washington's backing offer a realistic shot at meaningful change. The
USA itself still lacks "a coherent and long-term policy toward [Iran]."*

....

Memorandum for the President

From: Richard V. Allen
Subject: Iran

Recent events in Iran point to the growing need for formulating a
coherent and long-term policy towards this country.

Attached at Tab A is a memorandum from one of our NSC staff that
calls attention to "the advent of Islamic fascism." Even
Ayatollah Khomeini's grandson has now denounced the new regime.
According to our staff, "the new rulers of Iran are trapped in a
descending spiral of social disasters and escalating state
terror."

cc: The Vice President
Ed Meese
James Baker

....

Iran: The Advent of Islamic Fascism

The flight of Bani-Sadr and his allies to Paris symbolizes the
complete triumph of the Islamic extremists in Iran. Despite an
unprecedented wave of bombings and assassinations, the
dominant theocratic party was able to rely on mass arrests and
summary executions to intimidate the growing opposition, while
maintaining total control over the electoral process. Having
alienated most of its genuine support in its drive for power, the
survival of the new dictatorship will be determined solely by
its efficiency in deploying mechanisms of repression and terror.

Khomeini's Islamic Republic is a philosophical construct, not
a system of government, and neither Khomeini nor those who have
seized power in his name will be able to make it work. Two to four
million people are without jobs. More than one million others

are living in desperate circumstances as refugees from the war with Iraq. Rebellion is festering in the tribal areas surrounding the Persian plateau. In the capital, officials divide their time between political maneuver and grave debate over fine points of Koranic law, while the fabric of the nation unravels. The vast disparity between ideology and reality cannot be reconciled – it can only be suppressed. The new rulers of Iran are trapped in a descending spiral of successive social disasters and escalating state terror.

The 20-year old grandson of the Ayatollah recently described the situation in a remarkable public speech. "The new dictatorship established in religious form," he insisted, "is worse than that of the shah... Our country is governed by fascists more dangerous than the founders of fascism... The revolutionary courts are treating our people with more brutality than the Mongols did... The massacres committed in our country are worthy of the Middle Ages... God save our imam from those who have seized power in his name!" The young man is now under house arrest.

Khomeini himself is increasingly irrelevant. Originally, he provided the underlying vision and revolutionary legitimacy required to sustain the slow-motion coup by extremist forces. But now the coup is complete, Khomeini is as much a captive of the process as those who engineered it. The present ruthless leadership of Iran was swept into power on Khomeini's robes. At what point in the future, as they found themselves ground between political expediency and the old man's inflexible medievalism, will they conclude that he has outlived his usefulness to the revolution?

Iran is an ancient nation with 2500 years experience with mismanagement, corruption and tyranny. It has a collective tolerance for institutional chaos which is unimaginable in our society, and the present cycle of ever-increasing extremism, paranoia and repression may continue for quite some time. Nevertheless, the conditions are being created for a new explosion of social violence if and when the debts now being accumulated under the terror come to be settled.

[*Source: Ronald Reagan Library, Meese, Edwin: Files, Folder: Iran, Box: CFOA 160.*]

Document 18. White House, Memorandum, William P. Clark for President Reagan, "An Iranian Invasion of Iraq: Considerations for US Policy," TOP SECRET, circa July 10, 1982

The spring of 1982 marks a turning point in the Iran–Iraq War. Iraq's invasion, intended to take advantage of the disarray following the revolution, soon becomes mired in the mountains and marshlands of western Iran. Bumbling leadership from Iraqi commanders and a surprisingly swift response by the Iranians – comprising the increasingly important Islamic Revolutionary Guard Corps (IRGC) and remnants of the army backed by many thousands of volunteers – allow the Iranians to turn the tide and push the invaders back to the border. In one of the most important decisions of its young existence, the new government – specifically its leader, Ayatollah Khomeini – chooses to mount its own invasion into Iraqi territory, a fateful move that transforms Iran in the world's eyes from victim to aggressor.

This memo from the president's national security advisor to Reagan presents a dire account of the implications. Though far from supportive of Saddam and his regional ambitions, American policymakers find the idea of Iran's spreading revolution appalling. Choosing between the lesser of two evils, the USA sends a senior CIA official, named Thomas Twetten, unannounced to Baghdad bearing intelligence gleaned from satellite imagery showing Iranian forces massing on the border. According to Twetten, the Ba'athist officials who meet him, themselves intensely distrustful of Americans, are so stunned by his presence that they keep him waiting for hours while confirming his authenticity before they will even look at his invaluable information.[9]

US attempts at playing both sides of the Iran–Iraq War come under severe scrutiny in Tehran and play into condemnations by Iranian leaders over the years. But at the heart of this policy is Washington's perpetual fear of Soviet influence spreading in the Gulf. The USA does not want to allow Iran to attain "hegemony in the region," which will undermine US interests, but the Americans are equally afraid of "generating the perpetual enmity of the Iranians or moving them closer to the Soviets." Again, US policy toward Iran has to be seen in a global context.

....

Memorandum for the President

From: William P. Clark
Subject: An Iranian Invasion of Iraq: Considerations
                for US Policy

It appears that Iran will invade Iraq in the next few days. An invasion will create shock waves throughout the Gulf and pose further dangers for US interests in the Middle East, which are already threatened because of Lebanon. This memorandum summarizes the situation, reviews US interests and objectives, and outlines contingency measures which require your approval as we prepare to deal with the Iranian threat.

The Current Situation

The Iranians have made the necessary preparations to launch an invasion of southwestern Iraq. While attacks may occur at other points along the border, the Iranians are massing 100,000 troops opposite Basra, and their initial goal appears to be the destruction of the Iraqi army and the capture of Basra. The attainment of these objectives, coupled with the fomenting of Shia and Kurdish unrest, could succeed in bringing down the regime of Sadaam Hussein. In these circumstances, Iranian forces will sit astride Kuwait, leaving the Kuwaitis very vulnerable to direct or indirect Iranian threats. The Saudis, Jordanians, and Gulf states will be extremely alarmed, and can be expected to turn to us for protection. Faced with direct threats on their own territory, Iraqi forces may be invigorated and succeed in resisting Iran's invasion. However, given the past performance of the Iraqi army, it seems likely that Iran eventually will succeed in accomplishing its military objectives.

US Interests

- To deny Iran to the Soviet Union and keep open the possibility of US rapprochement with Iran.
- To protect moderate Arab states from overt or covert Iranian aggression and protect US economic interests (including oil access) in the region.
- To prevent a strengthening of Iraqi ties with the Soviet Union or the "capture" of Baghdad by Tehran or Damascus.
- To demonstrate the reliability and value of the US as an ally and the cynicism of the Soviet Union.

US Objectives

Political. Our principal objective is to help bring an end to the
war before Iran can assume hegemony in the region and undermines
[sic] our fatal interests. Simultaneously, we must act to
sustain and strengthen the confidence of Saudi Arabia and the
Gulf states in the US without generating the perpetual enmity of
the Iranians or moving them closer to the Soviets.

Military. Military instruments must be used carefully to
support our short-term needs without jeopardizing long-term
strategic requirements. First, US military actions should
deter direct Iranian aggression against friendly states
without constituting a provocative and counterproductive
direct threat to Iran. Second, our military posture should
convince our friends that they will not be forced to choose
Iranian subversion or Soviet guarantees, perhaps offered by
surrogates like Syria. Finally, we should use this situation as
an opportunity to foster enhanced strategic cooperation with
key states.

Economic. We must work with allies and friends to prevent the
widening of the war in a manner that would disrupt Gulf oil
supplies and/or international financial markets.

US Policy

Our response to an Iranian invasion will significantly influence
perceptions of American commitment and resolve. Doubts about
the US, stemming back to our failure to help the Shah, will be
enhanced or eroded, as will the value of strong association with
the US. If we are to convince the Saudis, in particular, that the
benefits of associating with us outweigh the costs, we must not be
perceived as wanting in our response. To prove our seriousness,
we must take steps that clearly demonstrate our readiness and
will to help defend our friends. This should be done in a manner
that does not enflame the Iranians or push them into the Soviet
orbit and that takes careful account of the political
sensitivities of our friends. In this vein, we should not force
measures on these states that are more overt than they feel the
traffic will bear. But neither should we seem reluctant to

respond nor willing only to take minimal measures. We must also bear in mind that the perception in the Arab world that we have colluded with Israel in Lebanon has further weakened our credibility. This may make some Arab leaders less inclined to turn to us for help in view of the internal threats to their regimes.

If you approve, the following measures would position us to act quickly to respond to requests from our friends in the area for assistance in the face of Iranian threats:

1. A Presidential letter to King Fahd, perhaps carried by a Special Emissary, that describes our concerns and states out [sic] readiness to cooperate in the defense of the kingdom.

2. Messages to Jordan, Egypt, the Peninsula states, and Pakistan expressing support and suggesting immediate consultations on the threat.

3. Public statements opposing acquisition of territory by force and raising the perception of the gravity of the situation.

4. Develop Congressional briefings that make clear the character of US interests in the region, threats to those interests, and feasible courses of action that the US may take to protect American interests.

5. Seek visible joint military exercises or demonstrations with Oman and/or Jordan and Saudi Arabia. Specifically, propose a bilateral air defense exercise with Saudi Arabia involving the deployment of a squadron of F-15s and/or an air defense HAWK battalion.

6. Move rapidly to establish the combined contingency planning group with the Saudis which is already approved in principle.

7. Develop specific combined contingency plans for the deployment of US aircraft and air defense units to Saudi Arabia in order to facilitate such a deployment if the Saudis request it.

8. Initiate consultation to see whether more frequent exchange of intelligence between appropriate services of both countries' armed forces, such as between MIDEASTFOR ships and units of Royal Saudi Navy, are desirable.

9. Consider providing airlift and logistic support for any Jordanian and/or Egyptian deployments to Gulf states.

10. Initiate with our allies an UNSC resolution calling for ceasefire, withdrawal, negotiations, and war relief measures.

11. Contingency press guidance at Tab A.

Recommendation

That you approve the above-listed measures.

[*Source: Ronald Reagan Library, NSC: Records, 1983–89, Near East and South Asia Affairs Directorate, IG (Interagency Group) Meeting 7/21/1982 Iran–Iraq, Box 91146.*]

Document 19. State Department, Cable, Lawrence Eagleburger Immediate for Embassy Baghdad, "Background on Iraqi Use of Chemical Weapons," SECRET, November 10, 1983

One of the ugliest developments of the Iran–Iraq War is the deployment of chemical weapons, begun by the Iraqi side shortly after Iran's counter-invasion. Despite its illegality under international law, the response by much of the world community is startlingly tepid and will become another of Tehran's deepest grievances relating to the war.

As this State Department report shows, the USA is aware of Iraqi chemical agents being used as early as October 1982. Yet US policymakers initially downplay the issue. Far from approving of the tactic, they have nonetheless "limited [their] efforts against the Iraqi CW program to close monitoring," citing "strict neutrality" in the war, the "sensitivity of sources" describing the program, and the "low probability of achieving desired results." The under-lying rationale is Washington's desire not to do anything that might further impede Iraq's dubious warfighting capability. As Secretary of State George P. Shultz writes in his memoir, "The United States simply could not stand idle and watch the Khomeini revolution sweep forward."[10] However, there is no direct evidence that Washington was actually complicit in Iraq's conduct at this stage.[11]

Late in the war, US intelligence reports assert that Iran has started to employ chemical agents, although at least one independent monitoring group would later challenge that conclusion. In 1987, Iranian diplomats reveal for the first time that the country has a development program but insist it is in response to Iraq's first use, a contention various CIA and Pentagon reports corroborate.[12]

....

[From NEA to Embassy Baghdad]

  11/10/83

  Subject: Background on Iraqi Use of Chemical Weapons

  [...]

3. [1 line redacted] oblique references in Iraqi public statements over the past year corroborate Iran's October 22 charge that Iraq has used prohibited CW in contravention of its treaty obligations. On November 8, Iran requested the UNSYG [UN Secretary General] to investigate. (Iran had made similar charges during the 1982 UNGA, which Iraq had denied.) [Half a line redacted]

4. [1-2 words redacted] as long ago as July 1982, Iraq used teargas and skin irritants against invading Iranian forces quite effectively. In October 1982, unspecified foreign officers fired lethal chemical weapons at the orders of Saddam during battles in the Mandali area. [Half a line redacted] In July and August 1983, the Iraqis reportedly used a chemical agent with lethal effects against Iranian forces invading Iraq at Haj Umran, and more recently against Kurdish insurgents.

5. Iraqi media have quoted Iraqi President Saddam Hussein as saying, "there is a weapon for every battle and we have the weapons that will confront great numbers." Military communications over the past year have referred to "all kinds of weapons" being used to repulse the Iranians. On December 18, 1982, Iraq claimed it would retaliate for an Iranian-claimed terrorist bombing in Baghdad "with more than one means... He who forewarns is excused." A military communiqué warned the Iranians against violating international norms and charters, perhaps trying to establish a pretext for using CW in violation of international protocols. In an interview published February 11, 1983, in Arabic in *al-Hawadith*, Defense Minister Khayrallah evaded the question on Iraq's

possession of a poison gas weapon. The *al-Hawadith* interview did not confirm Iraq's development of CW, but it put the question into the public domain. On April 12, 1983, Iraq again warned of "new weapons ... [to] be used for the first time in war ... not used in previous attacks because of humanitarian and ethical reasons ... that will destroy any moving creature."

6. Iraq has a limited indigenous capability to produce and deploy CW. For example, Iraq may be able to produce mustard gas from chemical intermediaries procured abroad. The Soviets have equipped and trained the Iraqi forces to fight in a CW environment. [Approximately 10 lines redacted]

8. Over many decades the U.S. has sought to deter the use of lethal and incapacitating CW when their use appeared to loom as a possibility. Iraq's use of lethal or incapacitating CW could further undercut an important agreement observed by nearly all nations against chemical warfare. Introduction of CW to the Gulf War represents an escalation of hostilities that could render still more remote the possibility of a ceasefire and negotiations. Furthermore, Iraq's use of CW gives the Iranians a powerful propaganda tool against the Iraqi regime, setting world opinion against Iraq at a time when Iran enjoys little international sympathy. Beyond the humanitarian and security/proliferation concerns, these facts should offset the attractiveness to Iraq of using prohibited CW.

9. Both Iran (in 1929) and Iraq (in 1931) have ratified the Geneva Protocol of 1925 prohibiting the use of chemical weapons. Iraq attached conditions to its succession, having the effect of a "no first use" clause, but its commitment not to use unless attacked with such weapons is unequivocal. Iran attached no conditions to its ratification of the protocols. There is some question whether Iran may have used chemical agents at one point early in the war.

10. The existing convention prohibits only the use RPT [repeat] use of lethal and incapacitating CW. No international treaty yet forbids development, production, or deployment of lethal and incapacitating CW. The U.S. and others have been negotiating for such a treaty for a number of years. Also, we do not interpret the Geneva Protocol as applying to

riot control agents as opposed to lethal and incapacitating chemicals. We limit their use to defensive military modes to save lives, e.g., controlling rioting POWs, dispersing civilian "screens" of attacks, rescue operations in isolated areas, and protecting convoys outside the combat zone.

11. Heretofore we have limited our efforts against the Iraqi CW program to close monitoring because of our strict neutrality in the Gulf War, the sensitivity of sources, and the low probability of achieving desired results. Now, however, with the essential assistance of foreign firms, Iraq has become able to deploy and use CW and probably has built up large reserves of CW for further use. Given its desperation to end the war, Iraq may again use lethal or incapacitating CW, particularly if Iran threatens to break through Iraqi lines in a large-scale attack. [5 lines redacted] Nonetheless, on the basis of open source reporting now available there may be steps we and others could take to deter further Iraqi use of prohibited CW.

12. Addressee should take no/no action on this issue until instructed separately.

[*Source: US Department of State, declassification release.*]

Document 20. Central Intelligence Agency, Memorandum, DDI Working Group on TWA Hijacking for Director of Central Intelligence *et al.*, "Iranian Involvement with Terrorism in Lebanon," TOP SECRET, June 26, 1985

The 1982 Israeli invasion of Lebanon provides an urgent motive for Iran to build a base of support among Lebanon's large Shia population and, seizing the chance, the Islamic Revolutionary Guard Corps sends 1,000 officers to train rebel fighters and help create what will become the terrorist group Hezbollah. Throughout the 1980s, Hezbollah, with funding and weapons from Iran and additional support from Syria, orchestrates some of the worst terrorist attacks against US targets. Iran's backing for radical groups in the region quickly becomes an enduring policy concern for Washington and escalates the animosity between the two countries.

This heavily excised document lists several of the major attacks already carried out in the short history of Iranian involvement in Lebanon, including the devastating 1983 bombings of the US Embassy and US Marine barracks in Beirut and a notorious TWA airliner hijacking in 1985. Left unmentioned, or perhaps redacted, is the fact that Majlis Speaker Akbar Hashemi Rafsanjani intercedes with the hijackers of the TWA flight to help end the crisis as part of his strategy to improve Iran's standing in the world.

The document goes further into the reasoning behind Iran's support for Hezbollah and others. This is about more than simply killing American targets. The Khomeini regime believes "it has a religious duty to export its Islamic revolution ... by whatever means necessary." Additionally, the authors recognize some of the complexity of the issue within Iran and point to the separation of the regime into two camps, the "radicals" and the "pragmatists" – though notably they assert both sides support the use of terrorism, just for different ends. Later attempts by the White House to make contact with so-called moderates in response to Lebanese terrorism will lead to the Iran-Contra Affair.

....

```
Memorandum for:  Director of Central Intelligence
                 Deputy Director of Central Intelligence
                 Deputy Director for Intelligence
From:            DDI Working Group on TWA Hijacking
Subject:         Iranian Involvement with Terrorism in Lebanon
```

The Iranian government is now trying to exploit the hostage situation, even though it does not appear to have been involved in planning or carrying out the hijacking. An overwhelming body of evidence, however, has implicated Iran in the Hizballah campaign of violence against Americans and other Westerners in Lebanon during the past two years. Iran provides substantial material and political support to the Lebanese radical Shias, but it does not control or have advanced knowledge of all of their operations. Senior Iranian clerics and Foreign Ministry officials are involved in supporting terrorism in Lebanon.
   [...]

Iran and the Hizballah

The Iranian Government maintains an intimate relationship with the Lebanese Shia fundamentalist groups that comprise the

Hizballah network. Iran has greatly strengthened Hizballah during the past two years by providing money, weapons, logistical support, training, and political and religious indoctrination. The Iranian Ambassador in Damascus and the Revolutionary Guard Commander in the Bekaa Valley work closely with the Council of Lebanon, the Iranian-created committee of Lebanese radical Shia leaders that tries to coordinate all fundamentalist activities in Lebanon.

Hizballah leaders have also worked in collusion with Iran on some terrorist operations. The Revolutionary Guards based in the Bekaa Valley are often colocated with Hizballah elements and share the same communications and support network. [6 lines redacted]

Despite Iranian efforts, however, the Hizballah remains largely a domestic Lebanese political movement with its own political agenda. While Iranian assistance may have been critical in 1982 and 1983, the Hizballah movement does not depend on Iran for its existence. Shia fundamentalism, whetted by decades of Shia deprivation and a brutal Israeli occupation, has firmly taken root in Lebanon and has achieved a momentum of its own. Hizballah elements can and often do conduct many of their activities without Iranian foreknowledge.

Hizballah terrorism is driven by the movement's internal goals. Lebanese Shia fundamentalists do not target Western officials primarily because Iran has ordered them to do so. Hizballah and Iranian cooperation on anti-Western terrorism arises from the shared belief that the first step in an Islamic revolution is the elimination of Western influence from Lebanon. Hizballah leaders share with Iran the ultimate objective of establishing an Islamic state in Lebanon and are therefore often receptive to Iranian encouragement and recommendations. Certain Hizballah elements, however, are also motivated by other concerns, such as a desire to free their Lebanese coreligionists in prison for terrorism in Kuwait and elsewhere.

The Lebanese Hizballah movement has grown increasingly independent as it has expanded in terms of membership and resources. Hizballah leaders are now serious competitors for the leadership of Lebanon's large Shia population and command the loyalty of perhaps as many as several thousand armed fighters. There is mounting evidence that the Lebanese Shias – although respectful of Khomeini and the Iranian revolution –

will no longer tolerate Iranian attempts to dictate their policies. Heavy-handed Iranian behavior and the competition between rival elements within the Iranian Government have also annoyed leaders of the Lebanese Hizballah.

In summary, the Hizballah network has become an autonomous terrorist problem in its own right. Iran supports and advises the Hizballah but cannot control it. It is no longer safe to assume that Iranian officials know in advance about all Hizballah operations.

Iranian Involvement in Past Terrorism

While Iran does not appear to be responsible for the current hijacking, there is considerable evidence of Iranian support for past terrorism in Lebanon. Circumstantial evidence indicates that the bombing of the US Embassy in Beirut in April 1983 was the work of pro-Iranian Lebanese Shias, but there is no hard evidence directly linking the act to Tehran.

[15 lines redacted]

The "Islamic Jihad Organization," which claimed responsibility for the bombing of the Embassy was probably an Iranian-supported Lebanese Shia group.

- The Jihad Organization had claimed responsibility for the attack in March on the US Marines assigned to the multinational peacekeeping force. It also said it carried out at least one other attack against the French contingent of the multinational force.

[3 lines redacted]

Evidence also pointed to Iranian-backed Lebanese Shias as perpetrators of the bombing of the US and French Multinational Force contingents in Lebanon during October 1983.

- [Several words redacted] members of the Shia Musawi family, associated with several pro-Iranian Shia splinter groups, were primarily responsible for the attacks.
- [1-2 words redacted] several pickup trucks of the type used in the attacks were seen parked in front of a Musawi office in Beirut.
- The Musawis are involved with the Islamic Amal group based in the Bekaa Valley and with the Husayni Suicide Forces based in southern Beirut.

[1.5 lines redacted] approximately 10 minutes after the bombings occurred, all of the officials of an Iranian Embassy office in West Beirut departed hastily by car. This Iranian office is believed to have engaged exclusively in intelligence activities.

- It is unlikely they could have been prepared to depart so quickly without prior knowledge of the attack.
- A high-ranking Iranian official stated publicly after the bombings that "the Muslim people" in Lebanon had acted in accordance with Khomeini's principles of revolution and that he hoped the US and France had "learned their lesson."

[Approximately 20 lines redacted]

We also suspect that Iran was involved in the bombing of the US Embassy Annex in East Beirut in September 1984, but we have less specific evidence in this case.

[Approximately 10 lines redacted]

Iranian Policy Regarding Terrorism

Tehran's support for terrorism stems primarily from the perception of the commanding regime that it has a religious duty to export its Islamic revolution and to wage, by whatever means necessary, a constant struggle against the non-Islamic world, particularly the US. Tehran's aim is to eliminate Western influence, overthrow pro-Western regimes, and establish Islamic Republics. Iranian leaders – both clerics and laymen – are convinced of the righteousness of Khomeini's brand of Islamic fundamentalism and believe that other Muslim societies would benefit from it. This religious motivation provides Iranian leaders with a moral justification for the use of terrorism.

Iranian leaders are divided between Islamic radicals and pragmatists who both support the use of terrorism – although for different reasons – and conservatives and moderates who generally oppose it. As long as radicals, such as Deputy Foreign Minister Sheikholeslam, a leader of the students who seized the US Embassy in Tehran, and Majid Kamal, who directs intelligence activities from an office in the Foreign Ministry, are major advocates of terrorism as a legitimate tool of state policy. In their view, the fusion of politics and religion justifies any means to export the revolution. Moreover, radical clerics in Qom who may hold no official position within the regime have independent sources of income and are able to finance and support terrorist operations without government approval.

Pragmatists – such as President Khamenei, Assembly Speaker Rafsanjani, and Ayatollah Montazeri – are willing to support whatever policies, including terrorism, that are likely to further Iranian interests. Each has been linked to the funding and support of Iranian-backed terrorist groups. They support terrorism because it can be a highly effective instrument of policy, but they also recognize the need for improved state-to-state economic relations and have sought to curb radical excesses. The pragmatists prefer to use terrorism selectively, choosing targets important to Iranian national interests rather than purely revolutionary goals.

Iranian policy on terrorism is now caught up in the internal power struggle among radicals, pragmatists, and conservatives as Iran moves toward the post-Khomeini era. So long as Iranian pragmatists perceive little cost in supporting terrorist operations, the Khomeini regime will continue its deep involvement in terrorism. Moreover, the US will remain a high-priority target for Iranian terrorism barring the unlikely accession of a conservative coalition.

[*Source: Central Intelligence Agency, CREST Database, CIA-RDP85T01058R000406550001–6 and CIA-RDP87T00434R000300240059–5.*]

Document 21. Ayatollah Hossein Ali Montazeri, Letter, for Ayatollah Ruhollah Khomeini, UNCLASSIFIED, October 7, 1985

The longest conventional war of the twentieth century, the Iran–Iraq War exacts an immense toll from both sides. The World War I–like trench combat of the frontlines soon falls into a stalemate. Child soldiers, human waves, and chemical weapons attacks become commonplace. New fronts open up and the horrors of war are inflicted on civilians and foreigners in attempts by both combatants – though more often initiated by Iraq – to make the war untenable for the other. The War of the Cities features missile attacks on civilian targets in both countries, while the Tanker War threatens to bring Persian Gulf oil shipping to a near standstill.

Within Iran, calls to end the war grow stronger as Khomeini repeatedly turns down peace talks with Saddam. Khomeini's heir apparent, Ayatollah Hossein Ali Montazeri, represents one of these "pragmatic" dissenting voices. In his candid and revealing letters to Khomeini, the widely respected Montazeri asks that the Supreme Leader consider the ever-growing cost of the conflict. He points to the self-destructive zealousness and cronyism rampant among IRGC commanders as a key cause for the continuation of the war, and bemoans the lack of "an authority to investigate the errors and weaknesses" of Iran's military structure and the "thousands of youths which are being lost cheaply due to negligence."

While it is tempting to leap at these comments and see Montazeri as condemning Khomeini and the IRGC, it is also important to understand the nuances at play. Montazeri is a true revolutionary who would be labeled a "radical" in some of his other beliefs. The IRGC's influence is certainly a concern for some in the regime, but there is never really a question among those in the power structure about the legitimacy of Iran's mission in the war or in the revolution. For these individuals, it is rarely a question of "why" but merely "how."

....

[...] Against my will, and considering the present sensitive condition of the country and the repeated referrals of people and administrators from different levels to me [...] I have pondered about reflecting these issues to you.

1. In the current state of affairs, despite the difficulties of the war and pressure from the world powers, there are no problems with our people, [they are] all concerned with the management of the country and the revolution. There is no doubt that the majority of administrators have good intentions. The main problem is in the key decision-making that has brought about the current situation, which [in turn] has put the revolution in grave danger. For instance, there may be no other way than to tolerate the current heart-wrenching conditions at the fronts; however, if two years ago the criticisms by the dear commanders and fighters, who mostly have been martyred, had been heeded, the course of progress would not have reached the level of impasse it has today. Alas, the self-regard and negligence of high-level administrators have brought us to this point. [...] I have

explained the mistakes and delinquencies of the leaders and high-ranking commanders in my private and public talks with the lower-ranking commanders who write to me. However when they say they have directly reminded the leaders of the problems, but the leaders have not paid the proper attention, what can one reply?

And what is the answer when experienced IRGC commanders say that the IRGC is at the point of self-destruction today? The main problem is that the fundamental task of the government is being performed by a limited number of people who are very busy. One hopes that important tasks have been given to the experts and that cronyism and partisanship do not exist. If there existed an authority to investigate the errors and weaknesses which have caused the continuous losses of the past two years and if we valued the lives of the thousands of youths which are being lost cheaply due to negligence, the situation of the war would be better than it is now.

The main backbone of the country's economy, Kharg Island, is regularly under attack. [...] Neither the stubbornness of our opposition to any possible alternative, nor the delinquency with which everyone treats every setback, is helpful to our cause. Instead of scrutinizing the conditions and their causes and making use of the opinions of the witnesses – commanders and soldiers – certain false announcements and imaginary victories are broadcast to the people, which surprises those who are at the fronts. All the mistakes are being hidden behind propaganda and the guilty do not fear the consequences and hold others responsible for their errors, and it is the revolution and the people who share the losses.

2. The political state of the country is no better than the situation at the fronts. Partisanship is affecting the issues of the war, which are the main problems of the country to the point that some ministers are becoming isolated from the prime minister. Ministers complain of not being aware of the decisions being made by the government and reading about them in the newspapers. The prime minister also claims that the ministers who don't accept him have been imposed on his cabinet. [...] I have given my opinion to both Mr. Khamenei and

Mr. Mousavi that the prime minister should not be under pressure when choosing the members of his cabinet, [...] so that the excuse of having a forced cabinet is not available to him.

3. Regarding your recent order establishing three forces divisions within the IRGC, it seems that in the current situation of war and the willingness of many Army personnel to cause trouble and flee, this decision may have undesirable consequences. It might have been possible to cleanse the Army without much exposure using young personnel and proper revolutionary and spiritual education, aside from retaining the military structure of the Army. However, unfortunately all our encouragement and investments were directed to the IRGC and due to our political partisanship and favoritism toward the IRGC, the Army was disparaged. And with your recent order, in addition to the economic problems, the last thread of the Army's hopes regarding the Islamic Republic has been lost. Hence, in the present difficult circumstances, we neither have an appreciative Army nor a strong IRGC. [...] With your current order, only God knows what will become of the competition between the Army and IRGC. The fact that many of our officers, especially pilots, have fled with airplanes and helicopters to Iraq and other places and that none of the Iraqi officers have fled to Iran, is evidence of our discouraged and untrusting officers versus motivated Iraqi officers.

4. Another important problem for the country is in the judiciary system and its disorder and its lack of appeal to more loyal and enlightened people. We are facing a shortage of judges, and even with those that we have in the judiciary, we are witnessing a loss of confidence in the capacity of the system to exact justice, given the increasing incidence of judicial malpractice and even bribery. The difficulties in the prisons are also due to the problems in the judiciary system.

5. Finally, at present, the problem of the war is the most important. I know that the Army and IRGC are not cordial, that neither accepts the leadership of the other, and preaching and advice are only temporarily effective. The war, more than anything else, requires a unified leadership that is accepted by all. [...] Since Mr. Khamenei is fairly aware of the state of the war and the fronts and the Army, what is standing in the

way of his taking responsibility for coordinated offensives against the enemy, the same way Bani-Sadr did, and directly monitoring them and leading? By witnessing conditions in person, he might solve the problems too. His leadership powers are better than Mr. Hashemi's. [...]

6. [...] The leaders of the three branches of the government are very busy and are not experts in every subject, and it is not appropriate to give them all the responsibilities. The prophet had ten advisers from different tribes, therefore it is fitting to gradually identify ten experts in different topics of war, the economy, culture and politics, and also choose two people loyal to Islam and the revolution, but with opposing views. [...] And seek their advice on important issues. [...]

[*Source: Hossein Ali Montazeri,* Khaterat *(Memoirs), Appendix 127, p. 770.*
www.amontazeri.com/Farsi/Khaterat/web/index.htm]

Document 22. White House, Memorandum, John M. Poindexter for the President, "Covert Action Finding Regarding Iran," Classification Unknown, attaching Presidential Finding, January 17, 1986

When Hezbollah begins kidnapping Americans, including CIA Station Chief William Buckley, in growing numbers in 1984, President Reagan reacts on a personal and political level. Touched by the pleas of hostages' families and recalling Carter's political nightmare, he makes clear to National Security Advisor Robert McFarlane the urgent need to get them back. (He later tells senior aides that he is even willing to risk breaking the law.[13]) The resulting decision in mid-1985 to sell arms to Iran in return for the release of hostages from Lebanon leads to the bizarre political scandal known as the Iran-Contra Affair.

Driven by wishful thinking and a poor understanding of Iran, the plan is initially for Israeli intermediaries to develop an opening to so-called moderates within the leadership using US weapons from Israeli stocks as currency. When one of the Israeli deliveries threatens a political firestorm, the White House decides to take over. The documents below record Reagan's approval of the new plan and include a rarely declassified presidential "Finding" to authorize the CIA to launch a covert operation.[14]

Beyond the legal, policy, and moral obstacles to selling weapons to Iran, the USA is working under several misapprehensions. The plan is "premised on the assumption that moderate elements in Iran can come to power if these factions demonstrate their credibility in defending Iran against Iraq." The idea that weapons sales will bring about this change comes from a notoriously shady Iranian arms dealer, endorsed by an advisor to the Israeli prime minister, who claims to represent members of the "pragmatic" faction. Ultimately, the operation manages to free three American hostages, only to have three more taken in the same period.

....

Memorandum for the President

From: John M. Poindexter
Subject: Covert Action Finding Regarding Iran

Prime Minister Peres of Israel secretly dispatched his special advisor on terrorism with instructions to propose a plan by which Israel, with limited assistance from the U.S., can create conditions to help bring about a more moderate government in Iran. The Israelis are very concerned that Iran's deteriorating position in the war with Iraq, the potential for further radicalization in Iran, and the possibility of enhanced Soviet influence in the Gulf all pose significant threats to the security of Israel. They believe it is essential that they act to at least preserve a balance of power in the region.

The Israeli plan is premised on the assumption that moderate elements in Iran can come to power if these factions demonstrate their credibility in defending Iran against Iraq and in deterring Soviet intervention. To achieve the strategic goal of a more moderate Iranian government, the Israelis are prepared to unilaterally commence selling military material to Western-oriented Iranian factions. It is their belief that by so doing they can achieve a heretofore unobtainable penetration of the Iranian governing hierarchy. The Israelis are convinced that the Iranians are so desperate for military materiel, expertise and intelligence that the provision of these resources will result in favorable long-term changes in personnel and attitudes within the Iranian government. Further, once the exchange relationship has commenced, a dependency would be

established on those who are providing the requisite resources,
thus allowing the provider(s) to coercively influence near-term
events. Such an outcome is consistent with our policy objectives
and would present significant advantages for U.S. national
interests. As described by the Prime Minister's emissary, the
only requirement the Israelis have is an assurance that they
will be allowed to purchase U.S. replenishments for the stocks
that they sell to Iran. We have researched the legal problems of
Israel's selling U.S. manufactured arms to Iran. Because of the
requirement in U.S. law for recipients of U.S. arms to notify the
U.S. government of transfers to third countries, I do not
recommend that you agree with the specific details of the Israeli
plan. However, there is another possibility. Some time ago
Attorney General William French Smith determined that under an
appropriate finding you could authorize the CIA to sell arms to
countries outside of the provision of the laws and reporting
requirements for foreign military sales. The objectives of the
Israeli plan could be met if the CIA, using an authorized agent
as necessary, purchased arms from the Department of Defense
under the Economy Act and then transferred them to Iran directly
after receiving appropriate payment from Iran.

The Covert Action Finding attached at Tab A provides
the latitude for the transactions indicated above to
proceed. The Iranians have indicated an immediate requirement
for 4,000 basic TOW weapons for use in the launchers they
already hold.

The Israeli's [sic] are also sensitive to a strong U.S. desire
to free our Beirut hostages and have insisted that the Iranians
demonstrate both influence and good intent by an early release of
the five Americans. Both sides have agreed that the hostages will
be immediately released upon commencement of this action. Prime
Minister Peres had his emissary pointedly note that they well
understand our position on not making concessions to
terrorists. They also point out, however, that terrorist
groups, movements, and organizations are significantly easier
to influence through governments than they are by direct
approach. In that we have been unable to exercise any suasion
over Hizballah during the course of nearly two years of
kidnappings, this approach through the government of Iran may
well be our only way to achieve the release of the Americans held

in Beirut. It must again be noted that since this dialogue with the Iranians began in September, Reverend Weir has been released and there have been no Shia terrorist attacks against American or Israeli persons, property, or interests.

Therefore it is proposed that Israel make the necessary arrangements for the sale of 4000 TOW weapons to Iran. Sufficient funds to cover the sale would be transferred to an agent of the CIA. The CIA would then purchase the weapons from the Department of Defense and deliver the weapons to Iran through the agent. If all of the hostages are not released after the first shipment of 1000 weapons, further transfers would cease.

On the other hand, since hostage release is in some respects a byproduct of a larger effort to develop ties to potentially moderate forces in Iran, you may wish to redirect such transfers to other groups within the government at a later time.

The Israelis have asked for our urgent response to this proposal so that they can plan accordingly. They note that conditions inside both Iran and Lebanon are highly volatile. The Israelis are cognizant that this entire operation will be terminated if the Iranians abandon their goal of moderating their government or allow further acts of terrorism. You have discussed the general outlines of the Israeli plan with Secretaries Shultz and Weinberger, Attorney General Meese and Director Casey. The Secretaries do not recommend you proceed with this plan. Attorney General Meese and Director Casey believe the short-term and long-term objectives of the plan warrant the policy risks involved and recommend you approve the attached Finding. Because of the extreme sensitivity of this project, it is recommended that you exercise your statutory prerogative to withhold notification of the Finding to the Congressional oversight committees until such time that you deem it to be appropriate.

Finding Pursuant to Section 662 of The Foreign Assistance Act of 1961 As Amended, Concerning Operations Undertaken by the Central Intelligence Agency in Foreign Countries, Other Than Those Intended Solely for the Purpose of Intelligence Collection

I hereby find that the following operation in a foreign country (including all support necessary to such operation) is

important to the national security of the United States, and due
to its extreme sensitivity and security risks, I determine it is
essential to limit prior notice, and direct the Director of
Central Intelligence to refrain from reporting this finding to
the Congress as provided in Section 501 of the National Security
Act of 1947, as amended, until I otherwise direct.

Scope   Description
Iran

    Assist selected friendly foreign liaison services, third
countries and third parties which have established
relationships with Iranian elements, groups and
individuals sympathetic to U.S. Government interests and
which do not conduct or support terrorist actions directed
against U.S. persons, property or interests, for the
purpose of: (1) establishing a more moderate government in
Iran, (2) obtaining from them significant intelligence not
otherwise obtainable, to determine the current Iranian
Government's intentions with respect to its neighbors and
with respect to terrorist acts, and (3) furthering the
release of the American hostages held in Beirut and
preventing additional terrorist acts by these groups.
Provide funds, intelligence, counter-intelligence,
training, guidance and communications and other necessary
assistance to these elements, groups, individuals,
liaison services and third countries in support of
these activities.

    The USG will act to facilitate efforts by third parties
and third countries to establish contact with moderate
elements within and outside the Government of Iran by
providing these elements with arms, equipment and related
materiel in order to enhance the credibility of these
elements in their effort to achieve a more pro-U.S.
government in Iran by demonstrating their ability to
obtain requisite resources to defend their country against
Iraq and intervention by the Soviet Union. This support
will be discontinued if the U.S. Government learns that
these elements have abandoned their goals of moderating
their government and appropriated the materiel for
purposes other than that provided by this finding.

The White House

Washington, D.C.   [*Signed: Ronald Reagan*]
Date January 17, 1986

[*Source: United States of America v. Oliver L. North, Criminal No. 88-00080-02,
United States District Court, District of Columbia, Defense Exhibit 73.*]

**Document 23. George Cave, Memorandum for the Record, [Report on
Mission to Tehran], TOP SECRET, May 30, 1986**

*Early in 1986, retired CIA Iran operations specialist and Persian-speaker
George Cave is brought into the secret negotiations with Iran. After several
inconclusive sessions in Europe, a decision is made to hold the next meeting in
Tehran so that senior Iranians can attend. Former National Security Advisor
Robert McFarlane, who brought the Reagan administration into the arms
initiative, is selected to lead the US mission, and it is seen as a potential
breakthrough, but turns out to be another disaster.*

*Contrary to promises by the intermediary, arms dealer Manucher
Ghorbanifar, no top-level officials are on hand to meet the delegation at the
airport. After four days isolated in a Tehran hotel meeting lower-ranked
functionaries, the Americans become even more exasperated to learn they
will not gain the release of the remaining hostages, as they have been led to
believe. McFarlane, convinced Tehran can simply instruct Hezbollah to let
them go, angrily refuses to give his hosts the additional time they plead for and
berates them for failing to live up to agreements. "The lack of trust will endure
for a long time," he declares. "An important opportunity was lost."[15]*

*As Cave records in this insightful – and judging by the many typos, hastily
written – report, the main problem is Ghorbanifar, who has repeatedly
misrepresented key facts to both sides. In retrospect, because of the lack of
Iranian internal sources, it is hard to tell where the Islamic regime (as opposed
to Ghorbanifar) may have actively misled the USA, but it is clear the
American side routinely deceived their counterparts. As the chief American
operative, National Security Council staffer Oliver North, told Congress in
1987: "I lied every time I met the Iranians." Insisting he had to "weigh in the
balance the difference between lives and lies," he declared, "I would have
promised them a trip to Disneyland if it would have gotten the hostages
released."[16] While some observers agreed about the sketchy circumstances, it*

*was arguably a questionable strategy if the overarching goal was to promote
better long-term relations with Iran.*

....

*[Authors' note: The excerpt is presented as it was written, without spelling or
other minor corrections. The text within brackets has been added for context.]*

[...]

This is an account of the U.S. mission to Tehran from May
25 through May 28, together with some comments and observations.
The U.S. team was headed by Mcfarland with Goode, Mcgrath,
Miller and O'neil[17] making up the rest of the team.
A communicator also accompanied the team on the trip
into Tehran.

The team arrived in Tehran at 0830 hours on 25 May and was left
to cool its collective heels for about two hours.

[...]

The first substantive meeting took place late in the afternoon
of 24 [*sic*] May. The Iranian side consisted of [Iranian First
Channel A: Kangarlou] named [1 line redacted] and a man named
[redacted] whom Gorba described as being in their intelligence
service. This initial meeting was hostile with the Iranians
listing past sins of the United States etc. The meeting ended
with what appeared to be little chance of any progress.
Basically the American side insisted on adherence to the
agreement as we understood it, and the Iranians inisisting that
America must do more to atone for its sins. At the end on the
Meeting, [redacted] set the tone by saying that even if no
progress is made during the discussions, we were their guests
and Iranians honored guests.

[...]

On Monday [26 May] we were left to our own devices throughout
most of the day. We finally had another meeting late in the
afternoon. At this meeting, another Iranian was introduced as
[redacted: Dr. Najafi (real name Ali Hadi Najafabadi)]. He is [1½
lines redacted] and very cultured. At this meeting, MacFarlane
outlined the reasons we were in Tehran. We wished to lay the
groundwork for a new political and strategic relationship
between our two countries. We considered the arms supplies as an

example of our good faith and we insisted on the release of the
hostages as an example of their good faith. [Najafabadi] made
the appropriate noises and said that Iran was prepared to have
normal relations with every country except two, Israel ans South
Africa.

[...]

During Tuesday's negotiations, all the demands of the
hostages holders evaporated except for the demand for the
release of the Shi'ite prisoners in Kuwait. Goode [North]
handled this part of the negotiations by firmly stating that the
United States would not interfere in the internal affairs of
Kuwait, particularly in an instance where Kuwaiti due legal
process had been carried out. [...]

The draft agreement [prepared on Tuesday by the Americans] was
the subject of intense negotiations with the Iranians making
some counter proposals which were designed to gain them more
time. Talks broke off around midnight with the Iranian
delegation saying it wanted to caucus. For the next two hours,
heated discussions were held within the Iranian delegation. [The
Iranian officials] both said that the other would be responsible
if nothing comes of the negotiations. Finally, shortly before
two on Wednesday morning, [Redacted] asked to see McFarland. He
wanted assurances that we would deliver the remaining spare
parts two hours after the hostages were released, and would stay
after the arrival of the spare parts to discuss additional
Iranian needs. He also asked for more time to get control of the
hostages. McFarland gave [Redacted] until 0630 wednesday
morning to arrange for the release of the hostages, The American
delegation retired to grab a couple of hours sleep knowing that we
had at least out-frazzled them.

[...]

Comments

1. If Gorba [Ghorbanifar] does appear, we must press him for
   positive identification of the people with whom we talked.
   Since [redacted] actually forget his alias during the course
   of one evening's discussions, we can assume that the others
   were using aliases ...

2. It is quite possible that the Iranian side was negotiating under the impression that we were only interested in a deal for the hostages. This would explain why they tried so hard to get us to do more in exchange for the hostages. [...] McFarland issued a stern warning that we are getting fed up with overatures from them that don't pan out. We are interested in a long term political and strategic relationship, and if Iran does not pick up on this opportunity it may be years before there is another one.

3. Ramadan was certainly a factor in how the negotiations went. also the problem caused by not being able to see anyone in a position of power. The people we were negotiating with were a couple of rungs down the ladder. The fact that [Kangarlou's] breath could curl rhino hide was no help either. On the positive side was the change in the attitude of the Iranian delegation. By tuesday they were begging us to stay.

4. We also may have the problem of the dishonest interlocutor. The Iranian side made it clear [...] that one of the problems in our negotiations was the fact that prior to our meeting, Gorba gave each side a different picture of the structure of the deal. [...]

5. [...] The serious problem we must address is whether the Iranians can gain control of the hostages. The French don't think they can. This could be our real problem. The Iranian side may be most willing, but unable to gain control.

Recommendation

Through hindsight it would have been better for Goode and O'neil to have gone in first to handle the initial negotiations. We should not have subjected a senior U.S. official to the indignities he was forced to endure. We have made the point to the Iranians that the draft agreement must be finally negotiated by senior responsible officials from both sides. If we have a subsequent response from the Iranian side it is strongly recommended that Goode and O'neil meet with the Iranian side somewhere in Europe to continue the negotiations.

[Source: S. Rept. No. 100-216, 100th Congress, 1st Session, Report of the Congressional Committees Investigating the Iran-Contra Affair, Appendix A: Vol. 1 (Washington, DC, 1988), pp. 1261–1265.]

Document 24. US Government, Transcripts [Meetings between US and Iranian Representatives in Frankfurt and Mainz, West Germany], TOP SECRET, October 1986

After the fiasco in Tehran [see Document 23], the US side explores a new inroad to the Iranians. Their main interlocutor turns out to be Parliament Speaker Rafsanjani's nephew, Ali Bahramani. Though apparently still in his twenties, he looks far more like the real deal than Ghorbanifar and the "first channel."

These transcribed excerpts come from rare tape recordings made by the American side and offer a highly unusual glimpse of how the secret negotiations unfolded. The discussions underscore, among other things, American desperation to have the hostages returned safely, and the curt tone reflects their impatience after months of largely inconclusive talks. Neither side wants to have the arms sales become public knowledge. North and his colleagues are anxious for them not to be tied directly to the hostages but instead to loftier political goals. Sprinkled throughout are references to moving past the hostages to engage with bigger policy issues, but it will never be known if that was a genuine aspiration. Even without a clear picture of Iranian intentions, the Americans' deceptions (e.g., North's false quoting of Reagan), coupled with Ghorbanifar's monumental earlier lies and the contempt for the Iranians evident in their reports to superiors, show little commitment to building trust.

These meetings also illustrate the scope of American wishful thinking and ignorance about Iranian politics. (Less can be gleaned about the Iranian side here.) Rafsanjani's nephew offers valuable insights into how decisions are made – for instance, describing the "shareholder" system and the specific roles of Khomeini and Rafsanjani. Contradicting a basic premise of the US operation (to engage with moderates), Bahramani explains that while there are "moderate" and "radical" elements within the leadership, they do not act unilaterally on foreign policy. Worse, it eventually dawns on the Americans that the new channel is more or less the same as the old channel, which was made up of not just hardliners but might even have included an individual who was behind the latest American kidnapping. CIA expert George Cave admitted later: "that really blew our minds."

Finally, Bahramani reveals a stunning development: reports of the secret deals have been circulating in Tehran thanks to opponents of cooperation with the United States. Within days, the story will make world headlines and grind to a halt the strangest bilateral discourse of the post-revolution period.

....

[*Authors' note: The American participants below are NSC staffer Oliver L. North, retired General Richard V. Secord, retired CIA official George Cave, and Secord's business partner, Albert Hakim, who mainly is interpreting for the Iranians. (Cave also speaks Persian and sometimes interprets.) The Iranian names are redacted but the participants are known from other accounts to include Ali Bahramani (mentioned above) and Ali Samii, a member of the Islamic Revolutionary Guard Corps, although his name is likely a pseudonym. The double parentheses and question marks indicate indistinct passages; they have been inserted by the government transcriber. The authors of this volume have provided additional text for context within brackets and in italics.*]

Frankfurt, October 6–8

((Tape begins with Hakim and [*Ali*] talking quietly together at times, even whispering. [...] Then U.S. parties enter the room and several conversations are taking place simultaneously. Then talks resume.))

Secord: [...] I'm going to address this list. There are some terrific practical problems here. There are a couple of real, as opposed to philosophical, problems with this list.

[...]

Secord: The first problem is political, based upon previous official requests of the Iranian government [...] and I would underline, desperate requests from him, for TOWs or HAWK parts and for high powered radars. We have achieved presidential authority for immediate air delivery of those items. [Redacted] can deny this or not deny this. It is irrelevant. We have documentary proof. It is not even worth discussing. And the president of the U.S. has approved a

secret operation to deliver these items immediately, and
we would have already delivered them except that we were
asked to hold up so that we could have these higher
level discussions.

[...]

North: Let me, Okay? Everything that the general [*Secord*] said
is entirely accurate. When we looked at this list, we
estimated that, excluding these two items, the HAWK and the
TOWs [*missile systems*], we are looking at a minimum of four
shiploads of equipment. Thousands of people in the U.S., at
a minimum, would know about that. If we are going to do
something like this, it has to be very clear that we are
doing this because we are working for a military balance in
the region and a political solution, and honorable
solution to the Iran-Iraq war.

[...]

North: That Saturday when [*Ali Bahramani*] was in Washington [*on
a visit arranged secretly by North that included a late night
tour of the Oval Office*] and I flew up to Camp David to talk to
the president, and I showed him the list, and he said, "Why
are you thinking so small?" He took the list, that list right
there, and he went like this with it – I was sitting across the
table – and he said, "For someone who has seen so much war as
you have, North, you should understand that I want to end
that war on terms that are acceptable to Iran ... I don't want
to simply help go out and kill more Iranian youngsters. What
about the 2 million people without homes? What about the oil
industry which is already in ruins? What about the
industrial base of Iran which is being destroyed? Stop
coming in and looking like a gun merchant." And he banged on
the table. "I want to end the war." And every time we get to
the point where we can act in that regard, we find this
obstacle sitting in the middle of the road.

[...]

Hakim: ((Interprets)) [*For "Samii," whom the Americans
nicknamed "The Engine"*] I think like you do in the

evaluation of the subject and its solution. And I also
understand that the main problem is what you just
discussed. But how can I defeat the prestige and honor of my
country while I am not convinced that I have something in
hand? I should be in a position when I go back and tell the
leaders of Iran that I want you to put at stake your honor in
trade for this which is the honor of the U.S. Add to this the
problem that we have in Lebanon. I want to tell you that if
these hostages were in our possession, like the matter of
the American hostages in Iran [in 1979] ((few words
missed)) we would have resolved it. He [Samii] wants you to
know that if they actually had their hands on the hostages
in Iran ((sic)) this should have been resolved the same day
that the other hostages were released. And I want you to
know that even today, as I'm sitting here, we do not have a
guarantee that the Lebanese would 100 percent listen to
what we have to say. We must put at stake the substance that
would be equal with our existence. And you know that even up
to this date, in connection with the Tehran hostages we are
still ((few words missed)) in a mess. Therefore, please
understand my problem. I cannot go to Iran and say forget
about the 500 million dollars in the Hague issue [regarding
the status of Iranian assets frozen by the U.S. after the
Tehran embassy seizure in 1979] . And I do not expect in this
meeting to resolve that.

[...]

North: Let me make just one last point, and then it's your turn.
[...] Ronald Reagan is going to be president of the U.S. for
two more years and will never again serve as president.
[...] This president would like to have - I can tell you
because I've listened to him - his vision is that when he
leaves office in 1989 we will have full diplomatic
relations between your country and ours. He would like to
be remembered as a man who helped to bring peace, if you
will, to the question and Muslim and Jewish people in this
world. That's why he [chose?] the phrase he did from our
Holy Book [a reference to Galatians 3:8, which Reagan
inscribed in a bible that North gave to Bahramani in
Germany as a token] . It isn't a [word indistinct] short-

term thing just to get reelected or to solve the immediate
problem and then forget about it. He really has a long-term
vision. He knows that Saddam Hussein is a ((expletive)).
Hakim: Do you want me to translate that?
North: Go ahead, that's his word, not mine.
[...]

Tape A3
(Meeting at Mainz, W. Germany, October 29-30, 1986)

[...]

Hakim: ((Interprets in Persian)) He was explaining that if we
are not successful, not only will this group's work come to
an end and ((few words missed)), but groups in the future
which want to make contact will use this as an example - that
Iranians ?are not reliable?. This will be studied.
[...]
Hakim: ((Interprets)) If you don't have any more [items] on
your side, he likes to let me explain what's happening on
their side.
North: Well, I do want to hear that. Let me just make one point
about that ... He ((Hakim)) works for me - you ((Cave))
translate this - he works for me as a consultant. I don't know
the Farsi word for consultant, but as a part-time contract
employee. He has been this for four, five years for me since
I have been at the White House and in the president's office. He
does translations. The VOA broadcast in Farsi which you asked
for and we gave, he translated those from my English to Farsi.
Secord: And if we fail, we are going to shoot him, because
somebody has to go. Like in Iran, somebody has to be shot.
[...]
Cave: ((In Persian)) Mr. North and I are lucky. They won't shoot
us, we'll just go to jail.
North: Fired.
Secord: The president may shoot North.
Hakim: OK, he wants to explain his case.
Hakim: ((Interprets)) I have addressed this issue earlier ?
that? he's bringing up. He wants to clarify his position
that people back home believe that a lot of times he talks
about things which he should not talk about. Therefore, it
is very important that whatever he tells us should not get

into the official channels and get back to ?them? Because
that would make life miserable for him and difficult for him.
He has no financial interest ((few words missed)). One
objective is to make sure that this thing is going to ((few
words missed)). He has full trust in this group, especially
in General Secord. He has been very truthful with him, very
helpful, and he wants to see that something good is going to
come out of this. Therefore, please, whatever he discusses
should not leave this room so he will feel comfortable to be
able to get back to us ((trails off)). I discussed that
earlier this week ((few words missed)).

[*The next passage relates to the Iranian political process*]
He says you have to understand that Iran just finished ((few
words missed)) and setting Imam Khomeini aside, the country
is managed by shareholding ((word missed)). And once you put
Khomeini aside, there are a number of people involved. There
are three basic groups of this shareholding company. One is
the radicals, and they are ((word missed)) radical and
((word missed)) radical within the same... Then the third
group is the right-wing and then there's two ((few words
missed)) who is headed by Hashemi Rafsanjani. And not only
do they follow their own line, but they are also the
connection in between the first and the third group.

[...]

He wants you to understand that the principle ... These three
groups have the same objective and they all agree in the
same way; when it comes to actual execution, they have
different approaches. And they are not purely political
((a few words missed)) religious ((a few words missed)). As
you probably know, Imam Khomeini has issued decrees ((few
words missed)). In public opinion he ((Rafsanjani)) is
considered the second man, second in command, basically
because of these ((word missed)). When [redacted] raised
the issue of establishing relations with the U.S. he was in
favor of it, but for his own politics he decided to get all
the groups involved and give them a role to play.

North: Wait a minute, who's "he?"

Hakim: Rafsanjani. He wants you to know who [redacted] is.
    [Redacted] works for [several words redacted] belongs to

the radical group, the radical group that they were the
university students who took the hostages in Iran. That's
the group. When [redacted] contacted [redacted] in this
approach to establish a relationship with the U.S., he,
[redacted] asked for representatives of the three groups
to be present and participate in this action, and ((two
words missed)) support. In other words, this idea of having
all groups participate in this is not new. It dated back a
long time ago, and still he's going to explain more and
still sticking to it. This issue as you can very well
understand is very sensitive. [3 lines redacted] This
approach of [redacted] was a double-edged sword – and
positive and negative points... The positive point being
that if it would be a failure and all parties are involved so
there would not be an internal war. And the negative part is
that because different views and opinions are under the
same roof, it's very difficult to manage.

....

Mainz, October 29

North: The big problem I've got is the whole damn appearance of
bartering over ... bodies. I mean if we're really sincere
about this whole friggin thing, what we ought to be doing
is, they ought to be exercising every possible amount of
leverage they've got to get these people out, and we agree
that as soon as they're out we can do all kinds of good
things, because that's where we are we're ?heading? [We?]
will have? a friggin FMS [Pentagon Foreign Military Sales]
contact ?team? [...] What we are trying to do is to close the
bridge [on?] this secret shit, and get on with the real
[reasons?]. You know, when we were in Tehran [see Document
23], okay, fouled up though it may have been, if you look at
the document that I wrote and [former National Security
Advisor Robert] McFarlane was prepared to sign, you will
see that that's what we were talking about way back then,
way back in May [1986] – is to get beyond the hostages and get
on with a formal relationship. Everything we have done
since the very first contact, whether it be step-by-step or
whether it be all at once, that's where we've been trying to

go. You guys don't trust us, and we don't trust you, and so we end up doing it a little bit at a time, and it takes forever.

[...]

North: I'm telling you, we are so close to having done the right thing – you and I and [Ali?] and the men in this room, and yet we are going to foul it up. I can see it coming.

[...]

North: When we were in Tehran, all McFarlane said was, "Look, we don't want you guys to lose the war, we want an honorable settlement and all you have to do is use your influence to get those hostages out, and we are going to do all kinds of things for you." in fact, he said don't limit yourself to this, there is much, much more that could be done. The hostages have to get beyond us, we have to get beyond them. ((time out for tea))

Hakim: They are convinced that we have ??good intentions?? He has said it before. He said, "After things broke up in Iran, and you left and then ?yet? you sent this stuff. That indicated to the Iranians that the Americans have good ((few words missed)). He has brought this up, but he says, in other words he's saying he knows that we have ??good intentions??

North: So how the hell do we get from where we are today to where we've got to go?

[...]

Hakim: ((Interprets)) He says a country like the United States – a superpower – is it not in their power to send two or three technicians Tuesday? I said, "Yes it is. We can send them on Monday, we can send them on Sunday." [...] Then I said, "An imam like Khomeini – the first Shiah Imam for the first government of Shi'ahs in the world – he doesn't have the power of going to Lebanon and telling those assholes to release the three hostages? Such a great religious power?

North: And his answer was?

Hakim: "No. He doesn't know the details." I said, "Well, our president doesn't know the details." I'm trying to make the point that it's the wrong attitude to sit back there and say the United States is a superpower, and we forget that [*Iran*] is a super religious country. It's very equal.

North: [*Well?*], it is and the influence that the Imam has over those who hold the hostages is near total.

Hakim: Of course. He can get those people back with one word. One word. I'm convinced. It's no bullshit. I think... He can. He can.

[...]

[*Source:* S. Rept. No. 100-216, 100*th* Congress, 1*st* Session, Report of the Congressional Committees Investigating the Iran-Contra Affair, *Appendix A: Vol. 1 (Washington, DC, 1988), selections from pp. 1571–1664.*]

Document 25. State Department, Flash Cable, Michael Armacost for Ambassadors, "Message on Military Operation," SECRET, April 17, 1988

It is 1988 and the Iran–Iraq War drags on. The War on Cities and the Tanker War continue to rack up civilian and economic casualties. Between 1984 and 1988, dozens of tankers and other merchant ships, sailing under international flags, are attacked by Iranian and Iraqi boats, missiles, or mines. The conflict reaches a turning point in April 1988 when the USS Samuel B. Roberts, *part of a months-long US Navy reflagging and escort operation for Kuwaiti tankers, runs into an Iranian mine, severely damaging it and injuring several American sailors.*

Reagan orders direct retaliation by US naval forces against Iranian targets, under Operation Praying Mantis. (The order is conveyed in this diplomatic cable to numerous American embassies so that certain foreign heads of state can have advance warning.) Bilateral relations have been worsening since the Iran-Contra scandal surfaced in late 1986, and this is certainly the lowest point since the Tehran hostage crisis – at least for now. Just four days after the Samuel B. Roberts *strikes the mine, US forces begin firing on Iranian naval targets, killing dozens and destroying significant Iranian assets. Iranian attempts at retaliation accomplish little and both sides quickly seek de-escalation. The USA is now directly engaged in the war and enmity toward Iran is near an all-time high.*

....

1. S – entire text
2. You are instructed, on an urgent basis as soon as possible after (0200 GMT) April 18, to convey the following oral

message from the president to the head of state or government
as appropriate (if necessary through the foreign minister to
ensure speedy delivery.) There will be no signed original,
and you should not rpt not leave the message as a non-paper.
Please report delivery, as well as any substantive
reaction, immediately.

3. In delivering this message, you should stress the need for
absolute confidentiality until the action it foreshadows is
public knowledge. Likewise you should not discuss this
message within your mission until the action has occurred.

4. Begin message.

 - I am today ordering U.S. military forces to strike certain
   Iranian military [] targets in the Persian Gulf. These
   targets have been used to attack non-belligerent shipping
   in the international waters of the Persian Gulf, [] the
   action which is a defensive measure designed and intended
   to deter further Iranian mining will commence within the
   next few hours. The U.S. commander in the Persian Gulf is
   coordinating with your commanders in the Gulf to assure
   they are forewarned and have time to take
   defensive precautions.

 - Because of our special political relationship, and the
   presence of your forces working alongside our own,
   I wanted to inform you in advance of our action and advise
   you on the reasons for my decision. I of course hope that
   you will support this decision privately and in your
   public statements.

 - We had hoped that actions the United States took last fall
   in response to various provocations by Iran would have
   served to convince Iran of the United States' seriousness
   of purpose and our resolve to continue to defend our
   interests in the Gulf.

 - Four times last fall, we informed the government of Iran
   that we could not accept Iran's minelaying in
   international waters, or in the waters of neutral states.
   We made clear we did not seek further confrontation with
   Iran, but indicated we would be prepared to meet any
   escalation of military actions by Iran with
   strong countermeasures.

 - The action I am ordering today is in direct response to
   Iran's recent mining of international waterways, one of

which struck and severely damaged the the [*sic*] USS Samuel
B. Roberts. Ten American sailors were injured during that
mining attack. The ship sustained significant damage.

- We have conclusive evidence that the mine which struck the
Samuel B. Roberts was one of several mines laid recently by
Iran in the international sea lanes off Bahrain. Iran
knows these lanes are regularly used by U.S. vessels, and
undoubtedly intended by its acts to damage or sink such
vessels, with serious potential loss of life or injury to
sailors or merchantmen on board.
- We know that the mines were manufactured in Iran in the
same factory that produced the mines found on the Iran AJR.
We believe that one of the mines was manufactured within
the last month. The place and approximate date of
production were determined from our inspection of the
external markings of the mine.
- We are making public photographs of additional mines U.S.
Navy divers located and exploded in the area where the
Roberts was struck. (for Rome, Brussels, London, the
Hague: we are most appreciative of your willingness to
participate in the clearing of this new Iranian mine field
in international waters.)
- The action we will be taking is an appropriate military
response to the unlawful use of force against the United
States, necessary to deter future mining by Iran aimed at
vessels in international waterways, including U.S.
vessels. It is a lawful exercise of the right of self-
defense enshrined in article 51 of the United Nations
charter. We are so notifying the president of the
security council.
- These belligerent actions by Iran, in reckless disregard
of neutral nations' right to free passage, underscore the
urgency of strong international measures in the United
Nations to pass a follow-on resolution to Resolution 598.
As the mining incident last week makes clear, Iran's basic
behavior remains unchanged. Regrettably, further action
was necessary for effective deterrence.
- I have instructed Secretary Shultz to raise with the
Soviets my concern about the deteriorating security
situation in the region. The root cause of this is the

continuation of the Iran-Iraq war. Secretary Shultz will underscore the need for rapid Security Council passage of a follow-on resolution. I count on your help with other members of the security council to break the deadlock.

- Last week's incident in the Gulf also further underscores the need for continued allied vigilance against Iranian threats to international shipping. We are determined to continue our naval protection and countermine efforts in the gulf. I trust you will do the same. We need to continue to send the Iranians (and others in the Gulf) a clear and unambiguous message of Western solidarity.

[*Source: National Archives and Records Administration declassification; Digital National Security Archive*, US Policy and Iran *collection, Document No. IU00889.*]

Document 26. Islamic Republic of Iran, Letter, Ayatollah Ruhollah Khomeini, [Announcing Agreement to a Ceasefire in the Iran-Iraq War], UNCLASSIFIED, July 16, 1988

Since 1982, Iraq has sought a means of ending the war it started but Iran has thus far flatly refused. National pride, hatred for Saddam, demands for compensation, and commitment to spreading the revolution drive Iranian hopes for total victory. But as the costly war continues, and with the United States now very visibly involved, that objective seems increasingly remote.

The final straw for Khomeini is the shooting down of an Iranian passenger plane by an American naval ship, the USS Vincennes. *The shocking event, coming on the heels of the US Navy's destruction of nearly a dozen Iranian naval vessels and operational bases a few weeks earlier, leads Khomeini to call a meeting of his top advisors to discuss a possible end to the conflict. Some, like Mohsen Rezaie who heads the IRGC, believe the war is still winnable, though admittedly at great cost, while others, like Rafsanjani, argue for its immediate termination. In the end, Khomeini chooses to "drink[] hemlock" and negotiate with Iraq after eight long years.*

The effects of war, terrorism, purges, and economic deterioration through the 1980s have been devastating to the country and its people. Yet, with Khomeini managing to retain his unchallenged authority, the Islamic leadership not only survives but solidifies its grip on the nation. When the Supreme

Leader dies less than a year later, however, the future of Iran becomes more uncertain.

....

In the Name of God, the Compassionate and the Merciful
   [Greetings and prayers...] Our military commanders in both the Army and the Revolutionary Guards, who are in charge of day-to-day operations in the war, have readily conceded that the Islamic Army will not achieve its victories any time soon. It is the view of these commanders (and also of the top political officers of the regime) that the war is no longer in the national interest, and they have expressed with much confidence their view that we cannot attain even one-tenth of the kinds of advanced military equipment and munitions that the Eastern and Western powers have provided to Saddam and the Iraqi Army. In light of the recent unsettling report sent to me by the Commander of the Revolutionary Guards [Mohsen Rezaie], and the receipt of tens of similar analyses and letters in the aftermath of our recent military defeats, the Commander of the IRGC is among the minority of voices still insistent on continuing the war. However, given the enemy's widespread use of chemical weaponry against our cities and civilians, I am now inclined to agree to a full-scale ceasefire, the reasons for which I shall outline in reference to the 23 June 1988 report of Commander Rezaie to me.
   This commander has written that within 5 years we will have no victory; it is possible that having resources/supplies - which we would have to acquire over the next 5 years - we would have the capability to resist and fight the enemy along our borders. He has instructed me that only if by the end of 1371 [1992] we are in possession of 350 mobile war stations, 2,500 tanks and 3,000 cannon/guns, 300 fighter planes and 300 helicopters, or even nuclear, chemical and biological weapons - which are among the necessities of war at this time - could we offset our losses and reach a fruitful victory. The commander has also noted that we must increase the Revolutionary Guards forces seven-fold and the Army by almost double its numbers today if we are to achieve these goals; in addition, he has brought to my attention that even if we were to soundly defeat the enemy in the battlefield,

victory would still not be possible without the expulsion of American forces from the Persian Gulf.

This commander has determined that the success of these plans would largely depend on our ability to pay for it out of the national budget, which it appears unlikely either the government or the office of central command of the armed forces would be able to do. Yet, in spite of all these grave realities, the commander insists that we continue the war, which amounts to sheer sloganeering on his part. After consulting with the ministers of treasury and budget, the prime minister has confirmed that our current budget already stands at a deficit. Moreover, the top decision-makers in charge of the war have informed me that the cost of military equipment and munitions that were expended in our recent military losses is the equivalent of the entire budget for the Army and the Revolutionary guards for the coming year. More importantly, top political officials have notified me that our recent military losses have given the public the impression that we cannot end this war in an expedited fashion, thereby weakening their willingness to join the frontlines and fight for their country.

I trust that you each know better than anyone else that this decision is like drinking hemlock for me; but I am only concerned with the satisfaction of God and with following His faith and the safekeeping of the Islamic Republic; if I have to sacrifice my dignity for Him, then I will. Dear Lord, we undertook the revolution out of our faith in you, we have fought this war out of our faith in you, and we shall accept this ceasefire out of our faith in you.

Dear Lord, you have witnessed that we do not reconcile ourselves to either the American or Soviet governments, and that we regard friendly relations with superpowers and great powers in this world to be against the fundamental principles of our Islamic faith. Dear Lord, in a world so full of corruption, greed, hatred, and deception we are but foreigners; we only have You as our companion [...]

[*Source: Sajed Online, IRGC (link no longer available).*]

Questions for further discussion

- How did Washington and Tehran react to the start of the Iran–Iraq War? How did each side view the role of the other?

- How did events in Lebanon during this period – from the 1983 Beirut bombings to the taking of hostages from 1982 to 1989 – influence Iran–US relations?

- What were the Reagan administration's motivations for pursuing covert arms-for-hostages deals with Iran? What did the episode reveal about each government's mutual attitudes, and how did it affect longer-term relations?

- What key events in the Iran–Iraq War contributed most directly to US and Iranian hostility? What factors or circumstances might have helped ameliorate this animosity had the other side been aware of them?

- What role did Majlis Speaker Akbar Hashemi Rafsanjani play in the Lebanese hostage events and what insights might this have given to American policymakers?

Notes

1. CIA memorandum, "Iran and the US Presidential Election," August 18, 1980.
2. See Malcolm Byrne, *Iran-Contra: Reagan's Scandal and the Unchecked Abuse of Presidential Power* (Lawrence: University Press of Kansas, 2014). For some administrations, the decision not to make regime change official US policy had more to do with practicalities than political ethics.
3. The proposal to use Western and even US arms shipments to Iran as leverage first surfaced within two weeks of Reagan's inauguration, during a meeting of the State Department-convened Iran–Iraq working group; see Chris Shoemaker, National Security Council staff, memorandum to Gen. Robert L. Schweitzer, "Iran – Iraq Meeting," February 4, 1981.
4. See, for example, Mark J. Gasiorowski, "The Nuzhih Plot and Iranian Politics," *International Journal of Middle East Studies*, Vol. 34, No. 4 (Nov. 2002), pp. 645–666.
5. Tom Twetten was director of Near East operations at the CIA; see his account in James G. Blight *et al.*, *Becoming Enemies: U.S.–Iran Relations and the Iran–Iraq War, 1979–1988* (Lanham, MD: Rowman & Littlefield, 2012), pp. 113–115; also interview with Patrick Lang, a senior Defense Intelligence Agency officer specializing in the Middle East who personally worked with the Iraqi military, June 24, 2009.
6. See for example Document 19; Patrick Lang interview, June 24, 2009 (note 5 above).
7. Reagan reportedly called it the saddest day of his career (Virginia Military Institute news release, November 4, 2014, quoting former Reagan military aide Charles F. Brower IV).
8. [Footnote from original document] *The Alert Memorandum is an interagency publication issued by the Director of Central Intelligence on behalf of the Intelligence*

Community. Its purpose is to ensure that senior policymakers are aware of impending potential developments that may have serious implications for US interests. It is not a prediction that these developments will occur. This memorandum has been coordinated at the working level with CIA, DIA, NSA, and State/INR, and the Strategic Warning Staff.

9. See Blight *et al.*, *Becoming Enemies*, pp. 113–115.

10. George P. Shultz, *Turmoil and Triumph* (New York: Scribner's, 1993), p. 237.

11. There is, however, documentation indicating some Western companies helped Iraq construct facilities that had dual uses – legitimate and weapons-related – and that Baghdad received chemical precursors from foreign sources. See, for example, Central Intelligence Agency, *Comprehensive Report of the Special Advisor to the DCI on Iraq's WMD*, with Addendums (Duelfer report), Vol. III, "Iraq's Chemical Warfare Program," September 30, 2004. There is also testimony from US ex-military intelligence officers that the Iraqis later utilized American targeting assistance for their own purposes; for example, interview with Patrick Lang, June 24, 2009 (note 5 above).

12. CIA, "Impact and Implications of Chemical Weapons Use in the Iran–Iraq War," April 1988; Defense Department, "Proliferation: Threat and Response," April 1996. But according to a specialist from the International Crisis Group, "no convincing evidence" yet exists "that Iran ever used chemical weapons" during the war with Iraq; see Joost R. Hiltermann, *A Poisonous Affair: America, Iraq, and the Gassing of Halabja* (Cambridge University Press, 2014, paperback), ch. 7, especially pp. 157–165.

13. Notes of a December 7, 1985, meeting of the president with top aides taken by the secretary of defense record that the president "could answer to charges of illegality but couldn't answer to the charge that 'big strong President Reagan passed up a chance to free the hostages.'" (Investigation of the Independent Counsel for Iran/Contra Matters, Caspar Weinberger notes, December 7, 1985, ALZ 0039831.)

14. As a side note, the cover memo intentionally distorts the timing of events to make it seem like the Israelis have just proposed this idea in early 1986 when in fact they did so in summer 1985, leading to three shipments of missiles to Iran. The problem, one of the core elements of the Iran-Contra scandal, is that the president never signed a Finding to cover any of those transactions. As subsequent investigations would discover, the president's aides are trying to give the appearance – falsely – that all appropriate legal steps have been taken prior to any arms shipment to Iran. (See, for example, Lawrence E. Walsh, *Final Report of the Independent Counsel for Iran/Contra Matters* [Washington, DC: US Court of Appeals for the District of Columbia Circuit, 1993], ch. 27 *passim*.)

15. Howard J. Teicher, memorandum of conversation, "U.S.–Iran Dialogue," circa May 28, 1986.

16. North, *Joint Hearings*, vol. 100-7, Part I, July 7, 1987, pp. 8, 335; July 9, 1987, p. 121.

17. The delegation used false Irish passports and pseudonyms: former National Security Advisor Robert McFarlane went as "Sean Devlin"; the White House's lead operative for Iran-Contra, Oliver North, as "Goode"; NSC staffer Howard Teicher as "McGrath"; Israeli government advisor Amiram Nir as "Miller"; and retired CIA Iran expert George Cave as "O'Neil."

Fig. 1 President Jimmy Carter and Rosalynn Carter (right) greet Shah Mohammad Reza Pahlavi and Shahbanu Farah Pahlavi at the White House, November 15, 1977. Moments later, tear gas from nearby clashes between pro- and anti-Shah demonstrators disrupted the ceremony. This image from an Iranian website superimposes a quote from Ayatollah Khomeini disparaging the then-departed monarch. (Official website of Ayatollah Khomeini, www.en.imam-khomeini.ir)

Fig. 2 Supreme Leader Ayatollah Ruhollah Khomeini (seated), seen here in the late 1980s surrounded by some of his longtime close advisors: Majlis Speaker Akbar Hashemi Rafsanjani, Foreign Minister Ali Akbar Velayati, President (and future Supreme Leader) Ali Khamenei, Intelligence Minister Mohammad Reyshahri, head of the judiciary Abdolkarim Mousavi Ardebili, and Prime Minister Mir-Hossein Mousavi (a future leader of the Green Movement). (Official website of Hashemi Rafsanjani, www.hashemirafsanjani.ir/en/node/134311)

Fig. 3 Iranian students clamber over the gates of the US Embassy in Tehran on November 4, 1979, determined, according to their own accounts, to prevent a repeat of the 1953 coup, which restored the Shah to the throne. The assault led to the seizure of dozens of hostages and a 444-day crisis that would have major repercussions for Iran's domestic politics and its position in the world. (STR/AFP via Getty Images)

Fig. 4 National Security Advisor Zbigniew Brzezinski briefs President Carter at the White House on the Iranian hostage crisis and its ramifications for US Persian Gulf strategy, January 4, 1980. (Presidential Assistant Frank Moore is at right.) The hostage saga would absorb administration energies until Carter's final day in office. Brzezinski's influence with the president on the subject of Iran usually overshadowed that of the more moderate Secretary of State Cyrus Vance. Brzezinski consistently pushed for a tough line and agonized over the Cold War implications of the crisis. (CSIS: Center for Strategic and International Studies)

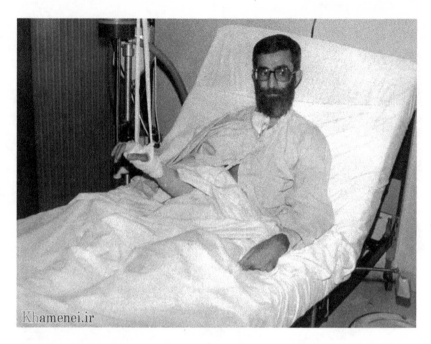

Khamenei.ir

Fig. 5 Ali Khamenei, Iran's future Supreme Leader, was a politically active cleric under the Shah who became a member of Ayatollah Khomeini's circle and held a variety of government posts in the often violent early years of the Islamic Republic. Here, he recovers in a hospital after a booby trap exploded at a mosque on June 27, 1981, causing him permanently to lose the use of his right arm, among other injuries. (Official website of Ayatollah Khamenei, http://farsi.khamenei.ir)

We undermined the vicious dominance of the superpowers, strengthened the roots of our revolution and promoted the sense of brotherhood.

Sahifeh-ye-Imam, Vol 21, page 285

Fig. 6 The 1980–1988 Iran–Iraq War was a crucible for the Islamic Republic, which emerged exhausted from the conflict. The experience solidified the regime's hold on power and hardened a sense of isolation from the world community, themes encapsulated in this scene from the war front with accompanying quote as displayed on Ayatollah Khomeini's official website.

Fig. 7 During the course of the eight-year war with Iraq, Iran's leaders came to believe they were battling not just the Iraqis but Western imperialists as well, especially the United States, which they accused (accurately) of backing Saddam Hussein. The moment that seared this belief into the thinking of Iran's leaders occurred on July 3, 1988, when the guided missile cruiser USS *Vincennes* shot down a civilian Iran Air passenger jet over the Persian Gulf. Here, mourners participate in a memorial service for the 290 victims. To this day, Tehran believes it was a deliberate attack while the US government insists it was a tragic mistake. (Photo by Norbert Schiller/AFP/Getty Images)

Fig. 8 The Iran-Contra affair in the mid-1980s was largely an outgrowth of President Ronald Reagan's intense desire to free American hostages held by Iran's ally, Hezbollah, in Lebanon. Here, Reagan meets at the White House on October 28, 1985, with relatives of captive Americans, whom he was anxious to reassure. To his right is National Security Advisor Robert C. McFarlane who spearheaded the initiative. The yellow ribbon on the table was a potent symbol – and pointed reminder by the families – of the hostage crisis that loomed over Jimmy Carter's presidency. (Ronald Reagan Presidential Library)

Fig. 9 President George H.W. Bush meets with United Nations Secretary General Javier Pérez de Cuellar to discuss the Middle East, January 5, 1991. Bush had inherited an unresolved hostage crisis from the Reagan administration in which he was vice president. Early in his own presidency, he reached out to Pérez de Cuellar to seek secret mediation with Tehran over the remaining American captives. Before he left the White House, they would all be back home, with Iran's help, but it would not be enough to produce the breakthrough in relations the presidents of both countries had hoped for. (George H.W. Bush Library and Museum)

Fig. 10 One of the most devastating direct attacks on US personnel attributed to the Islamic Republic was the truck bombing of the Khobar Towers military facility in Saudi Arabia on June 25, 1996. President Bill Clinton came under significant pressure to retaliate militarily, but by the time sufficient evidence emerged to convince him of Tehran's culpability, Iranians had gone to the polls and surprisingly elected a reformist president who seemed to offer a chance for a dramatic improvement in bilateral relations. (Photo by Scott Peterson/Getty Images)

Fig. 11 Upon entering office in 1993, President Clinton had little interest in improving ties with the Islamic Republic, focusing instead on containing the regime, largely through sanctions. On August 5, 1996, several weeks after the Khobar Towers bombing, he signed a tough new bill, the Iran and Libya Sanctions Act, remarking: "With this legislation we strike hard where it counts against those who target innocent lives and our very way of life." The following year, he would make a 180-degree turn in his views and pursue a rapprochement with Iran's new president. (Courtesy of William J. Clinton Presidential Library)

Fig. 12 On May 23, 1997, the Iranian people elected Mohammad Khatami president, signaling an acute desire to move the country toward reform – and away from the turbulence of revolution. Here, Supreme Leader Ali Khamenei (center) presides over Khatami's (right) inauguration on August 3 as outgoing President Akbar Hashemi Rafsanjani (left) looks on. Khatami's desire to engage the West in a "dialogue among civilizations" met with a positive response from President Bill Clinton but hardline resistance, especially in Iran, along with years of distrust, misunderstandings, and simple bad timing thwarted their efforts. (Official website of Ayatollah Khamenei, http://farsi.khamenei.ir)

Fig. 13 The day after the September 11, 2001, terrorist attacks, President George W. Bush looks over a briefing paper with Vice President Dick Cheney and National Security Advisor Condoleezza Rice outside the Oval Office. Even though 9/11 created surprising opportunities for cooperating with Iran against al-Qaeda and the Taliban, Cheney along with Defense Secretary Donald Rumsfeld led the opposition to engagement. Rice, who would take over from Colin Powell as secretary of state during Bush's second term, became more amenable to negotiating directly with Tehran after determining that the hardline approach had failed. (Courtesy of George W. Bush Presidential Library and Museum)

Fig. 14 President Mahmoud Ahmadinejad tours the uranium enrichment complex at Natanz on April 8, 2008. The facility's existence was revealed in 2002 and became a focal point of international concern over Iran's nuclear ambitions. Ahmadinejad enflamed Iran's adversaries by touting the country's capabilities, including making this highly publicized visit to the controversial site. The tactic backfired, however, giving Western intelligence an unexpected inside look at Iran's development of second-generation centrifuges. "This is intel to die for," a London-based analyst declared. (Photo by the Office of the Presidency of the Islamic Republic of Iran via Getty Images)

Fig. 15 Many Iranians, not just regime officials, have attached special significance to the country's nuclear program, which dates to the late 1950s under the Shah, two decades before the Iranian revolution. This print hanging in a quasi-government institution in Tehran is a revealing, idealized representation of the public image of the program – depicting Iranians in national garb lifting vials of uranium as doves hold up a banner celebrating the peaceful uses of the atom. (Photo by author)

Fig. 16 US policymakers and America's Middle Eastern allies have long seen Iran's backing of radical actors in the region as a core threat. The Islamic Republic, especially in its early years, was clear about its goal of spreading the revolution beyond the country's borders. Here in 2000, Supreme Leader Ali Khamenei meets with two leading figures in that campaign, Gen. Qasem Soleimani, commander of the Islamic Revolutionary Guard Corps's Qods Force, and Hassan Nasrallah, secretary general of Hezbollah, the Lebanese political party that has been tied to numerous terrorist attacks over the years. (Official website of Ayatollah Khamenei, http://farsi.khamenei.ir)

Fig. 17 The June 12, 2009, presidential elections in Iran, which returned hardliner Mahmoud Ahmadinejad to office, were widely viewed as rigged. Days of massive protests by the so-called Green Movement followed, often rallying around one of its leading candidates, former Prime Minister Mir-Hossein Mousavi (center). The elections and subsequent government use of brute force against the demonstrators damaged the legitimacy of the Islamic Republic. President Barack Obama at first held off condemning the regime, for which he was widely criticized in the West. (Photo by Getty Images)

Fig. 18 The Sultan of Oman (right) hosts President Hassan Rouhani during a visit to Muscat in February 2017. Oman for years enjoyed positive relations with both Iran and the West, including the United States, and the Sultan enthusiastically acted as an intermediary between Washington and Tehran. His ability to earn the trust of both sides helped prepare the way for secret bilateral talks in 2013 that made possible the 2015 Joint Comprehensive Plan of Action (JCPOA). (Photo by Mohammed Mahjoub/ AFP via Getty Images)

Fig. 19 President Barack Obama meets with Secretary of State Hillary Rodham Clinton and Under Secretary of State William Burns in the White House Situation Room on September 29, 2009, just before Burns departs for P5+1 nuclear talks with Iran in Geneva. (White House photo by Pete Souza; courtesy Barack Obama Presidential Library)

Fig. 20 Secretary of State John Kerry, joined by Under Secretary Wendy Sherman, Energy Secretary Ernest Moniz, and National Security Council staff member Robert Malley, exchanges pleasantries prior to a nuclear negotiating session with Iranian Foreign Minister Mohammad Javad Zarif, head of the Atomic Energy Organization of Iran Ali Akbar Salehi, Deputy Foreign Minister Abbas Araghchi (at far end), and others in Lausanne, Switzerland, on March 17, 2015. The P5+1 signed the JCPOA four months later, on July 14, 2015. (State Department photo)

3

Leaps of Faith: From Containment to Dialogue, 1990–2000

Introduction

After the tumult of the 1980s, most Iranians were ready for the restoration of peace and stability. The Islamic Republic had survived the brutal war with Iraq, and the *nezam* – Iran's system of theocratic government – had emerged in firm control despite years of domestic upheaval. With Khomeini's death in June 1989, leadership passed to his chosen successor, Ali Khamenei, a mid-ranking cleric who lacked "Imam Khomeini's" personal authority and political charisma. This opened the way for powerful voices – across society but also within the elite – to debate fundamental questions like the nature of the economy and the direction of Iran's foreign relations. In the United States, presidents from both major parties grappled with a "new world order" brought about by the collapse of the Soviet Union and the emergence of new challenges, notably the rise of different forms of Islamic radicalism for which they were largely unprepared. With the Cold War all but over, and new leaders in Iran, the 1990s evolved into a period of relative détente, though not before serious flare-ups threatened the possibility of open conflict.

George H.W. Bush began his term on an unusual note of optimism about Iran, embedding in his January 1989 inauguration address the message "goodwill begets goodwill" – a signal intended for Tehran, among other audiences. It was an auspicious time for Bush's gesture. Iran's new president, Akbar Hashemi Rafsanjani, had a plan to help rebuild his country by opening it up to the world, and Bush was cautiously intrigued [Document 29]. When disturbing videotapes of Americans taken hostage in Lebanon began to circulate, the White House cast about for options [Document 28], and in August took the groundbreaking step of approaching the UN Secretary General's office to deliver a message to Rafsanjani, a first since Carter.[1] Over the next two years, the remaining American hostages did gain their release; however, the hoped-for breakthrough with Iran never happened.

A bizarre episode in early 1990 revealed both the president's eagerness and something of the murkiness of Iranian politics. On February 5, the

White House communications office put through a phone call to Bush purporting to be from Rafsanjani himself. Bush took the call and was told that Iran wanted to make a deal for the hostages but that the USA should publicly announce it came at Rafsanjani's initiative. The call turned out to be a hoax, possibly aimed at embarrassing the Iranian president by tying him to another secret deal with Washington. Bush asked the UN Secretary General's office to alert Rafsanjani who a few weeks later reaffirmed that he was willing to help. Then, just as he had done a few years earlier when the Reagan administration arms-for-hostages scandal threatened him politically, he tried to get ahead of the story by disclosing it himself, mocking Bush at a Friday prayer service for getting hoodwinked. Bush, for his part, chose to deny to reporters that he had ever reached out to the Iranians.[2]

Ultimately, the aspirations of the two countries' presidents proved not to be enough. Like Reagan before him, Bush counted on the swift return of the hostages, but this was unrealistic. As Rafsanjani's nephew told Reagan's negotiating team in 1986 [Document 24], even the Iranian president could not simply order his Lebanese partners to comply. He did not have that kind of authority. Instead, he would have to bargain both with Hezbollah and his own domestic constituencies since each would demand something in return: Lebanese prisoners from Israel, the unfreezing of Iranian assets held since the revolution, guaranteed relief from sanctions, even an official acknowledgement that Iraq had been the aggressor in the recent war.

By the time the last American came home in December 1991, the White House had reconsidered the matter of reciprocity. Though kidnappings of Americans had stopped and Tehran's "positive neutrality" during Operation Desert Storm had impressed the president and his military commanders, Iranian agents meanwhile had taken to assassinating émigré dissidents in Europe in 1991, a development senior administration officials felt they could not "reward."[3] Compounding the problem were the unresolved 1989 religious fatwa against British author Salman Rushdie and a string of fresh terrorist incidents tied to the Islamic Republic in Buenos Aires, Berlin, and elsewhere. In spring 1992, when the UN intermediary checked back with Brent Scowcroft, Bush's national security advisor, he was told in effect that the deal was off. "Do you expect us to give something to Iran during a presidential election?" Scowcroft asked. "It can't happen." Rafsanjani, who had put himself at some risk politically, took the news badly.[4]

When Bill Clinton took over the White House in 1993, he had little interest in taking on Iran. His administration denounced it as a "rogue state" and an active sponsor of terrorism that continually undermined the Arab–Israeli peace process, pursued nuclear and other weapons technologies, and oppressed its population. To Clinton, the Islamic Republic radiated hostility and brought Washington nothing but frustration and embarrassment – Iran-Contra being a prime example. The Clinton White House was unmoved by Rafsanjani's outreach to the West and dismissed his efforts on the hostages as self-serving. Secretary of State Warren Christopher, who had formed his views of the Islamic Republic while negotiating for hostages during the Carter era, wrote it off as an "international outlaw."

In May 1993, the administration announced its official policy toward the Islamic Republic. The policy mostly carried on the Bush approach but paired Iran with Iraq under the rubric of "Dual Containment" [Document 30], reflecting a view that Washington did not need to move closer to either side and in fact wanted as little to do with them as possible. Policymakers assumed the Iranian leadership "had too strong an animus toward the United States" to justify even positive inducements, but also believed that Khamenei, unlike Saddam Hussein, was not likely to be overthrown. That left the option of containing the regime.[5] As often was the case when it came to Iran, Washington's thinking was conditioned by other priorities: in this case mainly the Arab–Israeli conflict, which policymakers thought would be easier to manage if Iran and Iraq, both seen as hostile to the peace process, could be kept from interfering.

The deep distrust at the root of this posture, certainly a regular feature on both sides of the relationship, left no room for the possibility that Iran's leadership – Rafsanjani in particular – genuinely sought an opening to the West for whatever mix of reasons. From the perspective of some Iranians who leaned in the direction of a better relationship, the Clinton adminis- tration's narrow attitude was likely to lead to a self-fulfilling prophecy.

Sanctions and other restrictive measures became the policy centerpiece for the rest of Clinton's first term. This required navigating both alliance and domestic politics. The Europeans, like Russia and China, did not see the Iranian regime as a serious threat and believed that trying to isolate it through sanctions or other means was counterproductive. On the other side of the debate, Republicans in Congress pressured the White House to be tougher, as did the Israeli government, going as far as to urge backing for "democratic forces" inside Iran.[6] During 1995, Clinton cajoled governments like Russia [Document 31] to stop supplying Iran's military and especially nuclear programs and imposed bans, first on oil deals and then all financial and commercial transactions with Iran. In the process, a lucrative petroleum contract Rafsanjani had approved for the American company Conoco went by the wayside. Clinton told the World Jewish Congress that contrary to the view "that the best route to change Iranian behavior is by engaging the country ... the evidence of the last two years suggests exactly the reverse."[7]

On June 25, 1996, a powerful truck bomb exploded at the Khobar Towers military compound in Saudi Arabia housing some 2,000 US Air Force personnel. The explosion killed nineteen American servicemen among other casualties [Document 32]. Within days, intelligence experts concluded Iran had been behind it. Clinton was incensed at the attack and declared "[t]hose who did this must not go unpunished," yet he balked at military retaliation. Instead, he insisted that before striking Iran, which vehemently denied its involvement, the government needed strong enough evidence to justify it to the public. In place of force, Clinton opted for more customary economic measures. Signing the sweeping Iran–Libya Sanctions Act [Document 33] a month later, he declared: "You cannot do business with countries that practice commerce with you by day while funding or protecting the terrorists who kill you and your innocent civilians by night."[8]

By the time the Saudis – in 1999 – finally turned over evidence they had gathered that implicated the Islamic Revolutionary Guard Corps, Iran's political circumstances had taken a dramatic turn. To near universal surprise, moderate candidate Mohammad Khatami handily won election to Iran's presidency in May 1997, promising a platform of reform and liberalization. Khatami's calls for a "dialogue among civilizations" electrified the West and sounded like a direct invitation to the United States. Clinton himself, now in his second term, was captivated by the prospect of a breakthrough with Tehran. Warm declarations from both governments followed, along with well-received gestures such as a celebrated US–Iran wrestling tournament.

Yet once again, good intentions were not enough to overcome a decade-and-a-half of antagonism. Neither side seemed able to take the concrete policy steps the other expected. While cultural exchanges were popular, initiatives in the political arena foundered. One contributing factor was the chronic problem of mutual ignorance. An embarrassing incident in September 1998 exemplified things. When Secretary of State Madeleine Albright tried to orchestrate a surprise face-to-face with Foreign Minister Kamal Kharrazi during the UN General Assembly session in New York – it would have been the first at that level in years – she could not recognize the person sitting across the table. "Are we sure this is Kharrazi?" she whispered to her aides who after a moment replied, "We don't know."[9] It turned out to be Kharrazi's deputy, Mohammad Javad Zarif, who would rise to global prominence fifteen years later. Almost a year-and-a-half after Khatami's election, State Department experts still could not identify his foreign minister.

A more serious handicap was the persistent inability by both sides to appreciate the constraints on the ability of either president to make commitments, usually because of pushback from domestic opponents. This led to disappointed expectations on more than one occasion. Another factor was time, perennially in tight supply in the context of a constantly evolving political environment. Khatami later regretted assuming he could just continue to work with whomever Clinton's successor might be and that he would have plenty of opportunity to make domestic hardliners more comfortable with the idea of developing closer US ties.[10]

The most significant attempt at direct political contact came in summer 1999, when Clinton dispatched a letter and oral message to Khatami intended to open a personal line of communication and offer assurances of goodwill [Document 35]. However, the plan had a major flaw: it assumed that an Iranian president had the authority to act unilaterally on a matter of such gravity. That Iran's leaders typically shared responsibility for sensitive decisions was a lesson the Reagan administration had already learned from Rafsanjani's nephew.

The Clinton team would make a similar misstep a year later, when Secretary of State Albright announced the lifting of restrictions on Iranian luxury imports like carpets and pistachios and acknowledged US culpability in the 1953 coup [Document 37]. These were the kinds of "deeds" Iranians had been demanding for years, but the speech, like Clinton's 1999 letter, could not escape the constraints of domestic politics. Albright's reference to power resting in "unelected hands" gave Supreme Leader Khamenei an easy opening to denounce the entire package and shut down a promising avenue to improved relations.

The Bush and Clinton presidencies overlapped with a period of reform within Iran. Presidents Rafsanjani and Khatami sought to rebuild their country's economy and international reputation, which encompassed closer relationships with the West. But the mutual mistrust and antipathy with the USA that had built up since the revolution could not be overcome in the limited time available, and with the turn of the millennium came a new president with very different priorities and unfamiliar realities for the two nations to face. When Tehran finally felt able to take the initiative beyond the cultural sphere, Washington was no longer interested.

Document 27. White House, Inaugural Address, George H.W. Bush, UNCLASSIFIED, January 20, 1989

When George H.W. Bush becomes president in January 1989, the Cold War is in a state of thaw but the elements of a "New World Order" are not yet in place. One piece of unfinished business from the Reagan presidency, in which he served as vice president, is Lebanon where Americans are still being held hostage by Islamic extremist groups. After the Iran-Contra affair, the common presumption is still that Iran has the power to bring about their release. Bush wants to see this happen, after which he seems ready to entertain an improvement in relations with Tehran. During his inaugural address, he hints at the possibility with the remark, "good will begets good will." If the Iranians are willing to work with Washington, they will find the US government cooperative.

To overcome this first hurdle, the White House looks to the United Nations. Assistant Secretary General Giandomenico Picco, a trusted intermediary among the various players – Western governments, Iranians, Hezbollah – agrees to deliver a request from Bush to Iran's President Akbar Hashemi Rafsanjani. According to Picco, Rafsanjani's first reaction is mild offense: "I'm the president of Iran, not Lebanon; why are the Americans talking to me about the Lebanese issue?"[11] Yet, in the mid-1980s the then-Speaker of the Parliament (or Majlis) put himself at political risk by advocating with Hezbollah for the release of Western captives, and in 1987 he publicly offered to work with the Americans, coincidentally calling for a show of "goodwill" on their part.[12]

....

[...]

I come before you and assume the Presidency at a moment rich with promise. We live in a peaceful, prosperous time, but we can make it better. For a new breeze is blowing, and a world refreshed by freedom seems reborn. For in man's heart, if not in fact, the day of the dictator is over. The totalitarian era is passing, its old ideas blown away like leaves from an ancient, lifeless tree. A new breeze is blowing, and a nation refreshed by freedom stands ready to push on. There is new ground to be broken and new action to be taken.

[...]

Great nations of the world are moving toward democracy through the door to freedom. Men and women of the world move toward free markets through the door to prosperity. The people of the world agitate for free expression and free thought through the door to the moral and intellectual satisfactions that only liberty allows.

[...]

To the world, too, we offer new engagement and a renewed vow: We will stay strong to protect the peace. The offered hand is a reluctant fist; once made – strong, and can be used with great effect. There are today Americans who are held against their will in foreign lands and Americans who are unaccounted for. Assistance can be shown here and will be long remembered. Good will begets good will. Good faith can be a spiral that endlessly moves on.

[...]

[*Source: The Miller Center, University of Virginia, Presidential Speeches: https:// millercenter.org/the-presidency/presidential-speeches/january-20-1989- inaugural-address*]

Document 28. White House, Memorandum of Conversation, "Telephone Conversation with Sultan Qaboos of Oman," CONFIDENTIAL, August 3, 1989

From early in his presidency, Bush is eager to feel out how serious Rafsanjani and his colleagues are about opening discussions. He repeatedly asks other world leaders who are in touch with the Iranians for their opinions, chief among them Sultan Qaboos of Oman. Qaboos, who is on good terms with both countries, provides the American president useful insights into Iranian thinking and character over a series of conversations in person and via telephone.

In this particular call, the two leaders speak following the news of American Lt. Col. William Higgins' murder by kidnappers in Beirut. The revelation, accompanied by "a brutal tape" documenting the killing, has shaken the Americans, and Bush worries that further violence toward the remaining hostages will "change the whole equation of what [I] must do." The Sultan is sympathetic and reassures the president that "he had to do what he had to do if things didn't improve." At the same time, both agree the Iranians are aware of this situation and are apparently "trying to be helpful in seeing there were no more killings of American hostages."

Bush's attitude toward the Iranians differs from the public posture of the previous administration. Though concerned about the well-being of US citizens held in Lebanon, he is not anxious to mete out punishment. Trying to understand the complexities of the situation, he shows a willingness, at least for now, to accept their support and resolve the problem.

....

Participants:	The President
Sultan Qaboos	
Notetaker:	Sandra Charles
Date, Time,	August 3, 1989, 11:31 – 11:42 EST
and Place:	
The Oval Office	

The President asked the Sultan how he was. Sultan Qaboos responded that he was fine.

The President said that he had not talked to the Sultan in a long time and that he was delighted this call had worked out.

Sultan Qaboos then said how shocked they were to hear of LTC Higgins' murder.

The President replied that this was one reason for his call. This tragedy had shaken our nation to the very core. LTC Higgins was a man wearing a uniform and a UN representative. He relayed what Sheikh Mohammed of Bahrain had said yesterday when he met with him: that made it the world's business. Everybody had expressed universal concern over this brutality.

Sultan Qaboos stated that he was really shocked, and that this was not good for international relations.

The President said that we presumed LTC Higgins was dead, but we didn't know for sure and we didn't know when he died, if he died. We were appealing to everybody – Prime Minister Thatcher, the Pope, and others – for the return of his body. He asked if there was any possible channel the Sultan could use to encourage, directly or indirectly, the hostage holders to send his body back, saying we did not want to leave any stone unturned.

Sultan Qaboos replied they would do their best, and he would get on the phone and get his men to do their utmost. At the moment, he was in Istanbul and was going to have dinner with the President, but he would telephone his country immediately.

The President continued saying we had another one hanging over our head – another American hostage – [Joseph] Cicippio. We had received a brutal tape, and they had suggested postponing the execution or murder for four hours. The President stated it was terrible to parade these men like this and we didn't know what they would do. We had reports the Iranians were trying to be helpful in seeing there were no more killing[s] of American hostages. The President said he knew Oman had some contacts with Iran and that the Foreign Minister was quite forward-looking in his dealings with them.

Sultan Qaboos replied that he would talk to his people immediately about what Iran was doing.

The President expressed his appreciation, saying he had always been comfortable talking frankly with the Sultan. Rafsanjani might turn out to be more reasonable, but he had some radicals in the government like Mohtashemi-Pur who might make things difficult. There might be a ray of hope, and we didn't want to mishandle our affairs if there might be a change in Iran.

Sultan Qaboos agreed on these points, saying as Rafsanjani came into power, things may be more hopeful.

The President was pleased they thought alike on that. He told the Sultan he was concerned that he may have problems explaining that to many from our side. Our problem would come if they killed another hostage which would change the whole equation of what he must do. Unfortunately, he said that would change the way we would conduct ourselves if it looked like every 24 hours they would kill a hostage. He thought Syria understood that, and Iran understood or was aware that this was our position. He said we were trying to be moderate, reasonable, and restrained.

Sultan Qaboos sympathized, saying the President couldn't be expected to watch his people be killed. He also had an international responsibility to consider. He had to do what he had to do if things didn't improve. The Sultan believed everybody would understand and support his actions.

The President said that was good to hear, but we would continue to use every diplomatic means we could. He concluded, saying that it was nice talking to the Sultan, if he ever had anything to pass on to please call, and then asked about his health.

Sultan Qaboos said he was fine and told him about his current trip, which had started in May in Kuwait. He was in Turkey now, and going to Egypt next week. He hoped to see King Fahd before he went home.

The President said the Sultan would probably see King Fahd before he comes to the U.S. and asked him to say hello to the King and President Mubarak. He added that he knew they appreciated the Sultan's friendship. He then recalled his visit to Oman, saying Barbara and he still remembered fondly the quiet little visit with the music and luncheon at the Sultan's palace in the south.

The Sultan appreciated his sentiments.

The President ended, saying a visit from the Sultan to our country would be most welcome.

[*Source: George H.W. Bush Presidential Library, Memcons and Telcons.*]

Document 29. White House, Memorandum of Telephone Conversation, "Telcon with Chancellor Kohl of Germany," SECRET, February 18, 1991

After his initial outreach to President Rafsanjani, Bush is still exploring ways to approach Iran and determine whether overtures from Tehran's leadership can be trusted. In this conversation with Helmut Kohl, the German Chancellor enthusiastically recounts his meeting with Iranian Foreign Minister Ali Akbar Velayati concerning Iraq following the US invasion several months earlier. Some of the Iranian's statements surprise Kohl and Bush, coming off as more collegial than expected. The president asks for Kohl's opinion of Velayati, "Is he a good man?" Kohl responds, "He is a man of quality, and a real Iranian."

Years later, Iran's former ambassador to Germany, Hossein Mousavian, would relate that Rafsanjani had a deliberate strategy to reach out to the West during the 1990s, focusing on the Germans as a kind of "pilot" case. Here, Kohl clearly recognizes that interest in improving ties and Bush seems to grasp it, too. But other factors ultimately intervene. One is the continued linking of Iran to assassinations of Iranian exiles and other terrorist events, which makes engaging with Tehran politically problematic. (Astonishingly, according to Mousavian, some Iranian officials cannot understand why the Americans are upset since the assassinations are not taking place in the USA but in Europe. Yet, the Europeans show none of the same outrage, leading some in Tehran to conclude that the Americans are exaggerating their concern![13])

Another intervening factor appears to be a simple misreading of intentions – or possibly a failure of imagination. Long after these events, a former senior diplomat under Bush's successor, Bill Clinton, responded to Mousavian that he had no idea about any such initiative by Rafsanjani and that the State Department routinely dismissed German approaches on Iran in the 1990s because they assumed the Germans were playing games with Iran and that the broader European approach – dubbed "critical dialogue" – was just an attempt to undermine American policy.[14]

....

Participants: The President
      Helmut Kohl, Chancellor
      Notetaker: Robert Hutchings, NSC Staff
      Interpreter: Gisela Marcuse
Date, Time February 18, 1991, 12:04 – 12:32 p.m.
 and Place:

      Camp David

Chancellor Kohl initiated the call.

The President: Helmut! How are you today?

Chancellor Kohl: Quite well. There is a lot of work, but things are going well.

The President: You are nice to call. What is going on?

Chancellor Kohl: There are three things I wanted to discuss. The first is a conversation I just had with the Iranian foreign minister, who was just here. What was quite interesting was that he reported that his side and yours started from the assumption that Iraq suffered substantial damage. He said that he had a conversation with the Iraqi foreign minister yesterday, before he went to Moscow. In the conversation, the Iraqi let the information seep through that there had been heavy damage. Obviously, the Iranian foreign minister has known his counterpart for a long time, and he said that this must have had the agreement of his government back home in Baghdad. Velayati is of the opinion that they are trying to find a face-saving option, a way out. I told him quite clearly that the declaration on Friday was clearly not in that direction, but he said that even in the face of what I told him he still believed they were trying for a face-saving option. He also told me they are pinning their hopes on the talks in Moscow. This morning I got a call from Gorbachev during a break in his conversation with the Iraqi foreign minister. This was because we had agreed on a date and hour before he knew of that meeting; we wanted to talk about the Two Plus Four in the Supreme Soviet. Incidentally, he assured me he wanted to push it through at all costs. He also said he would call tomorrow to report on the results of the Iraqi foreign minister's visit, and that he also intended to call you. So, I don't really know any specifics, but I have the impression that something is happening within Iraq. As to the outcome, we will have to wait and see.

The President: That is interesting. We have to see that Iraq will comply. I don't know about face-saving for Saddam Hussein. That doesn't interest me. The important thing, as you know, is compliance with the UN resolutions.

Chancellor Kohl: George, the Iranian foreign minister was very clear. He said they will have to comply with the UN resolutions demanding they withdraw.

The President: Helmut, did he mention reparations and other conditions?

Chancellor Kohl: No. What he did was try to explain that the conditions were not really conditions. What he wanted to tell me, and he considered this the most important point, was that Saddam Hussein did not make reference to Kuwait as his 19th province. He thought that meant he was preparing for withdrawal. I am only reporting, not assessing.

The President: I agree. It was the only thing that was new and encouraging. The rest of it was totally unacceptable.

Chancellor Kohl: Did Mikhail Gorbachev try to get in touch with you after his conversation?

The President: No, but I think Bessmertnykh will try to get in touch with Baker. On the other side, we cannot and will not permit Saddam Hussein to bring victory from the jaws of certain defeat.

Chancellor Kohl: I am in complete agreement with you, but if I understand the message coming out of the Iranian foreign minister correctly, Saddam Hussein has quite a lot of difficulties maintaining his foothold. He said something very interesting, that Iraq is not Saddam Hussein and that Iran wants to help Iraq but not help a certain individual. I thought it unusual.

The President: That is very interesting – a very interesting statement, Helmut. I hadn't heard it before.

Chancellor Kohl: As soon as I have anything new, I will get in touch with you. [...]

The President: Can I ask a question about Velayati? Is he a good man? I have heard positive things about him.

Chancellor Kohl: He is a man of quality, and a real Iranian. I remember when I studied I had fellow students from Iran. That is why I venture such an opinion. Second, from a religious viewpoint, his convictions are very strong. That is something to bear in mind. It was quite interesting when I said that it was a disgrace to see what was happening at the cradle of the three large religions of mankind. He was very glad to take up the subject. He also knows a lot about the West. He studied medicine in the U.S., I believe. I also have the impression, from something which Mikhail Gorbachev told me, that he has the ear of his President. Another thing, which I can't prove: my impression from the conversation is that once everything moves, once the dust settles, they are interested in improved relations with the U.S. – not right away, because there are still hostilities, but I do think there is a real possibility. He was addressing the future of the region, and who would play a role there. He said all relevant countries have to play a role, including the U.S.

The President: I think he is right. Given the pressures within Iran, this is not the time to restore full relations, but we keep hearing they want better relations. Yet here they are after an eight-year war with Iraq. I am very interested in what he said about the Iraqi people and not Saddam Hussein. My view is that if he got out we would all have a better time of it.

Chancellor Kohl: But unfortunately he is still there.

The President: Maybe not forever. Perhaps someday he will go. It has happened before.

Chancellor Kohl: Unfortunately it may take some time. You know we Germans have experience with that.

The President: Look at Romania, how people were dancing in the street after Ceausescu went. Thank you very much for the call, for keeping me informed.

[...]

[*Source: George H.W. Bush Presidential Library, Memcons and Telcons; obtained by the National Security Archive under the Freedom of Information Act.*]

Document 30. National Security Council, Speech, Martin Indyk, "The Clinton Administration's Approach to the Middle East," UNCLASSIFIED, May 18, 1993

By the time Bill Clinton enters the White House in early 1993, the Soviet Union's collapse has left the United States as the world's only superpower, while the Iran–Iraq War has heavily diminished the two combatants' military capabilities (all the more so in Iraq after Operation Desert Storm). These conditions, along with their shared hostility toward the United States, lead the new administration to conclude the USA does not need (and it no longer makes sense) to replay the old American strategy of balancing the two regimes against each other. Although the threats each poses are different, containment is the goal in both cases.

Rolling out the policy, National Security Council staff member Martin Indyk describes Dual Containment as one of three parts of a larger regional strategy. The other two center on the Arab–Israel peace process and stanching the spread of weapons of mass destruction, both long-standing staples of US Middle East policy. According to another senior NSC staffer at the time, the peace process is far and away Clinton's top Middle East priority in his first term.

Dual Containment is also interesting as an example of Iran and the USA misreading each other. Although the Americans view it as essentially a continuation of policy prior to the Gulf War, the Iranians see it as an intensification of antagonism. Not long afterwards, Tehran finds similar meaning in Clinton's scotching of an oil contract with Conoco. In that case, Washington is convinced it is an attempt to bypass containment whereas Rafsanjani and the Iranian leadership reportedly mean it as a gesture to encourage expanded engagement.[15]

[...]

A short-hand way of encapsulating the Clinton administration strategy is thus: "dual containment" of Iraq and Iran in the east; promotion of Arab-Israeli peace in the west; backed by energetic efforts to stem the spread of weapons of mass destruction and promote a vision of a more democratic and prosperous region for all the peoples of the Middle East.

[...]

Dual Containment in the East

The Clinton administration's policy of "dual containment" of Iraq and Iran derives in the first instance from an assessment that the current Iraqi and Iranian regimes are both hostile to American interests in the region. Accordingly, we do not accept the argument that we should continue the old balance of power game, building up one to balance the other. We reject that approach not only because its bankruptcy was demonstrated in Iraq's invasion of Kuwait. We reject it because of a clear-headed assessment of the antagonism that both regimes harbor towards the United States and its allies in the region. And we reject it because we don't need to rely on one to balance the other.

The coalition that fought Saddam remains together, as long as we are able to maintain our military presence in the region, as long as we succeed in restricting the military ambitions of both Iraq and Iran, and as long as we can rely on our regional allies Egypt, Israel, Saudi Arabia and the GCC, and Turkey – to preserve a balance of power in our favor in the wider Middle East region, we will have the means to counter both the Iraqi and Iranian regimes. We will not need to depend on one to counter the other. As Secretary of State Christopher has argued, we must not allow our efforts to press Iraq to comply fully with all UN resolutions to divert us from a recognition of the threat that Iran poses to our interests in the Middle East. And, by the same token, we must not allow our concern with the Iranian threat to divert us from our efforts to force Iraqi compliance.

[...]

Containing the threat from Iran is a more difficult though no less necessary undertaking. When we assess Iranian intentions and capabilities we see a dangerous combination for Western interests. Iran is engaged in a five-part challenge to the United States and the international community. It is the foremost state sponsor of terrorism and assassination across the globe. Through its support for Hamas and Hezbollah, Iran is doing its best to thwart our efforts to promote peace between Israel, the Palestinians and the Arab states. Through its connections with Sudan, Iran is fishing in troubled waters across the Arab world, actively seeking to subvert friendly governments. Through its active efforts to acquire offensive weapons, Iran is seeking an ability to dominate the Gulf by military means. And, perhaps most disturbing, Iran is seeking a weapons of mass destruction capability including clandestine nuclear weapons capability and ballistic missiles to deliver weapons of mass destruction to the Middle East.

I should emphasize that the Clinton administration is not opposed to Islamic government in Iran. Indeed we have excellent relations with a number of Islamic governments. Rather, we are firmly opposed to these specific aspects of the Iranian regime's behavior, as well as its abuse of the human rights of the Iranian people. We do not seek a confrontation but we will not normalize relations with Iran until and unless Iran's policies change, across the board. We are willing to listen to what Iran has to say, provided that this comes through authoritative channels. However, in the absence of dramatic changes in Iran's behavior, we will work energetically to persuade our European and Japanese allies, as well as Russia and China, that it is not in their interests to assist Iran to acquire nuclear weapons or the conventional means to pose a regional threat. Nor do we believe it is in their interests to ease Iran's economic situation so that it can pursue normal commercial relations on one level while threatening our common interests on another level.

We will pursue this effort of active containment unilaterally, maintaining the counterterrorism sanctions and other measures enacted by previous administrations to encourage a change in Iranian behavior. However, we recognize that success will require multilateral efforts since much of what Iran seeks in order to build up its military power is obtainable elsewhere. In this regard, we will seek to impress upon our allies the necessity for responding to the Iranian threat and the opportunity now presented by Iran's current circumstances.

The necessity to act now derives from the fact that Iran's threatening intentions for the moment outstrip its capabilities. But this moment will not last for long. If we fail in our efforts to modify Iranian behavior, five years from now Iran will be much more capable of posing a real threat to Israel, to the Arab world and to Western interests in the Middle East. The opportunity to act now, on the other hand, derives from the fact that Iran is no longer a good commercial proposition. It is $5 billion in arrears on its short term international loans and this figure is growing in leaps and bounds. Iran suffers from 30 percent inflation and 30 percent unemployment. In short, Iran is a bad investment in both commercial and strategic terms, not just for the United States but for all responsible members of the international community.

This argument should be compelling for another reason as well. Iran does not yet face the kind of international regime that has been imposed on Iraq. A structural imbalance therefore exists between the measures available to contain Iraq and Iran. To the extent that the international community, as a result, succeeds in containing Iraq but fails to contain Iran, it will have inadvertently allowed the balance of power in the Gulf to have tilted in favor of Iran, with very dangerous consequences. That imbalance therefore argues for a more energetic effort to contain Iran and modify its behavior even as we maintain the sanctions regime against Iraq.

[...]

[*Source: 1993 Washington Institute for Near East Policy Soref Symposium; reprinted with permission from The Washington Institute for Near East Policy © 1993.*]

Document 31. White House, Memorandum of Conversation, "Summary Report on One-on-One Meeting between Presidents Clinton and Yeltsin ... St. Catherine's Hall, The Kremlin," Classification Unknown, May 10, 1995

Since the fall of the Soviet Union, the new Russian Federation, headed by the eccentric Boris Yeltsin, has continued to play a significant role in world affairs and President Clinton has accorded the relationship due priority. The two leaders will meet eighteen times over seven years. One irritant that surfaces repeatedly is Russia's support for Iran's military and nuclear programs. CIA reports earlier this year have warned that Moscow's conventional sales of equipment – especially Kilo-class submarines, MiG-29 aircraft, and SA-5 missiles – will strengthen Iran compared to its Gulf neighbors and make it easier to interdict oil flows through the Strait of Hormuz.[16]

However, as this one-on-one conversation shows, the most serious point of contention is the nuclear issue. While Clinton (WJC) is determined to stop any progress by the Iranians, Yeltsin (BNY) is far less worried. For him, Russia's economic predicament is paramount and nuclear deals represent a valuable source of national revenue. When Clinton pushes for an end to support for Iran's program, Yeltsin pushes back: "You have $5.6 billion per year in trade of your own with Iran. We don't give you a hard time for that." He insists that nothing Russia is providing can be used to develop nuclear weapons. But allowing Iran's program to progress is anathema to US policy and Clinton admonishes that "even a country under IAEA safeguards can develop such a program over time."

The conversation eventually gets back on track and the two shake hands, promising to find a mutually agreeable solution. But Russia's economic and foreign policy interests will time and again clash with Washington's, and Iran will continue to feature regularly in their deliberations.

....

[...]

BNY: Before getting back to European security, I want to talk about the subject of our relations with Iran. What decisions did I take just before your visit? In our contract, we've left in place only the delivery of energy producing units for peaceful purposes. We have turned them (the Iranians) down on anything in the contract that has to do with military issues.

There are four points I want to make here:
First, no centrifuge – Nyet!
Second, the two silos – Nyet!
Third, we'll refuse delivery of military weapons-grade materials.
Fourth, only peaceful reactors will be delivered.

In light of what I've said, we should take it easy and stop torturing each other about Iran. You have outcries from your opposition, and so do I. Let's stop stirring them up.

You have $5.6 billion per year in trade of your own with Iran. We don't give you a hard time for that.

We don't give you a hard time for the fact that it was the U.S. and not Russia that gave them all they wanted; you armed Iran in the first place [in the days of the Shah].

We're giving them equipment for peaceful use, for electric power stations – not one iota more – even though we will lose financially because we'll have to cut back on the contract [to eliminate the gas-centrifuge].

WJC: First, let me say that I appreciate the fact that you are not going forward with the enrichment facility. That's a good decision.

But let me tell you about my own decision, which answers one of your points. Ten days ago I announced a total embargo on U.S. trade with Iran, so we'll be giving up the money you mentioned. I realize this is a sensitive economic and political issue for you and for me. Senator Dole and Speaker Gingrich have called for an aid cutoff if Iran is given this reactor. I don't agree with what they're saying, and I don't think that we should get into that kind of use of our aid program to punish Russia. I want to discuss this issue in terms of what is right for Russia and what is right for the world.

BNY: Bill, here's what I propose: let's have Gore and Chernomyrdin reach agreement on a protocol that will establish what deliveries can go ahead and which ones we should stop. You and I will then review the protocol.

WJC: Let me make sure we understand each other. If you'll let the GCC present arguments and evidence on why there should be no sale, then I agree. If you expect me to agree now that the sale should go forward, even in part, I cannot agree.

Our position is that nuclear cooperation of any kind with Iran is a mistake – from your standpoint as well as our[s]. We can also provide you with information to prove that.

We can also talk to you about how to minimize the economic cost to you for the loss of the sale.

BNY: Bill, what are you talking about? These are light water reactors! You're providing the same thing to North Korea.

WJC: There's a big difference. First, by building a nuclear reactor and getting money from South Korea and Japan, we're reducing North Korea's nuclear program from the level that already exists. Iran doesn't have LWR technology. So in North Korea, we're moving them drastically away from a program they have, while in Iran we're trying to persuade you not to help them start one up. Don't you see that difference?

BNY: No, no. All the cadres – all the atomic workers [in Iran] were trained by the U.S.! There are no Russian experts in Iran. We're refusing to provide experts, and we're letting them have only the LWR for peaceful purposes. That's why I urge that Gore and Chernomyrdin look into the matter and draw up a protocol. We'll provide only what we should. All other parts of the contract we'll cut out. We'll take the loss and maybe you will be able to make part of it up. The Gore-Chernomyrdin Commission will have to produce a protocol stating what is to be provided and what is not.

WJC: There's a point here you should understand. We have intelligence that we believe proves Iran is trying to develop nuclear weapons. I will share a copy with you. [Hands over Russian-language text.] Iran does not need nuclear facilities for energy because it has enough oil. It wants reactors for other purposes.

BNY: They are not capable of developing a nuclear-weapons program.

WJC: They are not capable of doing so now, but North Korea proves that even a country under IAEA safeguards can develop such a program over time. Also, Russia is closer to Iran than the U.S. is; that should make you all the more careful here. Moreover, you are a co-sponsor with us of the Middle East Peace process. Even the Arab states say that Iran is a principal force trying to disrupt peace – and that it would be a big mistake to build a power plant there. Think about that factor, too.

Now, Boris, I recognize that even if you believed I was
right, you could not announce today that you were ending the
sale. So I propose announcing today that the enrichment
facility and other military-related or potential aspect
[sic] are cancelled, and the Gore-Chernomyrdin Commission
will examine the issue of the reactor sale in the light of
our information. This is the kind of equipment that
requires maximum safeguards under any circumstances. But
we think the answer in this case is cancelling the sale
altogether, even though you can't say that today. So you say
you are reviewing the information we have given you, the
intelligence, and alternative proposals to deal with the
economic impact. I realize you can't say today, "I can't
sell the reactors." But you can say, "Let's look at the
report." So no centrifuge, no militarily useful
technology – that we'll announce today, and we'll turn the
rest over to the Gore-Chernomyrdin Commission to work hard
on a resolution. For our part, the resolution we'll be
arguing for is cancelling the deal, and trying to find ways
to help you the [sic] overcome the cost of the loss.

BNY: We've got a deal. [Offers his hand and they shake on it.]

[...]

*[Source: William J. Clinton Presidential Library & Museum, Clinton Presidential
Records, NSC Management, ([Yeltsin and Tel*...]), OA/Box Number: 582,
Folder Title: 9503774.]*

**Document 32. Director of Central Intelligence, National Intelligence
Daily, "Saudi Arabia: Bombing of US Military Barracks at Dhahran,"
TOP SECRET, June 26, 1996**

*While some of Iran's political elite continue to preach rapprochement, regime
support for terrorism remains a fundamental sticking point for the West.
A suicide bombing at the Israeli Embassy in Argentina, the killing of Kurdish
opposition figures in Berlin, and especially the bombing of Khobar Towers in
Saudi Arabia are all attributed to Iran or Iranian-backed agents. Tehran*

vehemently denies a connection to any of the attacks, however, and the Clinton administration struggles to find a way to hold Iran accountable.

The Khobar Towers bombing brings all of these issues to a head. The housing complex serves coalition forces enforcing a no-fly zone over Iraq – part of Clinton's Dual Containment policy – and as such becomes a natural target for militant groups seeking to strike symbols of US involvement in the region. On June 25, 1996, a truck carrying plastic explosives manages to drive close to the building and detonate near the first floor, killing nineteen US servicemen as well as a number of Saudis, and injuring hundreds more. Hezbollah Al-Hijaz, a Saudi branch of the Lebanese militant group, takes credit for the attack, but accusations of Iranian backing for the plot quickly swirl.

The Clinton administration is intent on finding the perpetrators and holding them accountable. The president orders retaliatory planning to be put in place, telling advisors, "I don't want any pissant half-measures." But absent concrete proof he can use to persuade the American people of Iranian involvement, he resists public and internal pressures to strike.

....

Developments

Saudi Arabia: Bombing of US Military Barracks at Dhahran

A gasoline truck carrying a bomb exploded outside the Khobar Towers military complex, a facility housing US, British, French, and Saudi military personnel at Dhahran Airbase last night. The four buildings that reportedly suffered the most damage almost exclusively housed US forces. [2 words redacted] two Arab males parked the truck at the northeast entrance to the facility and then fled in another vehicle. The explosion occurred three to four minutes later. [1 line redacted]

- [3-line paragraph redacted]

The attack was well executed and may have been planned for several months. Personnel at Khobar have reported several incidents of surveillance and harassment over the past eight months, *apparently efforts to test the facility's defenses and the guards' reaction times.* Security at Khobar, already heightened after a bombing incident in Riyadh last November, was further strengthened in response to incidents in the past several weeks.

No one has claimed responsibility for the bombing, but a number of groups reportedly have been contemplating attacks against US interests in Saudi Arabia. Before the execution on 30 May of four Saudis who were convicted for the Riyadh bombing, the Gulf Revolution Organization – a shadowy opposition group – sent several threat letters. [2 lines redacted]

- [3-line paragraph redacted]
- *The culpability of Iran and Iraq also cannot be ruled out.* [½ line redacted].

[*Source: Central Intelligence Agency, Document No. C06232031.*]

Document 33. State Department, Information Memorandum, Alan P. Larson for the Secretary of State, "Iran and Libya Sanctions Act of 1996," CONFIDENTIAL, July 26, 1996

Sanctions have been the United States' go-to weapon against Iran whenever diplomacy falters and because military action rarely seems viable. Starting with the hostage crisis in 1979, every president has resorted to restrictions or punitive action of varying kinds and scope. Previously, President Clinton has sought to underscore Washington's aversion for Iranian behavior by promulgating executive orders to clamp down on the oil sector and then all trade and investments. Now a year later, he takes a tougher step by signing the more sweeping – and statutory – Iran–Libya Sanctions Act (ILSA).

The administration has been feeling pressure from Congress, which passes ILSA unanimously in both houses, and from conservative Middle Eastern regimes to come down hard on Iran. But America's European allies are a different story and, as they often do over Iran, they present Washington with a dilemma. Most Europeans favor approaches the USA considers too soft. (In the 1990s the policy of choice for some in the European Union (EU) is known as "critical dialogue.") So when the White House expresses frustration at the resistance to multilateral sanctions by enacting measures such as ILSA, the EU, as predicted here by the State Department, pushes back, accusing the administration of imposing an "extraterritorial application of US law and a secondary boycott" – as well as having a double standard for opposing similar action against Israel and disregarding the profitable trade relationships some American companies enjoy with Tehran.

Clinton wants to avoid the "storm" anticipated in this memo, which will distract from larger objectives, and eventually agrees to waive implementation for some European investments in Iran. The experience points up the EU's importance as a player on Iran, although the next administration will not be so solicitous of them.

....

To: The Secretary
From: EB – Alan P. Larson, Acting
Subject: Iran and Libya Sanctions Act of 1996

Summary

The House passed the Iran and Libya sanctions Act on July 23 by unanimous consent. The President has indicated that he will sign it. The bill already has antagonized our allies, with the EU studying a possible blocking statute. The Act could conflict with U.S. trade and investment obligations. We expect Congress to monitor closely our implementation of the Act, with appropriate committee oversight hearings early next year. We are mapping a strategy to consult allies just prior to the bill signing to avoid reactions damaging to other areas of cooperation.

Discussion

A detailed summary of the Act's provisions and implications is attached. In general, the new law requires that the President impose sanctions against persons or entities investing $40 million or more in the Iranian or Libyan oil and gas sectors in a 12-month period (the Iran trigger drops to $20 million after one year in countries which fail to implement sanctions on Iran). Both provisions affect only new investment; implementing existing agreements will not trigger sanctions. The law also will require the President to impose sanctions on persons exporting to Libya particular goods and services proscribed by certain UNSC sanctions.

If the President determines that sanctions have been triggered as described above, he must impose at least two of the following sanctions on a sanctioned firm within 90 days:

- Prohibit Exim Bank assistance;
- Deny export licenses;
- Ban U.S. financial institutions from lending more than $10 million/year to a sanctioned firm;
- Ban a sanctioned institution from serving as a primary dealer of USG debt or as a repository of USG funds;
- Prohibit USG procurement from the firm; or,
- Ban imports of products selected by the President.

If imposed against nationals of certain countries, some of the sanctions would present possible bilateral or multilateral treaty violations, for which formal international dispute settlement mechanisms may be applicable. Concerns may be raised over the government procurement, import, and loan sanctions.

The legislation provides opportunities to delay imposition of sanctions while the President seeks to halt the objectionable activities. The President may waive the imposition of sanctions on a specific individual or entity if he determines this is in the national interest, or on nationals of countries that agree to take substantive measures against Iran.

Investment-related sanctions also are triggered only for investments under new agreements arrived at after enactment of the legislation. Investment under preenactment agreements may continue. Our interpretation of "existing agreements" will be an important issue with implications for how we deal with firms already operating in Iran and Libya.

Foreign Reaction

Coming on the heels of the Helms-Burton Act, passage of the Iran-Libya Act already is provoking very strong hostility from key allies, particularly France, Germany, Italy, and the UK. We expect that trading partners will argue strongly that the law is an extraterritorial application of U.S. law and a secondary boycott.

The investment trigger in Libya is the provision that will most anger our allies. Foreign investment in Iran's petroleum sector is limited to Total's development of the Sirri field, and

European investors were proceeding cautiously in any case. But our European partners have substantial interests in Libya, which supplies a significant amount of their oil imports, particularly for Italy.

EU officials have not yet indicated formally how they will respond to this new law, but we understand that the European commission may amend a proposed "blocking statute," originally designed to prevent European firms from complying with Helms-Burton, to include this Act. This proposal may go to EU ministers for approval by the end of July if UK concerns over sovereignty issues are resolved.

We have begun to develop a strategy to proactively engage our allies on this issue at high levels. We will emphasize our determination to press Iran and Libya to stop their unacceptable behavior, while expressing our desire to work with our allies to accomplish this. We also are formulating plans to implement the Act. The bill has had a chilling effect on European dealings with Iran, and we expect that it will continue to do so, if we can weather the storm of European reaction.

[*Source: US Department of State, Freedom of Information Act release, Case No. F-2014-15825, Doc. No. C06003503.*]

Document 34. White House, Memorandum of Conversation, "Meeting with Russian President Yeltsin …," CONFIDENTIAL, May 27, 1997

The Iranian presidential election in 1997 seems a lock for hardline Speaker of Parliament Ali Akbar Nateq-Nouri. With support from the Supreme Leader, he appears to be comfortably ahead of reform candidate and relative unknown Mohammad Khatami. But, with a remarkable 80 percent turnout, it is Khatami who comes out on top. His platform centers on reform and anti-corruption – a direct challenge to the revolutionary council. His election catches the world, and apparently himself, by surprise and opens wider the window of opportunity for rapprochement with the West.

Here, after discussing NATO, Afghanistan, and other topics, Clinton and the Russian president, accompanied by their foreign ministers and a few other top diplomats, exchange opinions on the sudden shift in Iranian politics.

Yeltsin sees no "upsurge in Islamic extremism and no desire to have nuclear weapons," and is hopeful the USA will "accord Iran better treatment." But while Clinton feels "positively," he is still skeptical about a real change in policy. "It is hard to know how much authority their president has under Khameni [sic]," he accurately points out. In a nod to the biggest political impediment on the American side, he declares that the "relationship with Iran is complicated by the investigation into the Khobar bombing."

Encouraged by Khatami's messages to the West, Clinton will begin to warm to the idea of dialogue with Iran. The Khatami–Clinton period of the late 1990s will become a high-water mark for bilateral relations, although it will fall well short of hopes on both sides.

....

Date, Time   May 27, 1997, 5:00–5:55 p.m.
and Place: The American Ambassador's Residence, Paris

[...]

The President: I have covered my issues. I want to ask if your
        people - your Foreign Minister - have any special insights
        into the Iranian election or Afghanistan.

[...]

President Yeltsin: ...As for the Iranian election, we assess
        it positively. We expect there will not be an upsurge in
        Islamic extremism and no desire to have nuclear weapons. We
        are waiting and for the time being will refrain from
        military and technical aid until the Iranians demonstrate
        their policies.
The President: The United States has agreed to try to set with
        the European Union benchmarks to measure Iranian behavior.
        Our position is that we are open to dialogue and ready to
        meet, but we have to be able to discuss the issues that
        divide us: support for terrorism, actions against the
        Middle East peace process and weapons of mass destruction
        proliferation. I expect that the mandate of the new
        president may not lead to change in these areas, but we're
        ready to talk if we can talk about these issues. It would be a

great thing if Iran were to change its external policies.
President Yeltsin: Of course.

[...]

President Yeltsin: Good. On Iran, now things may get quieter,
and I hope you can accord Iran better treatment.
The President: If their policies change. It is hard to know how
much authority their president has under Khameni [sic].
President Yeltsin: Did you send them a message, to the
president?
Mr. [Strobe] Talbott: Only through our press spokesman.
Secretary Albright: We stated that we are interested in what
will happen after the election.
Mr. [Samuel] Berger: We will judge by their actions.
President Yeltsin: But it was a press statement, not a message?
The President: Yes. Our relationship with Iran is complicated
by the investigation into the Khobar bombing. Some
evidence suggests Iranian involvement.
President Yeltsin: OK [...]

[*Source: William J. Clinton Presidential Library, Clinton Presidential Records, NSC
Management, ([Yeltsin and Tel*...]), OA/Box Number: 1623, Folder Title: 9703720.*]

Document 35. White House, Letter, President Clinton for President Khatami, "Message to President Khatami from President Clinton," Classification Unknown, June 1999

Clinton's second term, particularly following the surprise election of Mohammad Khatami as president of Iran, brings a major shift in policy toward the Islamic Republic. Whereas the first years of his presidency were characterized by sanctions and retribution for Iran's nuclear program and involvement in terrorist activities, by 1999 Clinton has become a convert to the gospel of dialogue. A presidential aide says later that Clinton "would have moved heaven and earth" to secure better relations if conditions had allowed, but two years of modest signaling have produced no meaningful results so far.

In June 1999, the White House attempts a "Hail Mary," transmitting a personal message from one president to another. Clinton enlists the ever-cooperative Omanis and sends two envoys to the Sultan to request that his foreign minister convey the written message along with an oral one directly to Khatami and no one else. Critically important, the oral message expresses Clinton's personal respects to Khatami and his desire for better relations. The hope is that these warm words will offset the sharp tone of the letter, reproduced below, which demands justice from Iran for the Khobar bombing, and which the White House feels is required to fend off domestic pressures to be tough with Iran.

Khatami seems very pleased with the oral presentation, according to the Omani foreign minister, but the plan goes awry when he unexpectedly dispatches the letter to the rest of his colleagues in the leadership [see Document 36]. The Americans have failed to grasp that Khatami as president does not have the standing on his own to take on an initiative as portentous as relations with the United States.

....

Message to President Khatami from President Clinton:

The United States Government has received credible evidence that members of the Iranian [*sic*] Revolutionary Guard Corps (IRGC), along with members of Lebanese and Saudi Hizballah, were directly involved in the planning and execution of the terrorist bombing in Saudi Arabia of the Khobar Towers military residential complex on June 25, 1996.

Nineteen American citizens were killed. The United States views this in the gravest terms. We acknowledge that the bombing occurred prior to your election. Those responsible, however, have yet to face justice for this crime, and the IRGC may be involved in planning for further terrorist attacks against American citizens.

The United States Government acknowledges the positive steps you have taken in seeing that those Iranians involved in corruption, drugs, domestic terrorism and international criminal activities are called to account for their actions. However, the involvement of the IRGC in terrorist planning and activity abroad remains a cause of deep concern to us.

The United States has no hostile intentions towards the Islamic Republic of Iran and seeks good relations with your government, but we cannot allow the murder of U.S. citizens to pass unaddressed.

In order to protect our citizens, which is the first responsibility of any government, and in order to lay a sound basis for better relations between our countries, we need a clear commitment from you that you will ensure an end to Iranian involvement in terrorist activity, particularly threats to American citizens, and will bring those in Iran responsible for the bombing to justice either in Iran or by extraditing them to Saudi Arabia.

[*Source: William J. Clinton Presidential Library & Museum, Clinton Presidential Records, National Security Council, Ken Pollack (Near Eastern Affairs), OA/Box Number: 2962, Folder Title: Iran – US*]

Document 36. Islamic Republic of Iran, Letter, Leadership for President Clinton, Classification Unknown, September 1999

This letter and the preceding document are the only direct exchange of communications between American and Iranian leaders that has yet been made public. Tehran takes almost three months to respond to President Clinton. The Iranians match the indignant tone of the American message. They strenuously deny any connection to the Khobar Towers bombing, and turn the tables by excoriating the USA for lending support to "terrorist elements and organizations" and for not only failing to prosecute those responsible for downing the Iranian civilian airliner in 1988, but for decorating them.[17] At the same time, the Iranians appear to leave the door open again. The Islamic Republic "[b]ears no hostile intentions towards Americans," they claim, and in fact has "respect for the great American people." The Iranian people will "vigorously pursue the policy of détente," but also "vigilantly and resolutely defend their independence, sovereignty and legitimate rights against any threat."

....

In the Name of God, the Compassionate, the Merciful

The allegations contained in the message attributed to President Clinton are inaccurate and unacceptable. The Islamic Republic of Iran views the recurrence of such unfounded allegations in the gravest terms.

Reliable investigations and serious scrutiny leave no doubt that this allegation, which has been repeated on several earlier occasions, is solely based on inaccurate and biased information. No agency of or entity connected with the Islamic Republic of Iran had any part, whatsoever, in the planning, logistics or execution of the said incident. Such allegations are fabricated solely by those whose illegitimate objectives are jeopardized by stability and security in the region.

The US Government – which has not only failed to prosecute or extradite the readily identifiable American citizens responsible for the downing of Iranian civilian airliner, but in fact has decorated them – is now seeking the trial or extradition of individuals totally unknown and without any connection whatsoever to the Islamic Republic of Iran. This behavior is unacceptable and must cease immediately.

It is also imperative that the US Government prevents further support of certain official US agencies and institutions for terrorist elements and organizations with irrefutable records of crimes against Iranian people. Any further assistance to these terrorists is indicative of inconsistency between US words and deeds, and shall remain a source of deep concern to the Iranian people and Government.

The Islamic Republic of Iran hears [sic: bears] no hostile intentions towards Americans and the Iranian people not only harbor no enmity, but indeed have respect for the great American people. At the same time, they shall vigilantly and resolutely defend their independence, sovereignty and legitimate rights against any threat.

As its irreversible and fundamental strategy, the Government of Iran, backed by a strong national consensus, shall vigorously pursue the policy of detente and institutionalization of the rule of law. The Government is confident and there exists no threat from the Islamic Republic of Iran against any other government or their nationals.

[Source: William J. Clinton Presidential Library & Museum, Clinton Presidential Records, National Security Council, Ken Pollack (Near Eastern Affairs), OA/Box Number: 2962, Folder Title: Iran – US.]

Document 37. State Department, Speech, Madeleine Albright, "Remarks before the American–Iranian Council," UNCLASSIFIED, March 17, 2000

With his time in office dwindling, Clinton and Secretary of State Madeleine Albright, who has a more receptive attitude toward Iran than her predecessor, Warren Christopher, decide to take another stab at reaching out to the Iranians. This time, rather than a secret message, it is a public announcement that comes during the Iranian New Year, Nowruz. Albright's speech is essentially a final attempted show of goodwill and as such is filled with admiring references to Iran's history, people, and national potential.

The gesture here is twofold. First, responding to perennial Iranian calls for "deeds not words," the USA will cut sanctions on luxury products like pistachios and Persian carpets. Second, on a political level, Albright admits to US involvement in the 1953 ouster of Mohammad Mosaddeq from power. For nearly fifty years this event has been a wedge between the two countries, regularly invoked by the regime as Exhibit A in a long list of injustices committed by the United States. Albright acknowledges other regrettable American actions, then follows with a recitation of "our own list of grievances, and they are serious."

This sort of cataloguing of criticisms is standard fare for politicians in both countries addressing domestic audiences, but much as Iranian leaders reacted badly to the mixed messages of Clinton's letter to Khatami a few months earlier, the Supreme Leader himself singles out Albright's disapproving comments. He homes in on a reference to power resting in "unelected hands," which he uses to slam the door on the US initiative. Two years later, George W. Bush will use almost the identical phrase in a State of the Union address to even more damaging effect.

Secretary Albright: [...]

As this audience well knows, Iran is one of the world's oldest continuing civilizations. It has one of the globe's richest and most diverse cultures. Its territory covers half the coastline of the Gulf and on one side of the Straits of Hormuz through which much of the world's petroleum commerce moves. It borders the Caspian Sea, the Caucasus in Central and South Asia, where a great deal of the world's illegal narcotics are produced, several major terrorist groups are based, and huge reserves of oil and gas are just beginning to be tapped. And it is currently chairing the organization of the Islamic Conference.

There is no question that Iran's future direction will play a pivotal role in the economic and security affairs of what much of the world reasonably considers the center of the world. So I welcome this opportunity to come to discuss relations between the United States and Iran. It is appropriate, I hope, to do so in anticipation both of the Iranian New Year and the start of spring. And I want to begin by wishing all Iranian-Americans a Happy New Year, Eid-e-shoma-Mubarak. (Applause.)

I extend the same wishes to the Iranian people overseas. Spring is the season of hope and renewal; of planting the seeds for new crops. And my hope is that in both in Iran and the United States, we can plant the seeds now for a new and better relationship in years to come.

That is precisely the prospect I would like to discuss with you today. President Clinton especially asked me to come to this group to have this discussion with you. It is no secret that, for two decades, most Americans have viewed Iran primarily through the prism of the U.S. Embassy takeover in 1979, accompanied as it was by the taking of hostages, hateful rhetoric and the burning of the U.S. flag. Through the years, this grim view is reinforced by the Iranian Government's repression at home and its support for terrorism abroad; by its assistance to groups violently opposed to the Middle East peace process; and by its effort to develop a nuclear weapons capability.

America's response has been a policy of isolation and containment. We took Iranian leaders at their word, that they viewed America as an enemy. And in response we had to treat Iran as a threat. However, after the election of President Khatami in 1997, we began to adjust the lens through which we viewed Iran. Although Iran's objectionable external policies remain fairly constant, the political and social dynamics inside Iran were quite clearly beginning to change.

In response, President Clinton and I welcomed the new Iranian President's call for a dialogue between our people. We encouraged academic, cultural and athletic content. We updated our advisory to Americans wishing to travel to Iran. We reiterated our willingness to engage in officially authorized discussions with Iran regarding each other's principal concerns, and said we would monitor future developments in that country closely, which is what we have done. Now we have

concluded the time is right to broaden our perspective
even further.

Because the trends that were becoming evident inside Iran are
plainly gathering steam, the country's young are spearheading a
movement aimed at a more open society and a more flexible approach
to the world.

Iran's women have made themselves among the most politically
active and empowered in the region. Budding entrepreneurs are
eager to establish winning connections overseas. Respected
clerics speak increasingly about the compatibility of
reverence and freedom, modernity and Islam. An increasingly
competent press is emerging despite attempts to muzzle it. And
Iran has experienced not one but three increasingly democratic
rounds of elections in as many years.

Not surprisingly, these developments have been stubbornly
opposed in some corners, and the process they have set in motion
is far from complete. Harsh punishments are still meted out for
various kinds of dissent. Religious persecution continues
against the Baha'i and also against some Iranians who have
converted to Christianity.

And governments around the world, including our own, have
expressed concerns about the need to ensure the process for
13 Iranian Jews, who were detained for more than a year without
official charge, and are now scheduled for trial next month. We
look to the procedures and the results of this trial as one of the
barometers of US-Iran relations.

Moreover, in the fall of 1998, several prominent writers and
publishers were murdered, apparently by rogue elements in Iran
security forces. And just this past weekend, a prominent editor
and advisor to President Khatami was gravely wounded in an
assassination attempt.

As in any diverse society, there are many currents swirling
about in Iran. Some are driving the country forward; others are
holding it back. Despite the trend towards democracy, control
over the military, judiciary, courts and police remains in
unelected hands, and the elements of its foreign policy, about
which we are most concerned, have not improved. But the momentum
in the direction of internal reform, freedom and openness is
growing stronger.

[...]

At their best, our relations with Iran have been marked by warm bonds of personal friendship. Over the years, thousands of American teachers, health care workers, Peace Corps volunteers and others have contributed their energy and goodwill to improving the lives and well-being of the Iranian people.

As is evident in this room, Iranians have enriched the United States as well. Nearly a million Iranian-Americans have made our country their home. Many other Iranians have studied here before returning to apply their knowledge in their native land. In fact, some were among my best students when I taught at Georgetown School of Foreign Service.

It's not surprising, then, that there is much common ground between our two peoples. Both are idealistic, proud, family-oriented, spiritually aware and fiercely opposed to foreign domination.

But that common ground has sometimes been shaken by other factors. In 1953 the United States played a significant role in orchestrating the overthrow of Iran's popular Prime Minister, Mohammed Massadegh. The Eisenhower Administration believed its actions were justified for strategic reasons; but the coup was clearly a setback for Iran's political development. And it is easy to see now why many Iranians continue to resent this intervention by America in their internal affairs.

Moreover, during the next quarter century, the United States and the West gave sustained backing to the Shah's regime. Although it did much to develop the country economically, the Shah's government also brutally repressed political dissent.

As President Clinton has said, the United States must bear its fair share of responsibility for the problems that have arisen in U.S.-Iranian relations. Even in more recent years, aspects of U.S. policy towards Iraq, during its conflict with Iran appear now to have been regrettably shortsighted, especially in light of our subsequent experiences with Saddam Hussein.

However, we have our own list of grievances, and they are serious.

The embassy takeover was a disgraceful breach of Iran's international responsibility and the [sic] trauma for the hostages and their families and for all of us. And innocent Americans and friends of America have been murdered by terrorist groups that are supported by the Iranian Government.

[...]

Neither Iran, nor we, can forget the past. It has scarred us both.

But the question both countries now face is whether to allow the past to freeze the future or to find a way to plant the seeds of a new relationship that will enable us to harvest shared advantages in years to come, not more tragedies. Certainly, in our view, there are no obstacles that wise and competent leadership cannot remove.

As some Iranians have pointed out, the United States has cordial relations with a number of countries that are less democratic than Iran. Moreover, we have no intention or desire to interfere in the country's internal affairs. We recognize that Islam is central to Iran's cultural heritage and perceive no inherent conflict between Islam and the United States.

[...]

The United States recognizes Iran's importance in the Gulf, and we've worked hard in the past to improve difficult relationships with many other countries - whether the approach used has been called detente or principle engagements or constructive dialogue or something else.

We are open to such a policy now. We want to work together with Iran to bring down what President Khatami refers to as "the wall of mistrust."

For that to happen, we must be willing to deal directly with each other as two proud and independent nations and address on a mutual basis the issues that have been keeping us apart.

[...]

[*Source: US Department of State Archive, https://1997-2001.state.gov/statements/2000/*
000317.html.]

Questions for further discussion

- What was President George H.W. Bush's attitude toward dealing with the Islamic Republic early in his term? What were the main stumbling blocks to engagement?

- What was the rationale underlying the Clinton administration's policy of Dual Containment? What was the general US attitude toward Iran at this point?

- How did the 1996 Khobar Towers bombing affect bilateral relations with Iran and how did domestic politics in the aftermath come into play on both sides?

- How did the election of President Mohammad Khatami change the prospects for improving US–Iranian ties?

- Why did President Clinton's attempt to reach out directly to President Khatami in 1999 fail? What does this episode say about each side's understanding of the other?

Notes

1. Giandomenico Picco, *Man without a Gun: One Diplomat's Secret Struggle to Free the Hostages, Fight Terrorism, and End a War* (New York: Times Books, 1999), pp. 110–114. Picco reports that one of the Iranian officials who helped with the hostage negotiations was a diplomat named Mohammad Javad Zarif, who would go on to play other significant roles over the next three decades.
2. "The President's News Conference," Public Papers, George H.W. Bush Presidential Library & Museum, March 13, 1990; Picco, *Man without a Gun*, pp. 120–121.
3. This viewpoint was described by a former official who worked in the White House at the time. See Bruce Riedel, quoted in James G. Blight *et al.*, *Becoming Enemies: U.S.-Iran Relations and the Iran–Iraq War, 1979-1988* (Lanham, MD: Rowman & Littlefield, 2012), p. 250.
4. Ibid., pp. 284–286.
5. Martin Indyk, *Innocent Abroad: An Intimate Account of American Peace Diplomacy in the Middle East* (New York: Simon & Schuster, 2009), pp. 39–40.
6. See Martin Indyk's comments in Glenn Kessler, "Rice Asks for $75 Million to Increase Pressure on Iran," *Washington Post*, February 16, 2006.
7. Associated Press, "USA: President Clinton: Plans to Cut Off All US Trade with Iran." May 1, 1995, AP Archive.
8. *New York Times*, August 6, 1996. Thinking outside the box, the US intelligence community decided to launch Operation Sapphire, a scheme to systematically confront Iranian agents around the world – essentially "outing" them – in order to send the very personalized message that the US could make life very difficult if it desired. See Richard A. Clarke, *Against All Enemies: Inside America's War on Terror* (New York: Free Press, 2004), pp. 120–121.
9. Madeleine Albright, *Madam Secretary: A Memoir* (New York: Random House, 2003), pp. 322–323.
10. See Khatami's comments in retrospect, *Financial Times*, September 5, 2006.

11. See Blight *et al.*, *Becoming Enemies*, p. 247.

12. *Jomhouri-e Eslami*, Reuters, April 22, 1987.

13. Hossein Mousavian, oral history conference, "Missed Opportunities? U.S.–Iran Relations, 1993–2001," Session 1, Musgrove Conference Center, St. Simons Island, GA, April 8–10, 2011 (files of the National Security Archive, Iran–U.S. Relations Project).

14. Exchange between Hossein Mousavian and Assistant Secretary of State Martin Indyk, oral history conference, "Missed Opportunities?" (see note 13).

15. Farideh Farhi (University of Hawaii–Manoa), oral history conference, "Missed Opportunities?" (see note 13), April 8, 2011.

16. CIA memorandum, "The Impact of Russian Arms Sales to Iran," February 3, 1995.

17. Captain Will Rogers III of the USS *Vincennes* received the Legion of Merit a year after the shootdown for "meritorious service." No mention was made of the incident.

4

Missed Opportunities: From 9/11 to Iraq to the Nuclear Impasse, 2001–2008

Introduction

The decade of the 2000s was an extraordinarily turbulent time in the Middle East that inevitably left a mark on US–Iranian relations. After the September 11, 2001, terrorist attacks, George W. Bush, a self-styled "gut player," claimed the mantle of global peace-maker, a role that envisaged reshaping the larger Middle East.

The Islamic Republic did not figure significantly in the calculations of US policymakers (beyond fervent hopes that it might be toppled in the course of events), but it would crop up in various roles over time – as collaborator, supplicant, and adversary. Iran's proximity to Afghanistan and Iraq, for example, made interaction inevitable, but cooperation also became a surprisingly viable option, at least initially. Failure to build on minor diplomatic achievements, however, allowed domestic politics to encroach further on foreign policy. Finally, Iran's repeated, demonstrable dissembling over its nuclear program isolated it even more from Western powers, who finally came together in their bid to pressure the regime.

At first, President Khatami saw grounds for optimism in the new US president and vice president's ties to the oil business, but the Bush team turned out to be fundamentally unreceptive. Secretary of State Colin Powell was a qualified exception in Bush's cabinet but often found his views eclipsed by Vice President Dick Cheney and Defense Secretary Donald Rumsfeld.[1] Bush himself had negative associations with Iran based on his father's frustrations and generally sided with the hardliners.

Once the administration satisfied itself that Tehran had no part in the 9/11 attacks (indeed Khatami made a point of being among the first foreign leaders to express condolences to the American people) [Document 39], a major opportunity for cooperation presented itself in Afghanistan. There, the Taliban had been protecting Osama bin Laden and al-Qaeda, the masterminds of the plot, and Tehran shared Washington's aversion for both groups. With the Supreme Leader's acquiescence, Iran's Supreme National Security Council authorized provision of logistical support for American military operations as well as mediation with their allies in Afghanistan's Northern Alliance.

In fact, a handful of representatives from both sides had already been meeting quietly for years, which helped prepare the ground for more open cooperation. The highlight of this interlude came at a conference on Afghanistan in Bonn, Germany, in late 2001, where American and Iranian diplomats, led respectively by Ambassador James Dobbins and Deputy Foreign Minister Mohammad Javad Zarif, collaborated remarkably smoothly to help the various Afghan political factions form a new government.[2]

The next month, however, during his State of the Union address, Bush erased hopes of building on that foundation by labeling Iran along with North Korea and Iraq as part of an "Axis of Evil" that posed a grave threat to world order [Document 41]. Many ordinary Iranians, not just supporters of the regime, were incensed. Some American officials were also infuriated because of the harm it brought to ongoing contacts. In particular, the head of the Islamic Revolutionary Guard Corps's Qods Force, General Qasem Soleimani,[3] who surprisingly supported what the Iranians termed the experiment of cooperating with Washington against the Taliban (and whose participation was considered critical to any success), went into a "tearing rage," according to Ryan Crocker, the chargé d'affaires in Kabul. In fact, the Afghanistan back channel did not immediately shut down [Document 38], but "the heart went out of the negotiations," Crocker recalled. "We were just that close," he said. "One word in one speech changed history."[4]

White House attention soon shifted to Iraq. Although Saddam Hussein also had no role in September 11, neoconservatives under Bush were eager to oust him from power, seeing it as a first step toward remaking the region.[5] Some Pentagon strategists theorized that a swift victory followed by political change in Iraq could even lead to change in Iran, either because of fears that an ascendant Baghdad would align with the USA, or because of popular internal pressure for political freedom.[6]

As it happened, within days of Bush declaring "mission accomplished" in Iraq in May 2003, the State Department received what was purported to be an Iranian offer of a "road map" for better relations [Document 42]. Flush with victory, US officials dismissed it as a desperate gambit that may not even have had the full approval of Iran's leadership. But some senior Americans have since seen the detailed and wide-ranging memo as a major missed opportunity that should at least have been explored.[7]

Within three years, American forces became deeply mired in Iraq's sectarian battles. The Islamic Republic, no longer feeling as threatened as in 2003, seized on the opening created by Saddam Hussein's overthrow to build ties to Iraqi Shiites and try to influence conditions in the country in their favor [Document 44].[8] The US military blamed the Qods Force for deadly IED (improvised explosive devices) and other incidents involving Americans. A US Army study in 2018 called the war potentially "one of the most consequential conflicts in American history" from which "[a]n emboldened and expansionist Iran appears to be the only victor."[9]

Even in those tense times, some officials on both sides sought to stabilize communications. Ambassadors Ryan Crocker and Zalmay Khalilzad, both widely experienced in the region, interacted with Iranians before and after the invasion. So did the commander of US forces in Iraq, Gen. David Petraeus, even though he thought Soleimani was "truly evil."[10]

The 2000s were also notable for a sharp rise in international concern over Iran's ambiguous nuclear program. Iranian officials have always claimed their objectives are civil not military – that they never intended to produce a nuclear bomb – and, harkening back to historical assertions of sovereignty over oil in the 1950s, insisted it was their inherent right to have such a program, a viewpoint that resonates deeply with ordinary Iranians.

The nuclear issue became a chronic crisis in 2002 when the Mujaheddin-e Khalq, a controversial opposition group in exile, disclosed the existence of two nuclear facilities, at Natanz and Arak, which Tehran had not reported to the IAEA. (Neither site was yet in operation and the Iranians claimed they were not required at that stage to report them, though in early 2003 the IAEA cited several other failures to meet related obligations.) Over the next decade, a cycle of delays, denials and justifications followed further discoveries of hidden facilities and suspicious evidence, leaving the world community with deep misgivings about the government's true intentions. The United Nations adopted half a dozen resolutions demanding Tehran take appropriate action. Several of these included sanctions provisions.

While critics and defenders of Iran's conduct had equally strong views, the picture was regularly clouded by the technical complexity of the science and by conflicting expert opinions. For example, the CIA concluded in 2007 that Iran had ended its weapons program four years earlier [Document 48]. This has led to disagreements over the meaning of certain evidence, the scope of legal obligations, and the interpretation of concepts and terms. It is not even clear what it means that Iran's religious leaders have declared nuclear weapons use forbidden ("*haram*") [Document 52].

For most of Bush's presidency, hardliners insisted on squeezing Tehran, particularly on the nuclear portfolio, through sanctions, international isolation, and even covert operations. During the presidency of the populist Mahmoud Ahmadinejad [Document 46], who alienated the West by denying the Holocaust and implying that Israel should be wiped off the map, the USA undertook an expanded clandestine program, according to media reports, funded by a $400 million congressional appropriation, to undermine the regime through support for dissident groups, but also to gather intelligence on the worrisome nuclear program. The latter concern prompted the launching of a stealth surveillance drone operation by the CIA and intensified electronic eavesdropping by the National Security Agency.[11]

During Bush's second term, pressure continued over gaining a clearer picture of Iran's nuclear activities. Bush told his new CIA director Michael Hayden he worried Tehran might soon surprise the world with a successful nuclear test, leaving the USA with two bad options: accept a new nuclear power in the Middle East or undertake military strikes. Both the CIA and State Department retooled and augmented their intelligence operations on Iran, including focusing on identifying and interacting with knowledgeable Iranians outside the country since they essentially had no access inside because of the lack of diplomatic relations.[12]

Meanwhile, as the influence of Cheney and Rumsfeld waned, former national security advisor and now Secretary of State Condoleezza Rice persuaded Bush that the confrontational neoconservative agenda for Iran had failed. Talks that had been taking place fitfully with Iranians, mainly on Iraq or Afghanistan, hewed exclusively to tactical issues. Bush himself resisted high-level negotiations because he thought they would amount to a "reward" for bad behavior. "These are assholes," he told his senior military commander for the Middle East. But Rice, partly out of a desire to mend fences with allies after Iraq, argued the United States needed to "take a risk"[13] by joining the European Union's nuclear talks with Tehran [Document 47]. It was a dramatic shift that caught the Iranians off-guard and succeeded in undermining their international position when they failed to take up the proposal.[14]

Over Bush's two terms, both sides passed up chances to exploit the promising conditions that followed 9/11. The Americans chose not to push on the open door provided by years of Afghanistan talks and snubbed a putative direct bid for a grand bargain in May 2003. Tehran chose not to engage with the United States in nuclear talks three years later. Even after a new president with a strikingly different attitude entered the White House in January 2009, it would take a full four-year term before the two governments finally settled down to serious diplomacy.

Document 38. State Department, Information Memorandum, Karl F. Inderfurth for the Secretary of State, "Iran Makes Positive Gestures to US on Afghanistan," CONFIDENTIAL, March 1, 2000

At the turn of the millennium, the USA and Iran make slow progress toward building trust and cooperation. Direct interactions remain elusive, but back channels like the 6+2 process on Afghanistan show the potential for dialogue. The informal group, consisting of the six countries bordering Afghanistan plus the United States and Russia, holds a series of meetings from 1997 to 2001, typically in Geneva, to discuss the future of the country, engulfed in a vicious civil war. The group's objectives include disrupting the flow of drugs being trafficked out of Afghanistan and blocking the Taliban with the help of Iran's ally, the Northern Alliance.

Since the Soviet invasion of the country in 1979, Afghanistan has remained a topic of mutual interest for Washington and Tehran. Both governments vehemently opposed a Soviet takeover and provided support for Afghan rebels. Neither wanted a continuation of the constant chaos and instability that the country's ongoing conflict produced. After 9/11 and the subsequent invasion led by the United States, Afghanistan's importance to the geopolitics of the region only increases.

This document, an information memorandum from Karl Inderfurth to the secretary of state, highlights the potential for using Afghanistan as a way to work more closely with the Iranians. For their part, the Iranians seem very open to the idea of working together, particularly on the issue of narcotics, for which they have a "zero-tolerance" policy. One of the key figures Inderfurth singles out is Iranian Deputy Foreign Minister Mohammad Javad Zarif, who will further impress his American counterparts at the upcoming Afghanistan reconstruction conference in Bonn in December 2001. More than a decade later, as foreign minister, he will play an instrumental role in the JCPOA nuclear negotiations. Diplomats like Inderfurth are eager to emphasize the promising behavior of the Iranians to the White House, but during the Bush-43 years – until well into the second term – there is no interest there.

```
To:          The Secretary
From:        SA – Karl F. Inderfurth
Subject:     Iran Makes Positive Gestures
```

Summary

During a February 28 Six-plus-Two meeting, the Iranian Deputy
Foreign Minister made several positive gestures towards the
U.S. He praised the U.S. initiating Six-plus-Two counter-
narcotics activities. In describing an Iranian-led OIC mission
to bring peace to Afghanistan, he emphasized Iran's desire to
include the U.S. and others if there is progress.

Discussion

On February 28, INL's [Bureau of International Narcotics and Law
Enforcement Affairs] Randy Beers and I led the U.S. delegation
to a special meeting of the Six-plus-Two group in New York to
discuss counter-narcotics cooperation. I was struck by the
efforts of Iranian Deputy Foreign Minister Mohamed Javed Zarif
(a former Iranian Deputy PermRep at the UN) to signal a positive
and open approach to the U.S.

Counter-Narcotics

I proposed in September that the Six-plus-Two, which has had no
success in bringing peace to Afghanistan, launch a counter-
narcotics initiative. Iran has been totally supportive of that
idea. The Iranians took the unexpected step at a working-level
meeting three weeks ago of formally nominating the U.S. to
coordinate the initiative. At Monday's meeting Zarif thanked
the U.S. for starting the process. He then noted Iran's "zero
tolerance" policy and its results – large drug seizures in Iran,
193 Iranian officials killed in battles with Afghan drug
smugglers, over 7600 Afghan drug traffickers in Iranian prisons.
And Zarif noted the key point, that narcotics trafficking helps
fuel the war in Afghanistan and finances terrorism.

Bringing Peace

Zarif also briefed the group on Iran's recently launched Afghan
peace initiative, using the Organization of the Islamic
Conference (OIC). He emphasized the initiative was designed to
complement UN/Six-plus-Two efforts, not to supplant them. An
OIC delegation had completed a tour of the region, and had

invited both the Taleban and the Northern Alliance to a meeting
in Jeddah on March 6. The Northern Alliance has agreed to come;
the Taleban have been "encouraging," but have not yet sent a
formal reply. An OIC delegation will meet the UN Secretary
General this week and ask him to send a UN observer.

Friendly Posture

Zarif's comments were positive and on the right track on
substance. His body language was also revealing. He spoke
directly across the table to the U.S. delegation, and seemed
clearly to welcome interaction with us. At the same time, we know
that Zarif still has some hesitations; he told UNDCP [UN
International Drug Control Program] head Arlacchi that he had to
postpone again an anti-narcotics meeting in Tehran which a U.S.
official from Embassy Islamabad was to attend.

Over the coming weeks, there will be continued working level
interaction with Iran on the Six-plus-Two counter-narcotics
initiative. We will discuss with NEA how to respond to Iranian
peace moves in Afghanistan. Looked at solely in terms of the
region, we believe this holds some promise. The Iranians have
made some cosmetic moves to smooth their relations with the
Taleban, but underneath they maintain a visceral dislike – and
provide as a result substantial assistance to the Northern
Alliance. We will discuss with NEA how we can interact with this
initiative without moving out in front of our overall
Iran policy.

[Source: US Department of State Freedom of Information Act release.]

**Document 39. Islamic Republic of Iran, Statement, President Khatami
for the American People, [Sympathy for the September 11 Attacks],
UNCLASSIFIED, September 12, 2001**

*To the surprise of many, the Iranian government is among the first to offer
public sympathy to the American people after the September 11 attacks.
Khatami goes a step further by issuing this personal statement. In it he
expresses genuine sorrow at the tragedy and denounces the perpetrators (as*

does Ayatollah Khamenei). But while sensitive to American suffering, the Iranians are distinctly aware of the potential consequences of direct American military involvement in the region, particularly so close to home. While Afghanistan continues to offer grounds for cooperation, the Iranians also warn that the USA should not get carried away in its desire for vengeance. In an interview two months later with CNN, Khatami emphasizes that the United States needs to make sure that the appropriate people are held accountable for "the ugliest form of terrorism ever seen."[15] Embedded in these comments is the fear that Washington may look for an excuse to strike against Iran and perhaps seek regime change there – as they do in Iraq two years later.

In the name of the Nation and the Government of the Islamic Republic of Iran, I condemn the terrorist attacks of hijacking airplanes, and attacking public centers in American cities, which sent a large number of defenseless people to their deaths; and I express my sincere condolences to the American nation, especially to those impacted, and the families of the victims of this incident. Terrorism is condemned and the international community must recognize its roots and dimensions and take fundamental steps to dry them out [eradicate them]. This is the principal intention of the Government of the Islamic Republic of Iran and it will not refrain from [taking] any action to bring this Islamic and humane belief to realization.

Seyyed Mohamad Khatami

[*Source: "President Mohammad Khatami Statement on September 11 Attacks,"* Hamshahri Newspaper, *September 12, 2001. Translated by Sina Azodi.*]

Document 40. State Department, Briefing Memorandum, William J. Burns for Deputy Secretary of State Richard Armitage, "US–Iran Relations – Next Steps," SECRET, January 16, 2002

After the conference on Afghanistan in Bonn in December 2001, Assistant Secretary of State for Near Eastern Affairs William Burns takes the opportunity to assess the relationship with Iran. Burns begins by noting that the "picture Iran projects has not been pretty lately." He points to their continued support for Hezbollah and "Rafsanjani's crude warnings to Israel about nuclear annihilation," and expresses frustration at their "aggressive angling for influence in Afghanistan," which directly counters Washington's own position in the country. He also remarks on the difficulty in properly assessing Iranian intentions because of "the opacity of Iranian political dynamics."

Despite all this, Burns recommends advancing the discourse currently in place: "whatever its limitations, the very limited dialogue we have now with the Iranians is more expansive than any we have had since the fall of the Shah." Furthermore, that communication turned out to be extraordinarily helpful at the Bonn conference. While there are a number of significant disagreements ahead, some dialogue is better than none, and the only way to accomplish US goals in the region is through "prudent engagement," not "dramatic moves."

Unfortunately, Iranian actions coupled with American mistrust and impatience do not allow for the "conservative, issue-specific engagement" Burns recommends. A few days earlier, the Israelis captured a freighter, the Karine A, carrying 50 tons of missiles, anti-tank rockets, and other heavy arms, reportedly meant to support the second intifada. Israeli authorities claim to track these weapons back to Iran and the affair is presented as evidence of Iran's continued "misbehavior" in the region. The baby steps toward a diplomatic arrangement, often taking place in backrooms and through back channels, are yet again undone by events on the ground.

....

To: The Deputy Secretary
From: NEA - Bill Burns
Subject: U.S.-Iran Relations - Next Steps

We have engaged the Iranians with some success on Afghanistan since September 11, but we have not changed the fundamentals of our policy. [1.5 lines redacted]

The picture Iran projects has not been pretty lately. [2 lines redacted] the leadership's support for Hizballah, involvement in terrorism and opposition to the peace process. Rafsanjani's crude warnings to Israel about nuclear annihilation reaffirmed the need to be concerned about Iran's quest for WMD. Despite stronger internal pressures for more freedoms, the ruling clergy continues to quash both the press and liberalizers in the legislative branch. Tehran's aggressive angling for influence in Afghanistan reflects an ongoing effort to counter our influence and to maximize its clout in the region. The Iranians tell us they have sealed their border with Afghanistan and are working to prevent the infiltration of terrorists. [3 lines redacted] We clearly need to press on both this issue and on the larger matter of support for the new Afghan central government.

Looking down the road, U.S. interests will compel us to work towards the long-term goal of improving relations with Iran, a country of immense strategic importance. At the same time, short-term management of issues will be complicated by the many serious differences between us and by the opacity of Iranian political dynamics.

The issue before us is whether to expand this engagement, and if so, how much and on what terms. Whatever its limitations, the very limited dialogue we have now with the Iranians is more expansive than any we have had since the fall of the Shah. It was also central to our ability to get agreement at Bonn and establishment of an Afghan interim authority. It will remain central to consolidating stability in Afghanistan. The balance of our long-term and short-term interests argues for continued, prudent engagement, but no dramatic moves. Major issues like economic sanctions, oil pipelines and the Hague tribunal claims, clearly are way down the road. We must continue to make clear that major steps in improving relations ultimately hinge on Iran changing its policies on issues of major concern to us. The prudent course at present is to maintain our conservative, issue-specific engagement, coupled with small moves that promote our longer-term interest in change in Iran. This would include lifting our block on WTO and expanding people-to-people contacts. [...]

Background on Issues

Since September 11, we have had a constructive, but very cautious engagement with the Iranians on Afghanistan. Although the results have been mixed, our dialogue has resulted in some positive Iranian actions, particularly Iran's contribution to the success of the Bonn Conference. We should maintain the same conservative and tough-minded approach to Iran for the next period, and not decide on any dramatic steps until we have a much clearer picture of the success of our policy in Afghanistan – and Iran's cooperation or lack of cooperation in achieving it. At the same time, there are some very small steps we can take that are not favors towards Iran, but are in our own interest, and consistent with this tough-minded approach. [2 lines redacted] Examples of such steps would be agreeing to Iranian accession to the WTO and expanding people-to-people programs.

Some recent Iranian actions raise doubts about the clerical regime's fundamental commitment to follow the moderate course projected by Khatami's condolences for the September 11 attacks, his Dialogue of Civilizations at the UN, and the constructive attitude displayed at the Bonn Conference. In Afghanistan, Iran has been aggressively asserting its influence in a potentially destabilizing way, despite its stated policy of support for the central government. [3 lines redacted] The Israeli capture of a ship smuggling weapons from Iran to the Palestinians highlights Iran's continuing support for terrorism and violence that undermines the peace process. In addition, the inflammatory rhetoric continually emanating from senior Iranian leaders such as Supreme Leader Khamene'i, and the Defense and Justice Ministers, among others, is also a concern. The recent speech by former President Rafsanjani, now Head of the Expediency Council, during which he raised the possibility of a nuclear attack on Israel, was a particularly radical example of this type of discourse engaged in by senior Iranians.

The heated rhetoric is indicative of the nervousness of many in the government over the internal Iranian conflict between those committed to maintaining the present system, and those who want to reform or outright change it – which has resulted in a brutal government crackdown on reformers. The harsh rhetoric is also a sign that the Iranian government is seized with the issue of ties to the U.S., which has in turn become part of the much larger internal conflict over the ultimate direction of the country.

Regional Stability and Terrorism:

Afghanistan: Our principal interest in the region at the moment is to nurture a stable and secure Afghanistan, which no longer serves as a host to terrorist organizations. As a long-time supporter of the Northern Alliance with much influence in the country, Iran must cooperate if Afghanistan is to have a chance to evolve in the proper direction. Despite its cooperation in Bonn, we remain concerned at Iran's aggressive efforts to promote its influence in Afghanistan. All of our communications with them must stress our common interest in the stability of Afghanistan. At the same time, we should avoid fueling Iranian paranoia about our longer-term intentions in the region, and emphasize that we have no plans to keep our forces in the area once the al-Qaida are uprooted and a stable Afghanistan is secured.

Iraq: As interagency discussions on Iraq unfold, we must consider if, when, and how to engage the Iranians on our Iraq policy. Should there eventually be a new government in Iraq, the Iranian role would largely mirror its present role in Afghanistan as a powerful neighbor whose influence could make or break the success of that government. Initiating a more formal dialogue with SCIRI would be one way to move on this issue.

The Peace Process and Terrorism: We must reaffirm that Iran's opposition to the peace process and support for terrorism are major obstacles to progress in bilateral relations between our countries. There is evidence that some Iranians are beginning to question why their government expends so many resources in support of the Palestinians when Iranian interests do not appear to be directly involved in the issue. However, the clerical rulers have made opposition to the existence of Israel such a fundamental tenet since the day Khomeini took power that they may view any backing away from this position as calling into question the very legitimacy of their regime. As long as they retain power, the very best we can hope for is that they refrain from interfering in any positive Palestinian moves on the peace process.

While Iran's leaders have condemned terrorism, and have pledged to combat it, some of the government's actions have been to the contrary. [4 lines redacted]

The Israeli capture of the *Karine A* arms smuggling ship highlighted Iran's continuing support for terrorism on the Arab-Israeli front as well. In addition to supplying Hizbollah in Lebanon with weapons and providing support for Hamas and Islamic Jihad, this latest incident indicates that the Iranians appear to be expanding their efforts to supply and influence the Palestinian Authority. Of particular concern is suspected Iranian harboring of terrorists on the U.S. most-wanted list. Finally, the Iranians have made no effort to implement any financial restrictions on the terrorist networks that are known to have operations in Iran.

At this point in the relationship, we need to continue to publicly press the Iranians to cease their obstruction of the peace process and their support for anti-Israeli terrorism, and press our allies to do the same in private. However, raising this issue in the dialogue would be counterproductive because it would likely lead to a quick impasse and ruin the chance for continued progress on other issues.

WMD and Ballistic Missile Development: Iran's development of missiles and WMD poses a destabilizing threat to the region, including the possibility of triggering a regional arms race. [2.5 lines redacted] We must continue to press other countries to refrain from selling Iran the equipment and know-how necessary for it to develop its programs. Also, we must press our allies to pursue their own dialogues with Iran on non-proliferation issues.

WTO: We do not see the WTO accession process as a reward, but rather as a tool that could serve our own interests by requiring significant Iranian internal reform. Iran will see a deferral as an indication that Washington is not prepared to reciprocate Iranian cooperation on Afghanistan. Lifting the U.S. block would send a signal to Iran that will be interpreted positively, but leave it no illusions about the hard issues that remain, including the major economic reforms that will be needed to accede to the WTO. This is one area where we need to move ahead.

Refugees and Narcotics: We have publicly praised Iran's actions with regard to refugee and counter-narcotics efforts. Iran has dealt fairly with the more than a million Afghan refugees who inundated the country as a result of the Soviet-Afghan War. During the present conflict, it has been instrumental in providing humanitarian assistance to Afghans fleeing from the fighting. In addition to setting up refugee camps just inside the Afghan border, Iran has allowed U.S. humanitarian assistance to transit Iranian territory. Our next step in this area should be to secure Iranian agreement to allow Americans affiliated with non-U.S. NGOs to work in Iran. This also promotes our goal of increasing people-to people contacts. Similarly, we should search for ways to encourage the Iranians to continue their productive anti-narcotics efforts, such as expanding our dialogue to specifically include this issue.

People-to-People Programs: Just as agreeing to WTO accession is not a favor to the Iranians, neither would facilitating more cultural and p2p exchanges be a reward. It is in our interest to bring as many non-government affiliated Iranians to the U.S. as possible. [2 lines redacted] Getting rid of the fingerprinting requirement for Iranians who enter the U.S. is one example of doing something that would address the concerns of the Iranian people and would be in our interest as well.

[*Source: US Department of State, Freedom of Information Act release, Case No. F-2011-00572.*]

Document 41. White House, State of the Union Address, George W. Bush, UNCLASSIFIED, January 29, 2002

President Bush takes American rhetoric against Iran to a new level in his 2002 State of the Union address. Just a few months after 9/11, the adminis-tration is still wrestling with how to define the nature of the new threat facing America and the West. At its center, say Bush administration strategists, is the prospect of a nexus between the development of weapons of mass destruction and purveyors of terrorism. The White House decides to use the State of the Union to outline the new challenges and how the United States will confront them. To "vivify" the point, as Secretary of State Condoleezza Rice puts it later, a speech writer inserts a key phrase that passes unnoticed through the editing process but will overshadow everything else about the speech.

Spotlighting three states that especially worry the United States, the presi-dent labels Iran, Iraq, and North Korea part of an "Axis of Evil" that aims to "threaten the peace of the world." Afterwards, Bush seems pleased with the reference but Rice admits she and the president are "stunned" at the reaction which helps "brand the Bush administration as radical and bellicose" and opposed to negotiation.[16] Iranians, leaders and ordinary citizens alike, show unusual unity in condemning it. Bush's reference to an "unelected few" adds to Tehran's resentment, recalling Albright's Nowruz *address in 2000* *[Document 37].*

The resulting damage to the relationship is significant. The dialogue on Afghanistan, one of the very few active areas of cooperation, sputters along briefly before shutting down entirely, indeed as the president's conservative advisors have hoped it would. Domestically, Iranian hardliners, citing national humiliation, pressure President Khatami to back away from his pursuit of rapprochement.

....

The President: Thank you very much. Mr. Speaker, Vice President Cheney, members of Congress, distinguished guests, fellow citizens: As we gather tonight, our nation is at war, our economy is in recession, and the civilized world faces unprecedented dangers. Yet the state of our Union has never been stronger. (Applause.)

[...]

Our second goal is to prevent regimes that sponsor terror from threatening America or our friends and allies with weapons of mass destruction. Some of these regimes have been pretty quiet since September the 11th. But we know their true nature. North Korea is a regime arming with missiles and weapons of mass destruction, while starving its citizens.

Iran aggressively pursues these weapons and exports terror, while an unelected few repress the Iranian people's hope for freedom.

Iraq continues to flaunt its hostility toward America and to support terror. The Iraqi regime has plotted to develop anthrax, and nerve gas, and nuclear weapons for over a decade. This is a regime that has already used poison gas to murder thousands of its own citizens - leaving the bodies of mothers huddled over their dead children. This is a regime that agreed to international inspections - then kicked out the inspectors. This is a regime that has something to hide from the civilized world.

States like these, and their terrorist allies, constitute an axis of evil, arming to threaten the peace of the world. By seeking weapons of mass destruction, these regimes pose a grave and growing danger. They could provide these arms to terrorists,

giving them the means to match their hatred. They could attack
our allies or attempt to blackmail the United States. In any of
these cases, the price of indifference would be catastrophic.
   [...]

[*Source: George W. Bush White House archived website, https://georgewbush-whitehouse
.archives.gov/news/releases/2002/01/20020129-11.html.*]

Document 42. Embassy of Switzerland, Memorandum, Tim Guldimann for the State Department, attaching "Roadmap" [Purported to be from the Iranian Government], UNCLASSIFIED, May 4, 2003

After the US military cruises to an easy victory over Saddam Hussein's forces in Iraq, an unusual signal appears out of the blue that Iran is ready to come to the table and discuss a full range of issues, from the nuclear program to the peace process. The message, said to come from responsible Iranian officials, is transmitted to the State Department by Tim Guldimann, Switzerland's ambassador to Tehran, who represents official US interests in the Islamic Republic. The document's reception in Washington says much about the obstacles to US–Iranian relations.

From the start, there are doubts about the document's authenticity because it bears no letterhead or signature – although non-papers are not unusual and Iran's desire for deniability strikes some officials as understandable. But discussions at the State Department lead the deputy secretary, Richard Armitage, and officials at the White House and Pentagon, to conclude it is not "in consonance with our state of relations [or] ... what we [are] hearing face to face" from other Iranian contacts. Guldimann maintains the document originated with, among others, Iranian Ambassador to Paris Sadeq Kharrazi, who has ties to the Supreme Leader.[17] But ingrained mistrust even among career diplomats and a clear "not interested" signal from political higher-ups all but guarantee it will find few takers on the American side.

Furthermore, the USA is riding the high of its march through Iraq and feels that it needs no help from Iran. Bad timing also once again plays a part. Just days afterwards, on May 12, a terrorist attack in Riyadh kills nine Americans among other victims. US intelligence quickly alleges a tie-in with al-Qaeda forces located in Iran. Although there is no proof Tehran is involved (and the government claims that al-Qaeda members within their borders are actually being detained), the Bush administration cuts off all contacts with Iranians, even through the productive channel on Afghanistan.

Almost two decades later, whether or not the "road map" was a genuine offer coming from Ayatollah Khamenei is still disputed and the episode is yet another "what if" in the relationship. The likelihood that top levels of the Bush administration would have been open to engaging with Tehran at that juncture is also far from given. Still, some senior diplomats, for example William Burns who oversaw Middle East policy for the State Department, later regret it was not explored more seriously.

....

1. On April 21, I had a longer discussion with Sadeq Kharrazi who came to see me (S.Kh. is the Iranian Ambassador in Paris, former Deputy FM [foreign minister] and nephew of the Foreign Minister, his sister is married to the son of the Religious Leader Khamenei). During this discussion, a first draft of the enclosed Roadmap was developed. He said that he would discuss this with the Leader and the Foreign Minister.

2. On May 2, I met him again for three hours. He told me that he had two long discussions with the Leader on the Roadmap. In these meetings, which both lasted almost two hours, only President Khatami and FM Kharrazi were present; "we went through every word of the [sic] paper." (He additionally had a series of separat [sic] meetings with both). The question is dealt with in high secrecy, therefore no one else has been informed. (S.Kh himself has become also very discreet in our last contacts). - S.Kh presented the paper to the Leader as a proposal which he had discussed with a friend in Europe who has close contacts with higher echelons in the DoS [Department of State]. The Leader explicitly hat [sic] asked him whether this is a US-proposal and S.Kh denied this, saying that, if it is accepted, this friend could convey it to Washington as the basis for opening the bilateral discussion.

3. Then S.Kh told me that the Leader uttered some reservations as for some points; the President and the Foreign Minister were very positive, there was no problem from their side. Then he said: "They (meaning above all the Leader) agree with 85%-90% of the paper. But everything can be negotiated." (By 'agree' he meant to agree with the points themselves referred

to as 'US aims' in the Roadmap, and not only to agree that the US puts these points on the agenda). – "There is a clear interest to tackle the problem of our relations with the US. I told them, this is a golden opportunity, one day we must find a solution." – then S.Kh. asked me whether I could present the enclosed Roadmap very confidentially to someone very high up in the DoS in order to get to know the US reaction on it. – He asked me to make some very minor changes in the Roadmap draft of our previous meeting, we re-wrote for instance the Iranian statement on the Middle East, and he said that he thinks that this statement would be acceptable – "the peace process is a reality."

4. Then he said: "If the Americans agree to have a discreet bilateral meeting on the basis of this Roadmap, then this meeting could be arranged very soon. In this meeting our remaining reservations could be discussed as well as the US would bring in their reservations on this paper. I am sure that these differences can be eliminated. If we can agree on a Roadmap to clarify this procedure, as a next step it could already be decided in this first meeting that the two Foreign Ministers could meet for starting the process" along the lines of the Roadmap "to decide on how to proceed to solve everything A till Z." Asked whether the meeting between the two foreign ministers has been agreed to by the Leader, he said "Look, if we can agree on the procedure, I believe honestly that it is O.K. for the meeting of the foreign ministers in Paris or Geneva, there is soon an occasion." – Asked whom he thinks would participate in the first discreet meeting, he mentioned Armitage, referring to the positive positions of the latter on Iranian democracy. – I told him that I think this is impossible, but then he mentioned a meeting these days between Khalilzad and Zarif (Ambassador to the UN) in Geneva on terrorism and said it could be on a similar level from the DoS and on their side maybe him or Zarif or both.

5. When I tried to obtain from him a precise answer on what exactly the Leader has agreed, he said that the lack of trust in the US imposes them to proceed very carefully and very confidentially. After discussing this problem with him I understood that they want to be sure that if this initiative

failed, and if anything about the new Iranian flexibility outlined in it became known, they would – also for internal reasons – not be bound to it. – However, I got the clear impression that there is a strong will of the regime to tackle the problem with the US now and try it with this initiative.

Roadmap

US aims: (Iran agrees that the US puts the following aims on the agenda)

- **WMD:** full transparency for security that there are no Iranian endeavours to develop or possess WMD, full cooperation with IAEA based on Iranian adoption of all relevant instruments (93 + 2 and all further IAEA protocols)
- **Terrorism:** Decisive action against any terrorists (above all Al Qaida) on Iranian territory, full cooperation and exchange of all relevant information.
- **Iraq:** coordination of Iranian influence for actively supporting political stabilization and the establishment of democratic institutions and a democratic government representing all ethnic and religious groups in Iraq.
- **Middle East:**
  1. Stop of any material support to any Palestinian opposition groups (Hamas, Jihad, etc.) from Iranian territory, pressure on these organizations to stop violent actions against civilians within borders of 1967.
  2. Action on Hisbollah to become an exclusively political and social organization within Lebanon.
  3. Acceptance of the two-states-approach.

Iranian aims: (the US accepts a dialogue "in mutual respect" and agrees that Iran puts the following aims on the agenda)

- US refrains from supporting change of the political system by direct interference from outside
- Abolishment of all sanctions: commercial sanctions, frozen assets, refusal of access to WTO
- Iraq: support of MKO, support of the repatriation of all MKO members, support of the Iranian claims for Iraqi reparation, no Turkish invasion in North Iraq, respect for the Iranian national interests in Iraq and religious links to Najaf/Kerbala

- Access to peaceful nuclear technology, biotechnolgy [*sic*] and chemical technology
- Recognition of Iran's legitimate security interests in the region with the according defense capacity
- Terrorism: action against MKO and affiliated organizations in the US

Steps:

1. Communication of mutual agreement on the following procedure
2. Mutual simultaneous statements "we have always been ready for direct and authoritative talks with the US/with Iran with the aim of discussing – in mutual respect – our common interests and our mutual concerns, but we have always made it clear that, such talks can only be held, if genuine progress for a solution of our own concerns can be achieved."
3. A direct meeting on the appropriate level will be held with the previously agreed aims
   a. Of a decision on the mutual first steps
      - Iraq: establishment of a common working group on Iraq, active Iranian support for Iraqi stabilization, US commitment to resolve MKO problem in Iraq, US commitment to take Iranian reparation claims into the discussion on Iraq foreign debts
      - Terrorism: Iranian commitment for decisive action against A Qaida members in Iran, agreement on cooperation and information exchange
      - Iranian statement "that it supports a peaceful solution in the Middle East, that it accepts a solution which is accepted by the Palestinians and that it follows with interest the discussion on the Roadmap, presented by the Quartett [*sic*]."
   b. Of the establishment of three parallel working groups on disarmament, regional security, and economic cooperation. Their aim is an agreement on three parallel roadmaps, for the discussions of these working groups each side accepts that the other side's aims (see above) are put on the agenda:
      1) Disarmament: road map, which combines the mutual aims of, on the one side, full transparency by

international commitments and guarantees to abstain
from WMD with, on the other side, access to western
technology (in the three areas),

2) Terrorism and regional security: road map for above
mentioned aims on Middle East and terrorism

3) Economic cooperation: road map for the lifting of the
sanctions and the solution of the frozen assets

c. and of a public statement after this first meeting on the
achieved agreements

[*Source:* Washington Post, *www.washingtonpost.com/wp-srv/world/documents/us_
iran_1roadmap.pdf; a transcribed "edited" version appears in Barbara Slavin,* Bitter
Friends, Bosom Enemies: Iran, the US, and the Twisted Path to Confrontation
(*New York: St. Martin's Press, 2007), Appendix, pp. 229–231.*]

**Document 43. International Atomic Energy Agency, Resolution, Board
of Governors, "Implementation of the NPT Safeguards Agreement in the
Islamic Republic of Iran," UNCLASSIFIED, September 12, 2003**

*The August 2002 disclosure of the Natanz uranium enrichment facility alarms
the international community and raises the nuclear issue to the level of a crisis
in Iran's relations with the rest of the world. A signatory of the nuclear Non-
Proliferation Treaty (NPT), Iran is required to disclose nuclear facilities to the
IAEA within certain timeframes and of course is prohibited from pursuing
nuclear weapons. Over the years, IAEA inspections uncover evidence that
alternately backs up and flatly contradicts Tehran's assurances that it has
always adhered to its international obligations.*

*This particular resolution by the IAEA's Board of Governors, one of many
during the 2000s, follows the troubling discovery in August 2003 of traces of
highly enriched uranium (HEU) at Natanz (later determined to have come
from recently transferred foreign equipment). The report expresses "grave
concern that, more than one year after initial IAEA inquiries to Iran about
undeclared activities, Iran has still not enabled the IAEA to provide the
assurances required by Member States that all nuclear material in Iran is
declared and submitted to Agency safeguards and that there are no
undeclared nuclear activities in Iran."*

*President Khatami defends Iran's behavior and denies the country needs a
bomb, but Tehran bows to pressure and in October signs on to the NPT's*

Additional Protocols and agrees to suspend uranium enrichment temporarily (although the definition of temporary becomes a problem later).

....

GOV/2003/69

Date: 12 September 2003

Implementation of the NPT Safeguards Agreement in the Islamic Republic of Iran

Resolution adopted by the Board on 12 September 2003

The Board of Governors,

(a) Recalling the Director General's report of 6 June 2003 (GOV/2003/40), which expressed concern over failures by the Islamic Republic of Iran to report material, facilities and activities as it was obliged to do pursuant to its safeguards agreement, and noted that the Secretariat continues to investigate a number of unresolved issues,

(b) Recalling also recent statements by Iranian authorities recommitting Iran to full NPT and IAEA safeguards compliance and renouncing Iranian interest in nuclear weapons,

(c) Acknowledging Iran's decision to start negotiations for the conclusion of an additional protocol, but noting it does not meet the Board's 19 June request that Iran promptly and unconditionally sign and implement such a Protocol,

(d) Noting with appreciation the Director General's report of 26 August 2003 (GOV/2003/63), on the implementation of safeguards in Iran, and acknowledging that as a result of intensive inspection activities in Iran by the Agency since February, the Agency now has a better, although still incomplete, understanding of Iran's nuclear programme,

(e) Commending the Secretariat for its continuing efforts to resolve all outstanding safeguards issues and sharing the view of the Director General that much essential work remains to be completed urgently to enable the Agency to draw conclusions on the programme,

(f) Noting the interim nature of the report of the Director General and calling on Iran to further enhance cooperation and provide full transparency to allow the Agency to fully understand and verify all aspects of Iran's nuclear programme, including the full history of its enrichment programme,

(g) <u>Concerned by</u> the statement of the Director General that information and access were at times slow in coming and incremental, that some of the information was in contrast to that previously provided by Iran, and that there remain a number of important outstanding issues that require urgent resolution,

(h) <u>Noting with concern</u>:
- that the Agency environmental sampling at Natanz has revealed the presence of two types of high enriched uranium, which requires additional work to enable the Agency to arrive at a conclusion;
- that IAEA inspectors found considerable modifications had been made to the premises at the Kalaye Electric Company prior to inspections that may impact on the accuracy of the environmental sampling;
- that some of Iran's statements to the IAEA have undergone significant and material changes, and that the number of outstanding issues has increased since the report;
- that despite the Board's statement in June 2003 encouraging Iran, as a confidence-building measure, not to introduce nuclear material into its pilot centrifuge enrichment cascade at Natanz, Iran has introduced such material;

(i) <u>Expressing grave concern</u> that, more than one year after initial IAEA inquiries to Iran about undeclared activities, Iran has still not enabled the IAEA to provide the assurances required by Member States that all nuclear material in Iran is declared and submitted to Agency safeguards and that there are no undeclared nuclear activities in Iran,

(j) <u>Mindful</u> of Iran's heavy responsibility to the international community regarding the transparency of its extensive nuclear activities,

(k) <u>Recognising</u> the basic and inalienable right of all Member States to develop atomic energy for peaceful purpose,

(l) <u>Stressing</u> the need for effective safeguards in order to prevent the use of nuclear material for prohibited purposes in contravention of safeguards agreements, and underlining the vital importance of effective safeguards for facilitating cooperation in the field of peaceful uses of nuclear energy,

1. Calls on Iran to provide accelerated cooperation and full transparency to allow the Agency to provide at an early date the assurances required by Member States;

2. Calls on Iran to ensure there are no further failures to report material, facilities and activities that Iran is obliged to report pursuant to its safeguards agreement;

3. Reiterates the Board's statement in June 2003 encouraging Iran not to introduce nuclear material into its pilot enrichment cascade in Natanz, and in this context calls on Iran to suspend all further uranium enrichment-related activities, including the further introduction of nuclear material into Natanz, and, as a confidence-building measure, any reprocessing activities, pending provision by the Director General of the assurances required by Member States, and pending satisfactory application of the provisions of the additional protocol;

4. Decides it is essential and urgent in order to ensure IAEA verification of non-diversion of nuclear material that Iran remedy all failures identified by the Agency and cooperate fully with the Agency to ensure verification of compliance with Iran's safeguards agreement by taking all necessary actions by the end of October 2003, including:

    (i) providing a full declaration of all imported material and components relevant to the enrichment programme, especially imported equipment and components stated to have been contaminated with high enriched uranium particles, and collaborating with the Agency in identifying the source and date of receipt of such imports and the locations where they have been stored and used in Iran;

    (ii) granting unrestricted access, including environmental sampling, for the Agency to whatever locations the Agency deems necessary for the purposes of verification of the correctness and completeness of Iran's declarations;

(iii) resolving questions regarding the conclusion of Agency experts that process testing on gas centrifuges must have been conducted in order for Iran to develop its enrichment technology to its current extent;

(iv) providing complete information regarding the conduct of uranium conversion experiments;

(v) providing such other information and explanations, and taking such other steps as are deemed necessary by the Agency to resolve all outstanding issues involving nuclear materials and nuclear activities, including environmental sampling results;

5. Requests all third countries to cooperate closely and fully with the Agency in the clarification of open questions on the Iranian nuclear programme;

6. Requests Iran to work with the Secretariat to promptly and unconditionally sign, ratify and fully implement the additional protocol, and, as a confidence-building measure, henceforth to act in accordance with the additional protocol;

7. Requests the Director General to continue his efforts to implement the Agency's safeguards agreement with Iran, and to submit a report in November 2003, or earlier if appropriate, on the implementation of this resolution, enabling the Board to draw definitive conclusions; and

8. Decides to remain seized of the matter.

[*Source: International Atomic Energy Agency, https://www.iaea.org/sites/default/files/ gov2003-69.pdf.*]

Document 44. US Central Command, Memorandum, "[Redacted]: SCIRI and the Badr Organization in Najaf Province," SECRET, June 11, 2005

Much as Lebanon was in the 1980s, Iraq becomes a proxy battleground between the USA and Iran in the 2000s. At first, indirect cooperation is the order of the day. After all, the US-led invasion handed the Islamic Republic a gift by toppling longtime enemy Saddam Hussein and marginalizing the Sunni elite, which opened up political space for the Shiite majority, and both sides share an interest in curbing terrorism and violent insurgencies. Within a year, however, the US military sours on developments as Iran increasingly buttresses Shia elements and engages in other forms of "interference," as Donald Rumsfeld asserts later, purportedly to establish "hegemony in the region."[18] For their part, Iranians point to growing fears of American military encirclement and their right to expand long-standing ties to their Iraqi co-religionists.

This document provides a US military assessment of one of the main Shia groups in the country, the Supreme Council for the Islamic Revolution in Iraq (SCIRI). Though established in Iran in 1982 during the Iran–Iraq War, SCIRI gains popularity in Iraq after the fall of Saddam Hussein through its humanitarian efforts in Shia-dominated regions and paramilitary victories by its militant wing, the Badr Organization. The US Central Command, which is running the occupation, keeps close watch on all political and military organizations in the country. This analysis points with unease to SCIRI's growing popularity and influence but also hints at the complexities behind Shiite power dynamics, noting the frictions with the rival Sadr Bureau and suspicions by ordinary citizens that these groups may be the subject of outside manipulation. Although the source of that manipulation is redacted, the four-letter word is almost certainly Iran.

....

[Redacted]: SCIRI and the Badr Organization in Najaf Province
11 June 2005

Background: [1–2 words redacted] in Najaf by utilizing SCIRI and its militant wing, the Badr Organization. SCIRI, or the Supreme Council for Islamic Revolution in Iraq, is a political organization that operated from [1 word redacted] during the Saddam era. The Badr Organization, previously the Badr Corps, is the [p]aramilitar[y] win[g] of SCIRI that received training and salary support from the [1 line redacted] SCIRI and Badr work within coalition-backed structures by placing members on town councils and in security forces. SCIRI has had a strong showing in national, provincial, and council elections, allowing many of its members into high level government positions, including the cabinet position for the Ministry of Interior. The Badr

Organization has taken a more political approach since the elections of late January and has increased in favor across southern Iraq. Together, these two organizations are attempting to shape Iraq according to their agendas by infiltrating Iraqi Security Forces (ISF) and purging members of the ISF not loyal to SCIRI, a method used during the Saddam era to maintain power and control.

Influence in Najaf Province: SCIRI continues attempts to control the security forces at the local and provincial level by recruiting SCIRI sympathizers. Despite announcements to the Najaf security forces made by the SCIRI-affiliated Minister of Interior (MOI), the Najaf governor (Assad Altase Abu Gilal) and chief of police are installing their own appointments. In one case, MOI-appointed [1-2 words redacted] was arrested in April for mutiny and human rights violations, after reportedly complaining of payroll corruption to the MOI. The deputy governor of the province, reportedly sympathetic to SCIRI, is now the acting chief of police.

The Badr Organization has distanced itself from its militant heritage since the success of the elections, even toning down its name from Corps to Organization to prevent being associated as a militia. Badr members, with help of SCIRI leadership, are filling both high ranking and mid-level provincial security positions within the ISF in order to expand their influence.

SCIRI and Sadr: The Sadr Bureau, an increasingly influential Shi'a organization led b[y] Mu[k]tada Al Sadr, has generally been in opposition to SCIRI despite strong [1-2 words redacted] Friction exists between both organizations as they vie for public support for their organizations. Sadr is reaching for greater support by increasing his religious stature and adopting legitimate political measures. Most recently Sadr acted as a mediator between SCIRI and the MUC.

Assessment: Citizens in Najaf are suspicious of [1 word redacted] causing SCIRI and Badr members to hesitate on relying too heavily on [1 word redacted] for support. Both organizations have taken measures to assure the citizens of Najaf province that they are not being manipulated by [1 word redacted] While [1 word redacted] does provide funding for the organizations, reporting indicates that the organizations are looking to move away from [1–2 words redacted] as the emerging Iraqi government matures.

One way SCIRI may try to gain more popularity among the Shia may include a name change. If SCIRI decides to change names it would likely happen before upcoming December elections in order to change public perception of [1–2 words redacted] among SCIRI members. Another possible COA could involve dissolving the Badr Organization with members filling security positions throughout the province and other Shia dominated areas in order to show non-supporters they are no longer [1–2 words redacted]. SCIRI will continue to influence government and security positions by placing more members in mid level governmental positions throughout An Najaf. The Badr organization will conduct more positive public activities in order to increase support for their organization. Future Badr operations against MNF and ISF IVO An Najaf will be limited to covert intelligence collecting.

MNI-C2 CACE, Future Intelligence Section, DSN [Redacted]
Sources:
[5 lines redacted]

[*Source: US Central Command, Freedom of Information Act release, based on a FOIA for a fully redacted version that appears as item no. 0598 in a compendium of documents attached to the two-volume study: Col. Joel D. Rayburn and Col. Frank K. Sobchak, eds.,* The US Army in the Iraq War *(Carlisle Barracks, PA: United States Army War College Press, 2019).*]

Document 45. Iranian Supreme National Security Council, Speech, Hassan Rouhani, "Beyond the Challenges Facing Iran and IAEA Concerning the Nuclear Dossier," UNCLASSIFIED, circa September 2005

The lack of transparency of Iran's nuclear program and evidence of official deception about it have long been worries for the West. That is what makes relatively unguarded discussions like this from future President Hassan Rouhani so valuable and intriguing. Rouhani is still serving as secretary to the Supreme National Security Council (a post he has held since 1989) and Iran's lead nuclear negotiator. In the audience is President Khatami who is about to be replaced by Mahmoud Ahmadinejad.

In these remarks to the Supreme Cultural Revolution Council, Rouhani admits Iran has conducted secret tests and not reported some of its activities to the IAEA. The reason, he says, is pressure from the United States. "My basic discussion with the three European ministers was that if we presented a full picture of our nuclear program, according to the regulations, what would the Americans do, given that the Americans insist on taking us to the UN Security Council? If they were going to promise to resist the American pressure, we thought, we would cooperate. But if they were not going to resist, then we would choose a different path."

Among other points of interest, Rouhani acknowledges that "the IAEA was fully informed about most of the cases we thought were unknown to them," thanks in part to reports provided by Russia and China but also to information found in a dissertation and a scientific paper written by Iranian scholars that the IAEA inadvertently stumbled upon. He also asserts that Iranian authorities themselves had no idea about high levels of uranium contamination at certain facilities until the inspectors arrived.

....

Hassan Rouhani: [...] The Islamic Republic of Iran 15 or 16 years ago - that is, in 1366 [1987-1988] or 1367 [1988-1989] - started to pursue fuel cycle technology. We pursued this technology because we always wanted to make use of nuclear energy, wanted to have nuclear power plants, and wanted to be able to produce the needed fuel for those plants ourselves.

We tried very hard to purchase the technology and nuclear fuel cycle capabilities from other countries. In those years, we mostly went to the Soviet Union and China to buy technology, but no country agreed to give us that technology.

Countries have a natural right to possess the fuel cycle, but because of the capabilities that accompany such a technology, they avoided giving it to us. Thus, we started our efforts to obtain this capability through different means. We started our activities inside the country, things that we had to do to develop a national capability in this area. We also started to go to the black market and contact different individuals and networks. We took steps inside the country to address this issue and built up some capabilities through different means.

In more recent years, that is to say since 1378 [1999-2000], a decision was made to become more active and upgrade our capabilities. To this end, we redoubled our efforts in the country and granted the Atomic Energy [Organization of Iran] authorities that it did not have before. That is to say, we gave the agency a freer hand with new credits and a more liberal spending procedure, new facilities, and special regulations. This allowed them to become more active, without being forced to go through bureaucratic and regulatory labyrinths. It was after these activities that the uproar started in the Western media in the summer of 1381 [2002-2003], which argued that Iran is in the process of building an atomic bomb.

You may remember that this uproar started in Mordad 1381 [July-August 2002]. Reacting to this outcry in the Western media, the International Atomic Energy Agency (IAEA) asked Iran questions about this matter to determine whether Iran's actions were legal, to see if these activities were secret or open, to see if Iran had violated the terms of the NPT or if it had done anything against the rules.

You also may remember that after this great uproar in the international media, [IAEA Director General Mohamed] ElBaradei visited Iran in the winter of 1381 [2002-2003]. During that visit, he also visited [the enrichment facility at] Natanz. After that visit, the argument was put forward that Iran's case must be sent to the IAEA Board of Governors. Because the Americans at that time were determined to attack Iraq, they temporarily ceased to pursue the matter and put this issue on the back burner. But even under those conditions, the debate continued in the United States: Should they attack Iran first or Iraq? In the end, they decided to attack Iraq. So, America was getting ready to invade Iraq in Bahman [January-February], it appeared completely ready for action in Esfand [February-March], and began its attack on the last day of the month of Esfand [19 March].

Naturally, because of the issue of Iraq and the invasion of that country, the arguments over the Iranian issue subsided during the months of Farvardin and Ordibehesht [March-May]. Nevertheless, starting in Khordad [May-June], when America's victory in Iraq became evident and, as they themselves said, they succeeded in occupying Iraq – and the resistance that we see today and the kind of pressure currently on the American troops had not materialized yet – they revisited this issue. They started to think that conditions were right for them to raise the issue of Iran at the meeting of the IAEA Board of Governors and to pave the way for sending the case to the UN Security Council. The idea was to plan sanctions or even military operations against Iran, or at least put political and economic pressure on this country.

It was for this reason that Iran's case, for the first time, was officially addressed in the meeting of the IAEA Board of Governors in Khordad 1382 [May–June 2003]. Of course, no resolutions were issued at that meeting. The director general of the International Atomic Energy Agency, Mohamed ElBaradei, presented his report, and the chairman of that meeting summarized the discussions by way of a statement, which was not a particularly good summary. It was then that we felt a threat, a sense of danger in the country. We thought that we might be facing a plot against Iran and that we might encounter some problems.

Until that time, the Atomic Energy Organization of Iran was the authority that was basically handling all political and technical issues concerning this case. That is to say, the Iranian Atomic Energy Agency was the authority that, with the president's approval, used to appoint the Islamic Republic of Iran's representative to Vienna to deal with the IAEA. Therefore, the Atomic Energy Agency Organization of Iran handled both the political and technical aspects of the issue. Of course, the Foreign Ministry also provided support at different junctures. Nonetheless, it was felt that this issue must be addressed at a higher level. Therefore, the Supreme National Security Council came to discuss the issue for the first time to determine our course of action. We held several meetings until we got closer to the next meeting of the IAEA Board of Governors, which was in September (Shahrivar 1382). Strong differences emerged between the Iranian Atomic Energy Agency and the Foreign Ministry over how to handle this issue. The Atomic Energy Organization of Iran argued that Iran's nuclear case was not an important issue and that we could successfully solve the problem at the Board of Governors' meeting. The Foreign Ministry, on the other hand, issued a strong warning that this case might have a very difficult road ahead. These two bodies, in fact, held exactly opposite views.

In the meetings that we held in the Secretariat of the Supreme National Security Council, it was very clear that we were dealing with differences of opinion. It was at this point that we engaged in a public argument in the country about what to do regarding the Additional Protocol [to the NPT]. If you remember, we had huge outcries in the country: should we accept the protocol or shouldn't we? Is accepting the protocol a necessity or an act of treason? The reason was that ElBaradei (the head of the IAEA) stated in his report, which was prepared for the September meeting and which was made public, declared that he would not be able to determine the truth of Iran's claims or carry out a verification, unless Iran accepted the Additional Protocol.

At the September [2003] meeting, the IAEA Board of Governors approved a strongly worded resolution against Iran based on consensus (without taking a vote). Of course, at that time, we were a member of the IAEA Board of Governors, too. The statement was prepared in such a way that it took us to the doorstep of the UN Security Council. It was very clear that this statement was a very carefully contemplated move that was planned behind closed doors to take us to the UN Security Council. It was under these conditions that a new discussion started in this country: What were we supposed to do under these circumstances?! One assumption was that we would end up going to the UN Security Council. Another argued that the problem could be solved somehow. At that juncture, when we reviewed the matter from a technical and legal point of view – by then we had created a committee in the Secretariat of the Supreme National Security Council that included ministers whose ministries were involved in this matter, and we held lengthy discussions – we concluded that even if we fully cooperate with the IAEA to address all the concerns raised in their resolution, we still would be sent to the UN Security Council come November (Azar 1382). Therefore, we had to find other solutions to cooperate with the IAEA and not to go to the UN Security Council. The issue was not to guarantee that we would never go to the UN Security Council. Instead, the issue was that, at that time, the United States was at the height of its pride and our country also was not yet ready to go to the UN Security Council, so the issue was for the case not to be referred to the UN Security Council. At the same time, we had not yet tried all the ways available to us. We had not tried to see if we could solve the problem through other means. Therefore, we held numerous meetings and reviewed the issue from different perspectives and at different levels.

At the present time, too, we discuss and make decisions about the nuclear issue at four different levels. One is the technical level, considering the technical aspects of the issue. This is headed by a Foreign Ministry executive, and all of the relevant departments participate in these discussions. Technical discussions also take place at a higher level, during the meetings of the Supreme National Security Council Secretariat. The third level is a ministerial committee that also meets in the Supreme National Security Council Secretariat. The fourth is at the level of the heads of the ruling system.

All of the major fundamental decisions are made there. In the meeting of the heads of the ruling system, the issue was raised that, according to the September resolution of the IAEA Board of Governors, we were to present the IAEA with a complete report on our nuclear activities in previous years. The main discussion was this: Would presenting a complete picture of our past nuclear activities solve the problem? If we presented a complete picture, that picture itself could take us to the UN Security Council. If we did not present a complete picture, this would have been considered a violation of the resolution, and we would go to the UN Security Council on the grounds that we had violated the resolution. Therefore, no matter which option we chose, it was argued, our case would end up at the UN Security Council. Thus, we had a discussion at the lower, technical level: Should we start cooperating with the Europeans in this regard, and would such cooperation be effective? Some believed that cooperation with Europe would not have any effect on the situation, because Europe is not independent and the United States is determined to take us to the UN Security Council; so, they argued, Europe would not be able to do anything. There also were those who believed that cooperation with Europe could bear fruit. All these arguments were presented to the heads of the ruling system at their meeting.

You should also keep in mind that the three European countries sent a letter to the Iranian Government in the summer of 1382 and proposed a plan to deal with Iran's nuclear case. Of course, they raised different issues in that letter. One was that Iran should abandon its fuel cycle program. The Russian Government sent a similar letter to the Iranian Government. They also said Iran should abandon its fuel cycle program. So the issue was now this: Should we invite the three European ministers to visit Tehran? Those who opposed inviting the ministers to visit Tehran did so essentially from two different perspectives. Some argued that discussions with Europe would be fruitless, that the Europeans would not be able to do anything in front of the United States, even if they wanted to do something. There were others who believed that the Europeans, if we invited them to come to Iran, would not accept our invitation. Their reason was that three important European ministers had never joined together before to visit a non-European country on any mission and that such a thing was practically impossible. Our Foreign Ministry also believed that, even from a ceremonial point of view, this could not be done. That is to say, even if we invited the three ministers to visit Tehran, they would not come. Nevertheless, it was decided during that meeting that we should invite those ministers to visit Tehran. If they declined, we would hold the meeting in one of the European countries. This discussion coincided with another discussion about the need for one person to take charge of the nuclear case and have all departments operate under his supervision. All of the participants in the meeting of the heads of the ruling system decided that I should take charge of this case.

It was at that time that we invited the three [European foreign] ministers [to visit Tehran]. The objective was to find a way to present a complete picture of our past nuclear activities, without being sent to the UN Security Council. If we did not make our past activities public, the IAEA would clearly take that as a sign of noncooperation. Most of the activities that we had not reported to the IAEA had already been reported to the IAEA by other countries that had worked with us and that were party to those activities, such as China. We had certain projects with China in the past that, according to the regulations, we had to report to the IAEA and had not done so. The Chinese, on the other hand, told us that they had reported all of those activities to the IAEA. In addition, we had purchased some equipment from the Russians, and they too, had reported all of it to the IAEA. It also became evident that the IAEA knew about some secret tests we had conducted a number of years earlier. For instance, we had conducted a test in Tehran. The person in charge of that project was a university professor. One of his students that year had written a dissertation, and several copies were made of that dissertation. The IAEA had accidentally taken possession of a copy of that dissertation, and we did not know anything know about it. It was only sometime later that the IAEA produced a copy of that dissertation and said: You have conducted that test. Or, for example, in another case that we thought nobody knew anything about, one of the scholars who participated in that project wrote a scientific paper about it and had it published in an international journal. The IAEA had a copy of that paper. Therefore, the IAEA was fully informed about most of the cases we thought were unknown to them. Moreover, in one instance – a test that we carried out 10 or 12 years ago – as we prepared to submit the report on our past activities to the IAEA, one of the IAEA officials told our people that we should be sure to include that test in our report! In fact, he wanted to tell us that they knew all about it! My basic discussion with the three European ministers was that if we presented a full picture of our nuclear program, according to the regulations, what would the Americans do, given that the Americans insist on taking us to the UN Security Council? If they were going to promise to resist the American pressure, we thought, we would cooperate. But if they were not going to resist, then we would choose a different path.

When we invited the three ministers, they all declared themselves ready to come to Iran, but they said that first the directors general of their respective foreign ministries must come to Iran on an unofficial visit to conduct technical negotiations to see if there was a way for us to move ahead or not. The directors general from the three European countries came to Tehran and talked with the experts from the Foreign Ministry and myself. In the end, the three foreign ministers decided to visit Tehran. Of course, until the last minute before the actual visit took place, we had not agreed on the final text of the accord. But they came to Tehran anyway. The working groups had first discussed the important issues but had failed to solve the problems. Therefore, inevitably, the issues were raised in the discussions between the three ministers and me. That meeting was very long. It started in the morning and lasted until about 1500, when we finally reached an agreement.

At that meeting, the Europeans promised us that if we presented a complete picture of the country's nuclear activities to the IAEA, as the resolution called for, they would resist the American pressure to take us to the UN Security Council and would not allow that to happen. Of course, we might have been operating under unique conditions. The Americans were at the height of their pride and victory in Iraq, and the Europeans did not want to see that case go to the UN Security Council and cause another crisis in the region. There, they promised us that they would resist and would not allow that case to go to the UN Security Council. As a result, we presented the IAEA with a complete picture of our nuclear activities and also announced that we would sign the Additional Protocol. Of course, all the agreements that we made with the Europeans were agreements that the system had embraced beforehand. That is to say, even if we did not reach an agreement with the Europeans, we still would have unilaterally declared that we would sign the Additional Protocol. We would present the IAEA with a complete picture of our nuclear activities, and we would declare that we would suspend parts of our fuel cycle program. That is to say, decisions had been made beforehand that we would unilaterally take those steps even in the absence of an agreement with the three [European] countries. Nevertheless, we made a deal. The deal was for us to take those steps in exchange for some commitments by the Europeans.

The most important promise that they made to us was that they would stand firm against attempts to take this case to the UN Security Council and work to solve the problem within the framework of the IAEA. The Europeans upheld that commitment at the November meeting [of the IAEA Board of Governors]. Even though the Americans, backed by Australia, South Korea, and Japan, insisted on sending the case to the UN Security Council, the three European countries stood firm and did not allow the American proposal to go forward. This was a noteworthy development. The Russians even told us that this was an interesting scene in political history that we were witnessing, the United Kingdom going against the United States. We had not seen anything like that before, and it was beautiful to see. We

put the November meeting behind us, but later we had some
problems with our confidence-building measures with
the Europeans.

[...]

Overall, it is clear that Europe is not our friend and that it
does not have a good relationship with Islam. Nevertheless,
because of Iran's strategic position, Europe does not want to
lose Iran. Under the present conditions, Iran is the only
breathing space that Europe has in this region. It is for this
reason that they do not want to lose this space. We think that in
some instances they have cooperated with us and have not done so
in other cases. There are also some differences between the
United States and Europe, although when it comes to the nuclear
issue, they generally agree and follow the same objective.

2. As for the question of what we can do now that they all
disagree with our having the fuel cycle, I submit to you that we
require an opportunity, time to be able to act on our capability
in this area. That is, if one day we are able to complete the fuel
cycle and the world sees that it has no choice, that we do possess
the technology, then the situation will be different. The world
did not want Pakistan to have an atomic bomb or Brazil to have the
fuel cycle, but Pakistan built its bomb and Brazil has its fuel
cycle, and the world started to work with them. Our problem is
that we have not achieved either one, but we are standing at the
threshold. As for building an atomic bomb, we never wanted to
move in that direction and we have not yet completely developed
our fuel cycle capability. This also happens to be our
main problem.

3. One of the members indicated here that all this should have
been done in secret. This was the intention; this never was
supposed to be in the open. But in any case, the spies exposed it.
We did not want to declare all this. Some of you say that if we had
said from the start that we wanted to have the fuel cycle, the
situation would have been easier. Yes, if we had decided to
declare our intention at the beginning, if we had told the IAEA
that we intended to build a UCF plant at the same time that we
started construction at Esfahan, if we had announced our
facilities at Natanz from the start, we would not have any
problems now, or our problems would have been far less than they
are today. In fact, this is the very reason that our case has

become so complicated. They ask: If you truly were after fuel cycle, why did you do it secretly?! This is the root of all problems. If we had done it openly, the problem would have been far simpler. In the beginning, we decided not to go public for a number of reasons. For example, pressure from the West to deny us primary materials, and reasons like that. We wanted to keep it secret for a while. Of course, we all knew at that some point this would become public knowledge. I do not want to get into the history of this issue at this time.

4. Some have pointed to a number of difficulties. In any case, there have been a number of problems, and today we are facing these conditions. The West is against us having the fuel cycle, and this happens to be our main problem. If the Russians had agreed that we should have the fuel cycle, our job would have been much easier. Even if China or Japan had agreed, we would have had an easier time. All these countries are against this. The powerful countries are all against this, and the United States and Israel also provoke them. Europe is against this, too, so it is not easy for us to carry on with our activities. If we can reach a political agreement to work with the world and activate our fuel cycle, that would be very desirable. We think there is a chance we would be successful in this undertaking. If we can, it would be a great, artful deed for the Islamic Republic of Iran. If we fail to reach our objective, that is, if the situation develops into a confrontation instead of cooperation, then the country must decide whether it wants to activate the fuel cycle – even if we go to the UN Security Council and they place sanctions against us – or it wants to continue the suspension.

[...]

Not only I or our politicians did not know, but even our technical people were not fully informed that our imported machines were contaminated. When the IAEA inspectors came to take their samples, we were happy. We thought that these inspections would show that our activities had been within the framework of the NPT.

[...]

As far as we are concerned, we are not sure about any of the promises that the Europeans are making, unless we ultimately reach a final agreement and see in practice whether they remain true to what they say. We do not have any trust in them. Unfortunately, they do not trust us, either. They think we are out to dupe them, and we think in the same way, that they want to trick and cheat us. Therefore, we should build trust, step by step and in practice.

This is a very, very complex and difficult effort. Personally, I am not very optimistic, but I am not without hope, either. In fact, I cannot even say that I am pessimistic and think that there is no way and that we are at an impasse. We must go forward. We may not achieve everything that we want 100%, and what the Europeans want may not come true, either. In the end, we – the Europeans and us – might compromise, accept something less than 100%, and reach an accord.

Well, apparently, the call to prayer [Azan] has been made. We must get ready to say our prayers and break our fast [iftar].

Peace and God's blessing upon you.

[*Source: Tehran* Rahbord *in Persian, September 30, 2005, translated by Foreign Broadcast Information Service.*]

Document 46. Islamic Republic of Iran, Letter, President Ahmadinejad for President Bush, UNCLASSIFIED, circa May 8, 2006

The most controversial Iranian leader of the 2000s is Mahmoud Ahmadinejad. The populist former mayor of Tehran wins the presidency in 2005 largely on a platform of economic justice. He quickly gains notoriety for his inflammatory statements about the Holocaust and the need to eliminate the state of Israel and returns Iran to a hostile policy toward the United States. He also pointedly beefs up the country's nuclear program at a time of enormous global pressure to do the opposite. These actions make it nearly impossible politically for Washington to engage diplomatically with Tehran.

In this letter to President Bush (he later writes to President Obama, too), Ahmadinejad mainly succeeds in cementing his reputation abroad as little short of a crackpot. But buried beneath the extraordinarily abrasive language is a declaration of interest in a dialogue with the United States. In fact, aside from the severity of the tone, some of the content does not read terribly differently from earlier US demands – cloaked as propositions – that Iran recognize its wrongdoing [Document 35, for example].

While most observers ridicule the letter, an Iranian government spokesperson goes so far as to call it "a new doctrine" and declares the "door of dialogue with the world is open."[19] But Americans cannot get past the aggressive attacks. Secretary of State Condoleezza Rice tells the media: "This letter is not the place that one would find an opening to engage on the nuclear issue or anything of the sort." Yet, according to knowledgeable Iranians later, that is exactly what it is[20] – albeit perhaps the most ineptly conceived invitation of its kind in the post-revolutionary period – and it almost certainly required the approval of the Supreme Leader himself.

....

Mr. George Bush,
President of the United States of America

For some time now I have been thinking, how one can justify the undeniable contradictions that exist in the international arena and which are being constantly debated, especially in political forums and among university students. Many questions remain unanswered. These have prompted me to discuss some of the contradictions and questions, in the hopes that it might bring about an opportunity to redress them.

Can one be a follower of Jesus Christ (peace be upon Him), the great Messenger of God, feel obliged to respect human rights, present liberalism as a civilization model, announce one's opposition to the proliferation of nuclear weapons and [other] weapons of mass destruction, make "War [on] Terror" his slogan, and, finally, work toward the establishment of a unified international community – a community which Christ and the virtuous of the Earth will one day govern, but, at the same time, have countries attacked; have the lives, reputations, and possessions of people destroyed; and on the slight chance [that there are] criminals in a village, city, or convoy, for example, set ablaze the entire village, city, or convoy?

The War in Iraq

[...]

On the pretext of the existence of WMDs, this great tragedy came to engulf both the peoples of the occupied and the occupying country. Later it was revealed that no WMDs existed to begin with. Of course Saddam was a murderous dictator. But the war was

not waged to topple him. The announced goal of the war was to
find and destroy weapons of mass destruction. He was toppled
along the way toward another goal. Nevertheless, the people
of the region are happy about it. I point out that throughout
the many years of the war on Iran, Saddam was supported by
the West.

[...]

Israel and the Holocaust

[...]

Students are saying that 60 years ago such a country did not
exist. They show old documents and globes and say, "Try as we
might, we have not been able to find a country named Israel."
I tell them to study the history of World War I and World War II.

[...]

After the war, they claimed that 6 million Jews had been
killed. Six million people that were surely related to at least
2 million families. Again, let us assume that these events are
true. Does that logically translate into the establishment of
the state of Israel in the Middle East or support for such a
state? How can this phenomenon be rationalized or explained?

[...]

Another big question asked by people is, why is this regime
being supported? Is support for this regime in line with the
teachings of Jesus Christ (PBUH) or Moses (PBUH) or liberal
values? Or are we to understand that allowing the original
inhabitants of these lands – inside and outside Palestine –
whether they are Christian, Muslim, or Jewish, to determine
their own fate runs contrary to principles of democracy, human
rights, and the teachings of the prophets? If not, why is there
so much opposition to a referendum?

[...]

Monotheism

[...]

We believe a return to the teachings of the divine prophets is
the only road leading to salvation. I have been told that Your
Excellency follows the teachings of Jesus (PBUH) and believes in
the divine promise of the rule of the righteous on Earth. We also
believe that Jesus Christ (PBUH) was one of the great prophets of
the Almighty. He has been repeatedly praised in the Koran. Jesus

(PBUH) has been quoted in Koran as well: "And surely Allah is my Lord and your Lord, therefore serve Him; this is the right path, Marium."

[...]

Judgment Day

[...]

Mr. President, history tells us that repressive and cruel governments do not survive. God has entrusted the fate of man to them. The Almighty has not left the universe and humanity to their own devices. Many things have happened contrary to the wishes and plans of governments. These tell us that there is a higher power at work and all events are determined by Him.

[...]

World Turning to Religion

The people of the world have no faith in international organizations because their rights are not advocated by these organizations. Liberalism and Western-style democracy have not been able to help realize the ideals of humanity. Today these two concepts have failed. Those with insight can already hear the sounds of the shattering and fall of the ideology and thoughts of the liberal democratic systems.

We increasingly see that people around the world are flocking toward a main focal point – that is the Almighty God. Undoubtedly, through faith in God and the teachings of the prophets, the people will conquer their problems. My question for you is: "Do you not want to join them?"

Mr. President, whether we like it or not, the world is gravitating toward faith in the Almighty and justice and the will of God will prevail over all things.

> Peace to him who follows the rightfully guided,
>
> Mahmud Ahmadinejad
> President of the Islamic Republic of Iran

Document 47. State Department, Statement, Condoleezza Rice, [Proposal to Meet with EU-3 and Iranians], UNCLASSIFIED, May 31, 2006

During the Bush administration's first term, Vice President Dick Cheney, Defense Secretary Donald Rumsfeld, State Department official John Bolton, and other hardliners consistently oppose high-level engagement with Iran for policy and moral reasons. Only when Condoleezza Rice, having replaced Colin Powell as secretary of state, tells the president that his approach to Iran is "dead in the water" does the United States declare its readiness to join the Europeans' direct nuclear talks with the Islamic Republic.

Rice's aim is not to develop warmer ties with Tehran, but to rein in a regime the USA sees as a nuclear proliferator and leading state sponsor of terrorism. Her offer to join talks, moreover, hinges on the prerequisite of Tehran abandoning its uranium enrichment, which ignores a basic Iranian conception – that enrichment is their right. The two sides' inability to overcome this difference in interpretations partly explains the prolonged negotiating stalemate.

With this public statement, Rice calls out Iran for defying the IAEA and the UN Security Council by accelerating its nuclear program, then puts forward both carrot and stick. The first of two possible "paths" she identifies for Iran is the pursuit of nuclear weapons, for which the regime "will incur only great costs," including international isolation. The second path is cooperation with the USA and Europe, resulting in promises of assistance with economic development, open discussion of a civilian nuclear program, and more.

....

As Prepared

The pursuit by the Iranian regime of nuclear weapons represents a direct threat to the entire international community, including to the United States and to the Persian Gulf region. In defiance of repeated calls from the IAEA Board of Governors and from the Security Council, the Iranian government has accelerated its nuclear program while continuing to conceal its activities from international inspectors.

Working with our international partners, the United States is making every effort to achieve a successful diplomatic outcome, but the international community has made clear that the Iranian regime must not acquire nuclear weapons. The vital interests of the United States, of our friends and allies in the region, and of the entire international community are at risk, and the United States will act accordingly to protect those common interests.

Today, the Iranian regime can decide on one of two paths – one of two fundamentally different futures for its people and for its relationship with the international community.

The Iranian government's choices are clear. The negative choice is for the regime to maintain its current course, pursuing nuclear weapons in defiance of the international community and its international obligations.

If the regime does so, it will incur only great costs.

We and our European partners agree that path will lead to international isolation and progressively stronger political and economic sanctions.

The positive and constructive choice is for the Iranian regime to alter its present course and cooperate in resolving the nuclear issue, beginning by immediately resuming suspension of all enrichment-related and reprocessing activities, as well as full cooperation with the IAEA and returning to implementation of the Additional Protocol providing greater access for the IAEA.

This path would lead to the real benefit and longer-term security of the Iranian people, the region, and the world as a whole.

The Iranian people believe they have the right to civil nuclear energy. We acknowledge that right. Yet the international agreements Iran has signed make clear that Iran's exercise of that right must conform with its commitments. In view of its previous violations of its commitments and the secret nuclear program it undertook, the Iranian regime must persuasively demonstrate that it has permanently abandoned its quest for nuclear weapons.

The benefits of this second path for the Iranian people would go beyond civil nuclear energy, and could include progressively greater economic cooperation.

The United States will actively support these benefits both publicly and privately. Furthermore, President Bush has consistently emphasized that the United States is committed to a diplomatic solution to the nuclear challenge posed by the Iranian regime.

We are agreed with our European partners on the essential elements of a package containing both the benefits if Iran makes the right choice, and the costs if it does not. We hope that in the coming days the Iranian government will thoroughly consider this proposal.

Our British, French and German partners have rightly required that Iran fully and verifiably suspend its enrichment and reprocessing activities before the sides can return to negotiations. This is the condition that has been established by the IAEA Board of Governors and by the UN Security Council.

The United States is willing to exert strong leadership to give diplomacy its very best chance to succeed.

Thus, to underscore our commitment to a diplomatic solution and to enhance the prospects for success, as soon as Iran fully and verifiably suspends its enrichment and reprocessing activities, the United States will come to the table with our EU-3 colleagues and meet with Iran's representatives.

This morning US representatives have conveyed my statement to Iran through the good offices of the Swiss government, and through Iran's representative to the United Nations.

Given the benefits of this positive path for the Iranian people, regional security, and the nuclear nonproliferation regime, we urge Iran to make this choice for peace – to abandon its ambition for nuclear weapons.

President Bush wants a new and positive relationship between the American people and the people of Iran – a beneficial relationship of increased contacts in education, cultural exchange, sports, travel, trade, and investment. The nuclear issue is not the only obstacle standing in the way of improved relations.

The Iranian government supports terror, is involved in violence in Iraq, and is undercutting the restoration of full sovereignty in Lebanon under UN Security Council Resolution 1559. These policies are out of step with the international community and are barriers to a positive relationship between the Iranian people and the people of the United States and the rest of the world.

Iran can and should be a responsible state, not the leading state sponsor of terror. The United States is ready to join the

EU-3 to press these and other issues with the Iranian government in addition to our work to resolve the nuclear danger.

At the same time, we will continue to work with our international partners to end the proliferation trade globally, to bar all proliferators from international financial resources, and to end support for terror. We also intend to work with our friends and allies to strengthen their defensive capacity, counterproliferation and counterterrorism efforts, and energy security capabilities.

Those measures present no threat to a peaceful Iran with a transparent, purely civil nuclear energy program, but provide essential protection for the United States, our friends and allies if the Iranian regime chooses the wrong path.

If the Iranian regime believes that it will benefit from the possession of nuclear weapons, it is mistaken. The United States will be steadfast in defense of our forces, and steadfast in defense of our friends and allies who wish to work together for common security.

The Iranian people have a proud past, and merit a great future. We believe the Iranian people want a future of freedom and human rights – the right to vote, to run for office, to express their views without fear, and to pursue political causes. We would welcome the progress, prosperity, and freedom of the Iranian people.

The United States looks forward to a new relationship between our peoples that advances these goals. We sincerely hope that the Iranian regime will choose to make that future possible.

[*Source: 2001–2009 Archive for the US Department of State, https://2001-2009.state.gov/ secretary/rm/2006/67088.htm.*]

Document 48. National Intelligence Council, National Intelligence Estimate, "Iran: Nuclear Intentions and Capabilities," (Key Judgments Only), UNCLASSIFIED, November 2007

Most intelligence experts consider it self-evident that Iran has been in hot pursuit of a nuclear weapon for several years. Tehran's refusal to allow IAEA inspectors unfettered access to its facilities and the 2002 revelations about Natanz and Arak [Document 43] seem ample corroboration of illicit activity. More recent occasional threats aimed at Israel by Rafsanjani and Ahmadinejad have added to concerns, and in 2005 the National Intelligence Council (NIC), which is charged with analyzing high-interest national security issues on behalf of the US intelligence community, reinforced these assessments.[21] But just two years later, the NIC conducts an "extensive reexamination" of the issues. The resulting National Intelligence Estimate (NIE), excerpted here, reverses several of the earlier judgments, stating with "high confidence" that the Islamic Republic in fact halted its nuclear weapons program in 2003, as Iran has been claiming.

The NIE concludes that Iran made the decision after the Mujahedin-e Khalq's disclosures in August 2002. It will now take at least until 2015 before it can produce and reprocess enough plutonium for a weapon. This finding runs directly counter to official US thinking, thereby undercutting the case for tougher sanctions or even military strikes against Iran. Critics from the president on down decry the report. One of the main arguments derives from a footnote defining the report's focus as the country's "nuclear weapons program" – weapon design, weaponization, and covert uranium-related activities – rather than its "declared civil work" on uranium, which the administration says is its core concern. "The NIE had a big impact," Bush remarks, "and not a good one."[22]

On a broader level, the report illustrates the difficulty of gathering and assessing intelligence on a target like Iran's nuclear program. The science is highly complex, and evidence can be open to multiple interpretations. As a general matter, Iran itself is not as closed off from the world as North Korea, but US officials regularly remark that Tehran's decision-making process is a "black box," a problem exacerbated by the lack of diplomatic relations which sharply constrains direct access to the country.[23] So, gauging regime intent, especially through the welter of confusing signals, deception, and pitched rhetoric, is a huge challenge. With the political stakes as high as they are, one of the tests for intelligence analysts is how to present a chronically fluid and uncertain situation in a form that has value for policymakers.

....

Key Judgments

A. We judge with high confidence that in fall 2003, Tehran halted its nuclear weapons program;[24] we also assess with moderate-to-high confidence that Tehran at a minimum is keeping open the option to develop nuclear weapons. We judge with high confidence that the halt, and Tehran's announcement of its decision to suspend its declared uranium enrichment program and sign an Additional Protocol to its Nuclear Non-Proliferation Treaty Safeguards Agreement, was directed primarily in response to increasing international scrutiny and pressure resulting from exposure of Iran's previously undeclared nuclear work.

o We assess with high confidence that until fall 2003, Iranian military entities were working under government direction to develop nuclear weapons.

o We judge with high confidence that the halt lasted at least several years. (Because of intelligence gaps discussed elsewhere in this Estimate, however, DOE and the NIC assess with only moderate confidence that the halt to those activities represents a halt to Iran's entire nuclear weapons program.)

o We assess with moderate confidence Tehran had not restarted its nuclear weapons program as of mid-2007, but we do not know whether it currently intends to develop nuclear weapons.

o We continue to assess with moderate-to-high confidence that Iran does not currently have a nuclear weapon.

o Tehran's decision to halt its nuclear weapons program suggests it is less determined to develop nuclear weapons than we have been judging since 2005. Our assessment that the program probably was halted primarily in response to international pressure suggests Iran may be more vulnerable to influence on the issue than we judged previously.

B. We continue to assess with low confidence that Iran probably has imported at least some weapons-usable fissile material, but still judge with moderate-to-high confidence it has not obtained enough for a nuclear weapon. We cannot rule out that Iran has acquired from abroad – or will acquire in the future – a nuclear weapon or enough fissile material for a weapon. Barring such acquisitions, if Iran wants to have nuclear weapons it would need to produce sufficient amounts of fissile material indigenously – which we judge with high confidence it has not yet done.

C. We assess centrifuge enrichment is how Iran probably could first produce enough fissile material for a weapon, if it decides to do so. Iran resumed its declared centrifuge enrichment activities in January 2006, despite the continued halt in the nuclear weapons program. Iran made significant progress in 2007 installing centrifuges at Natanz, but we judge with moderate confidence it still faces significant technical problems operating them.

o We judge with moderate confidence that the earliest possible date Iran would be technically capable of producing enough HEU for a weapon is late 2009, but that this is very unlikely.

o We judge with moderate confidence Iran probably would be technically capable of producing enough HEU for a weapon sometime during the 2010–2015 time frame. (INR [State Department Bureau of Intelligence and Research] judges Iran is unlikely to achieve this capability before 2013 because of foreseeable technical and programmatic problems.) All agencies recognize the possibility that this capability may not be attained until *after* 2015.

D. Iranian entities are continuing to develop a range of technical capabilities that could be applied to producing nuclear weapons, if a decision is made to do so. For example, Iran's civilian uranium enrichment program is continuing. We also assess with high confidence that since fall 2003, Iran has been conducting research and development projects with commercial and conventional military applications - some of which would also be of limited use for nuclear weapons.

E. We do not have sufficient intelligence to judge confidently whether Tehran is willing to maintain the halt of its nuclear weapons program indefinitely while it weighs its options, or whether it will or already has set specific deadlines or criteria that will prompt it to restart the program.

o Our assessment that Iran halted the program in 2003 primarily in response to international pressure indicates Tehran's decisions are guided by a cost-benefit approach rather than a rush to a weapon irrespective of the political, economic, and military costs. This, in turn, suggests that some combination of threats of intensified international scrutiny and pressures, along with opportunities for Iran to achieve its security, prestige, and goals for regional influence in other ways, might - if perceived by Iran's leaders as credible - prompt Tehran to extend the current halt to its nuclear weapons program. It is difficult to specify what such a combination might be.

o We assess with moderate confidence that convincing the Iranian leadership to forgo the eventual development of nuclear weapons will be difficult given the linkage many within the leadership probably see between nuclear weapons development and Iran's key national security and foreign policy objectives, and given Iran's considerable effort from at least the late 1980s to 2003 to develop such weapons. In our judgment, only an Iranian political decision to abandon a nuclear weapons objective would plausibly keep Iran from eventually producing nuclear weapons – and such a decision is inherently reversible.

F. We assess with moderate confidence that Iran probably would use covert facilities – rather than its declared nuclear sites – for the production of highly enriched uranium for a weapon. A growing amount of intelligence indicates Iran was engaged in covert uranium conversion and uranium enrichment activity, but we judge that these efforts probably were halted in response to the fall 2003 halt, and that these efforts probably had not been restarted through at least mid-2007.

G. We judge with high confidence that Iran will not be technically capable of producing and reprocessing enough plutonium for a weapon before about 2015.

H. We assess with high confidence that Iran has the scientific, technical and industrial capacity eventually to produce nuclear weapons if it decides to do so.

[*Source: Office of the Director of National Intelligence, National Intelligence Council, public release.*]

Document 49. State Department, Email, William J. Burns for the Secretary of State, "Meeting with Iranians, July 19," SECRET, July 19, 2008

After Secretary of State Rice persuades the president in May 2006, talks with Iran eventually restart. This report from Under Secretary of State William Burns puts the reader right in the room with Iranian representatives and gives a clear picture of the complexity and personal aspects of these interactions. While direct engagement is certainly a step toward bettering relations, the many obstacles rapidly become apparent.

Burns' frustrations come through in his wry comment that "we may not have been missing all that much over the years." The Iranians are didactic and meandering in their responses. Their offers are "intentionally confusing" and do not propose "anything . . . that really matters." He finds the Europeans and Russians helpful but the Chinese "a little squishy." After a full day of discussions, they are rewarded with a "brief tiny opening" until the lead Iranian diplomat, Saeed Jalili, "veered off into the ether again." The scene is reminiscent of CIA expert George Cave's experience in Tehran twenty years earlier [Document 23].

Clearly, decades of mistrust cannot be dismantled in a single afternoon. For the Iranians, the frequent references to their own history and significance in the region, which Americans typically see as tedious and wasteful, signify how important these issues are to them. Respect is a perennial sticking point, and the dismissiveness Iran often perceives from Americans and Europeans reinforces old stereotypes and fears of Western intentions, as Iranian officials repeatedly make clear in public statements. At times, it might appear as though neither side has managed to get past the same cultural differences that manifested in 1979. Yet, the discussions and openings being carved out late in the Bush presidency do help set the stage for future, more consequential meetings.

....

Madam Secretary,

As I mentioned on the telephone, five and a half hours with the Iranians today were a vivid reminder that we may not have been missing all that much over the years. They were infuriatingly vague and indirect, refusing to be pinned down on an answer to the clear proposition that the P5+1 have put to them. I think an American presence was slightly unnerving for them; I got lots of sidelong glances from Jalili during the meeting, and he seemed uncertain about what this all meant for the Iranian position. It certainly seemed to have a positive effect on the P5+1, all of whom were effusive in their emphasis to Jalili about the significance of the meeting, the unity of the international community, and the importance of the choice before Iran. Solana was uncharacteristically firm, and even the Russians and Chinese made noises about the UNSC sanctions track.

Solana began the opening plenary with a strong presentation about the incentives package and the way forward paper, and the need to get an unequivocal reply from Iran. Jalili responded with nearly 30 uninterrupted minutes of philosophizing about Iran's culture and history, and the constructive role it can play in the region. (There was a heavy element of Rodney Dangerfield in all this, and much emphasis on the need to be treated with respect.) Jalili's tone was up on the high-road; he never recited any grievances about the U.S. or Israel or anyone else. But he studiously ducked Solana's direct question.

Needed to reload, [*sic*] Solana then turned to each of the Political Directors to make brief remarks. I said I was there to convey a simple message: the United States is serious about its support for the package we've all put on the table, the unity of the P5+1, and the need to resolve the Iranian nuclear issue on the basis of UNSC resolutions. I emphasized that Iran had a rare choice before it; we could only hope that it would take advantage of it. Jalili took very careful notes, and smiled faintly throughout, but otherwise had nothing to say in response. The other Political Directors were straightforward in their support for Solana, with the Chinese a little squishy and the Russians more resolute than usual.

Jalili then wandered off on another meandering monologue, but ended by offering a new Iranian "non-paper." (The English version was mistakenly headed "None Paper," which is an apt description of its substance.) It offers an intentionally confusing phased framework for negotiations, which basically avoids any mention of a "freeze" or "suspension" or anything else that really matters. The tactical goal seems clearly to be to start negotiations without giving away anything up front, and dragging things out as long as possible (certainly beyond our elections). Solana and the rest of us looked at it quickly (my French colleague helpfully groaned and muttered "bullshit" as he looked at the paper, which caused Jalili to look somewhat startled). Solana suggested that we break for lunch. He took a bullet for the team and ate one-on-one with Jalili; the rest of us ate in another room, with the two Iranian aides sitting by themselves at one end of the table. (I shook hands at the outset with Jalili and his delegation, before the cameras came into the room, but otherwise had no direct conversations with them. They didn't exactly seek me out anyway.)

We regrouped with Solana before going back into the afternoon session. He explained that he had given up trying to understand Jalili's explanation of the Iranian paper, and had told Jalili simply that we could talk about how to organize negotiations as much as the Iranians wanted during the six week "freeze for freeze" pre-negotiating phase – but we weren't going to engage on any of that until the Iranians agreed to the basic measures we had outlined for that phase, meaning no new UNSC resolutions on our side for six weeks, and no new nuclear activity (no additional centrifuges) from the Iranians during that same period. We all agreed that the Iranian paper was a deliberate non-starter, and suggested no willingness at all to suspend enrichment activity at any point.

Solana did a very good job in the afternoon hammering away at Jalili on the need for a clear answer on "freeze for freeze." He did repeat a couple of times that suspension was still the condition for actual negotiations, but focused mainly on the importance of getting into the prior phase first. The Russians were especially good at emphasizing that the Iranians owed us a clear answer, with the French, Brits and Germans all chiming in supportively. The Chinese were more reticent, but after I reminded my colleague that we were going the extra mile diplomatically by taking part in the Geneva meeting, he later spoke up more assertively.

Jalili offered a brief tiny opening at one point late in the afternoon and suggested that the Iranians might be willing to live temporarily with "the current circumstances" as we explored how to begin negotiations, but when Solana pressed him about whether that meant Iran could accept "freeze for freeze," Jalili veered off into the ether again. Exasperated, Solana concluded that "we have talked enough about all this," and said the time had come for an Iranian answer. Jalili acknowledged that he had neither a "yes" nor a "no" to offer in Geneva. As we had agreed ahead of time, Solana then said the P5+1 needed a reply one way or the other in two weeks. The Russians added that they hoped Iran would think very carefully about this. The alternative would likely be a move back to New York for new sanctions over the next few months, "even if that's not Russia's first preference." The Brits jumped on that energetically, causing Jalili to bristle for the only time in the day's discussions. "We don't respond to threats," he replied. Interestingly, Jalili followed that by repeating for the third time over the course of the day that Iran is ready to engage in diplomacy because it is in a strong position "at home, in our economy, and in the region." (The first time he mentioned this sounded inconsequential; by the third time, I began to wonder why he was belaboring the point if his regime was so self-assured.)

Jalili conceded that he would get back to Solana "in a couple of weeks," but gave little indication that his reply would be crisp or unequivocal. Solana was solid in the subsequent press conference, repeating the two-week deadline and making clear that we had not yet gotten an acceptable answer.

We gathered briefly afterward, once the Iranians had left, to review the bidding. While deeply frustrated (if not surprised) by the Iranians, it was the most united I've seen the P5+1 in quite a while. The Russians, and even the Chinese, acknowledged that a negative or non-answer from the Iranians would require new forms of diplomatic and economic pressure, and that we would have to head back to New York early in the fall to try to hammer out a new resolution. The Europeans renewed their promise to pass a strong EU package of measures that go beyond 1803 implementation before the end of July. We have additional designations ready to launch in the same time frame. The French and British are also quite interested in separate, even more substantial, economic measures that we might pursue with other interested Europeans, and perhaps the Japanese and Australians. These could include some of the good ideas Stuart Levey has been developing, including in insurance.

I have no illusions that the glow of P5+1 unity that we saw at the end of today will last indefinitely. It will surely dim when the Iranians throw out chaff to seem constructive, or when the Chinese in particular start looking at specific economic sanctions. A new resolution will be an exceedingly tough project. But UNSC resolutions do seem to focus Iranian minds, less because of their content than because they upset Iran's narrative that it is a victim of American hostility and has the international community increasingly on its side.

Without exaggerating its impact, I think our presence today put us back on the diplomatic offensive with the Iranians, took them off guard, and certainly bolstered our standing with our partners. Whichever choice the Iranians make about "freeze for freeze" - and I'd guess that the chances of a clean acceptance are well under 10% - we're better positioned to keep the diplomatic initiative. It gives us a little capital to draw on in New York, and a better means of pressuring the
Iranians internationally.

Jalili mentioned that he still lectures part time at Tehran University. I don't envy his students.

I spoke to the Italians this evening, as you requested, and also to Sallai Meridor, who was appreciative. I also touched bases with Sean McCormick and David Welch, as well as Jim Jeffrey. I'll talk to the Russians and Chinese again tomorrow morning (both are scheduled to see Jalili, before he returns to Tehran).

Look forward to seeing you in Abu Dhabi.

> Best regards,
> Bill

[*Source: "The Archive":* Collection of documents released in tandem with William J. Burns, The Back Channel: A Memoir of American Diplomacy and the Case for Its Renewal *(New York: Random House, paperback, 2020),* Carnegie Endowment for International Peace, *https://carnegieendowment.org/publications/interactive/back-channel/.*]

Questions for further discussion

- What was Iran's public reaction to the September 11, 2001, terrorist attacks and what were its motivations?
- How did the Iranian delegation contribute to the talks on the future of Afghanistan in late 2001? What did the American side conclude from that about the potential for improved ties with Tehran? How did senior administration officials respond?

- What did the reference to an "axis of evil" in the 2002 State of the Union address imply about US views on Iran? What was the speech's impact?

- What was the reaction of Iranian leaders to the 2003 invasion of Iraq? How did Iran's role in Iraq evolve and how did US officials interpret Tehran's intentions?

- How did Iran justify its nuclear program during this period? In what ways did the nuclear issue color each side's views?

Notes

1. Powell felt further undercut by the hawkishness of John Bolton and others on his staff whose presence, he told the British foreign secretary, "had been 'the price' he'd had to pay for insulating himself from the neocons." Jack Straw, *Last Man Standing: Memoirs of a Political Survivor* (London: Pan Books, 2013), p. 454.

2. Dobbins raved to his superiors about the helpfulness of the Iranians but the president's top advisors showed no interest in pursuing opportunities. See James Dobbins, "Negotiating with Iran: Reflections from Personal Experience," *Washington Quarterly*, Winter 2009/2010, Vol. 33, Iss. 1, pp. 156–157. Reflecting the schizophrenia in administration thinking, while the Afghanistan conference was underway and unbeknownst to Dobbins, other US officials, with White House and Pentagon blessing, were meeting in Rome with Manucher Ghorbanifar, the discredited Iran-Contra figure, to hear his latest plans for undermining the regime. (For one account of this, see George Tenet, *At the Center of the Storm: My Years at the CIA* [New York: Harper Collins, 2007], pp. 311–314.)

3. The Qods Force served (and still does) as a kind of paramilitary vanguard for spreading the Islamic revolution abroad and has long been associated with attacks on US forces in the region. Soleimani attained legendary status as their commander. He was targeted and killed in a US drone attack in Iraq early on January 3, 2020 (Baghdad time).

4. The comments on Soleimani come from former Iranian diplomat Hossein Mousavian, oral history conference, "U.S.–Iran Relations, 2001–2009," Massachusetts Institute of Technology, June 14, 2012 (files of the National Security Archive's Iran–U.S. Relations Project); Ryan Crocker, interviewed in Dexter Filkins, "The Shadow Commander," *New Yorker*, September 23, 2013; Crocker again in Barbara Slavin, "34 Years of Getting to No with Iran," *Politico*, November 19, 2013; and Dexter Filkins, "The Shadow Commander."

5. President Clinton appeared to go along with calls for regime change, which was an explicit objective of the Iraq Liberation Act, signed on October 31, 1998 (https://nsarchive2.gwu.edu/NSAEBB/NSAEBB326/doc02.pdf). But his administration insisted the idea was to encourage Saddam Hussein's removal by working with opposition groups over time, not by overthrowing Saddam. (Defense Secretary

William S. Cohen quoted in Vernon Loeb, "Saddam's Iraqi Foes Heartened by Clinton," *Washington Post*, November 16, 1998.)

6. Among those who subscribed to such views were Under Secretary of Defense Douglas Feith, Chairman of the Joint Chiefs of Staff Richard B. Myers, and his deputy General Peter Pace. See David Crist, *Twilight War: The Secret History of America's Thirty-Year War with Iran* (New York: Penguin Books, 2012), p. 453; and Douglas Feith, *War and Decision: Inside the Pentagon at the Dawn of the War on Terrorism* (New York: Harper Perennial, 2009), pp. 230–233.

7. Ironically, the memo gibes with the speculation of those Pentagon strategists who thought Tehran might reach out to Washington to try to avoid becoming America's next military target. This presumes the offer was genuine and not a partial fabrication by the Swiss ambassador, as some American officials said it was. (See note 13 below.)

8. For a rare window into these activities, see excerpts from a collection of documents obtained from an operative within Iran's Ministry of Intelligence and Security and reported on by *The Intercept* and the *New York Times* in November 2019 (https://theintercept.com/2019/11/18/iran-cables/).

9. Col. Joel D. Rayburn *et al.*, *The U.S. Army in the Iraq War, Volume 2: Surge and Withdrawal, 2007–2011* (Carlisle Barracks, PA: United States Army War College Press, 2019), p. 639.

10. For his part, Soleimani denied killing Americans. After five US soldiers were killed in Karbala, Iraq, he wrote to the American ambassador: "I swear on the grave of Khomeini I haven't authorized a single bullet against the U.S." Filkins, "The Shadow Commander."

11. Seymour Hersh, "Preparing the Battlefield: The Bush Administration Steps Up Its Secret Moves against Iran," *New Yorker*, online posting June 29, 2008. The expanded covert program reportedly began in late 2007 when Bush presented a Presidential Finding to members of Congress. In 2012, Hersh reported that the US Joint Special Operations Command had started training the controversial opposition group Mujahedin-e Khalq (MEK) in 2005. The MEK had been on the State Department's foreign terrorist list since 1997 but was later removed under political pressure during the Obama administration. See Hersh, "Our Men in Iran?," *New Yorker*, April 5, 2012.

12. Joby Warrick and Greg Miller, "U.S. Intelligence Gains in Iran Seen as Boost to Confidence," *Washington Post*, April 7, 2012; Jillian Burns, "The Iran Watcher Program: A Different Kind of Teleworking," *Foreign Service Journal*, March 2015.

13. Condoleezza Rice, *No Higher Honor: A Memoir of My Years in Washington* (New York: Crown Publishers, 2011), pp. 461–463; CENTCOM commander Adm. William Fallon is quoted in Bob Woodward, *The War Within: A Secret White House History, 2006–2008* (New York: Simon & Schuster, 2009), p. 334.

14. Tehran's reasoning was somewhat opaque although the West's insistence that they give up enrichment was certainly an obstacle. Another possibility is that Rice's claim to want engagement conflicted with her request to Congress earlier in the

year for $75 million to promote democracy inside the Islamic Republic. (Glenn Kessler, "Rice Asks for $75 Million to Increase Pressure on Iran," *Washington Post*, February 16, 2006.) Of course, sending mixed signals was something both sides could be accused of.

15. CNN, "Iranian President Condemns September 11 attacks," November 12, 2001, http://edition.cnn.com/2001/WORLD/meast/11/12/khatami.interview.cnna/.

16. Condoleezza Rice, *No Higher Honor*, pp. 148–151.

17. Both diplomats later said Ayatollah Khamenei himself had approved the concept. See, for example, Barbara Slavin, *Bitter Friends, Bosom Enemies: Iran, the U.S., and the Twisted Path to Confrontation* (New York: St. Martin's Press, 2007), pp. 204–206; also, Zarif interview with Malcolm Byrne, New York, May 10, 2007, and Kharrazi interview with Malcolm Byrne, Tehran, December 2014.

18. Donald Rumsfeld, Memorandum to President George W. Bush, December 8, 2006.

19. Gholam-Hoseein Elham, quoted in IRNA, May 15, 2006.

20. See discussion in Seyed Hossein Mousavian with Shahir Shahidsaless, *Iran and the United States: An Insider's View of the Failed Past and the Road to Peace* (New York: Bloomsbury Academic, 2015), p. 233.

21. The May 2005 estimate appears to still be classified but other sections of this NIE detail some of the earlier findings.

22. Quoted in Gregory F. Treverton, "CIA Support to Policymakers: The 2007 National Intelligence Estimate on Iran's Nuclear Intentions and Capabilities," CIA Center for the Study of Intelligence, May 2013.

23. Martin Indyk, oral history conference, "Missed Opportunities? U.S.–Iran Relations, 1993–2001," Session 1, Musgrove Conference Center, St. Simons Island, GA, April 8–10, 2011 (files of the National Security Archive, Iran–U.S. Relations Project), April 8, 2011.

24. [Footnote in original:] *For the purposes of this Estimate, by "nuclear weapons program" we mean Iran's nuclear weapon design and weaponization work and covert uranium conversion-related and uranium enrichment-related work; we do not mean Iran's declared civil work related to uranium conversion and enrichment.*

5

Breakthrough: Long Road to a Short-Lived Deal, 2009–2016

Introduction

Barack Obama entered the White House determined to depart from conventional foreign policy by engaging directly with America's enemies – Iran prominently among them. In his inaugural address in January 2009 he signaled: "To those who cling to power through corruption and deceit and the silencing of dissent, know that you are on the wrong side of history, but that we will extend a hand if you are willing to unclench your fist."[1]

Two months later, to mark *Nowruz*, the Persian New Year, he posted a videotaped message [Document 51] to the people and leaders of Iran filled with words and phrases – "engagement," "respect," "the true greatness of the Iranian people and civilization" – designed to resonate. He broke precedent by specifically naming "the Islamic Republic of Iran." At the same time, he pointed out that for Iran to gain its rightful place in the world "comes with real responsibilities, and ... cannot be reached through terror or arms." Other presidents had sent messages to Iranians but not with the same impact. Supreme Leader Khamenei responded within days with much of the usual rhetoric but expressed a guarded willingness to see what "the new US president and government" would do next [Document 52].

More signs of progress followed. The administration completed a remarkably speedy Iran policy review by early April; the government confirmed the USA would join the P5+1 nuclear talks without preconditions; Obama delivered a landmark address in Cairo reaching out to the world's Muslims; and he wrote a personal letter to Khamenei pledging not to pursue regime change. The Supreme Leader surprised the Americans by writing back – another first. Obama quickly responded, this time proposing to hold covert talks at a suitable level.

How Khamenei might have answered cannot be known because a major crisis intervened. On June 12, the mercurial Mahmoud Ahmadinejad was declared the winner of Iran's presidential elections. Evidence of blatant irregularities brought widespread condemnation from his rivals and from across society, including several senior clerics. When large-scale protests began, the authorities suppressed them violently; armed with cell phones, demonstrators transmitted powerful images to the world, the first time social media had ever been used this way on such a large scale. The crisis gave rise to the Green Movement and marked Iran's worst political rupture since 1979.

Rather than a clear opportunity to score political points, the uprising put the Obama administration in a quandary. The president had to balance the natural inclination (and strong pressure from all sides) to denounce the crackdown against the urge to keep open the possibility of direct nuclear talks. Despite the advice of some aides, he chose to soft-pedal public criticisms, in part to avoid historical charges of American interference, an explicit concern of many Iranians, including Mir-Hossein Mousavi, Ahmadinejad's closest presidential rival and the Green Movement's presumptive leader.

The White House faced significant fallout for the decision, but arguably it paid off when the opportunity arose for a quick nuclear arrangement with Iran. That same summer, the country's atomic energy agency approached the IAEA seeking fuel for the Tehran Research Reactor, an American-made facility used for medical purposes. With US backing, the IAEA suggested a fuel swap involving Russia and France that would have satisfied other aims for each side – greatly reducing the low-enriched uranium available to Iran to produce a bomb while implicitly acceding to Tehran's long-standing insistence on the right to enrich its own nuclear fuel. However, after first agreeing, the Iranians suddenly backed away from the plan. Ironically, part of the reason was domestic, but with a twist, as Ahmadinejad's disgruntled rivals joined to block him from notching a political victory.

Obama's first-year expectations for Iran thus ended on a low note. US attitudes had steadily hardened over the political persecutions in Iran, the IRGC's seizure of three American hikers who reportedly wandered into Iranian territory, and the discovery of another major, unreported nuclear facility at Fordow. When its December 2009 deadline to start negotiations with Iran passed, the administration – urged on by Congress and regional allies Israel and Saudi Arabia – began imposing sanctions. Their preferred venue was the United Nations Security Council, which meant persuading chronically averse Russia and China not to veto any resolutions.

While that complex diplomatic process played out, two new players came onto the scene with a fuel swap plan of their own. In spring 2010, the leaders of Turkey and Brazil approached Ahmadinejad – believing they had Obama's encouragement [Document 56] – and proceeded to work out a trilateral agreement. But more powerful forces – the USA, the Europeans, Russia, and China – had their own agendas, and the day after the three-way

Tehran Declaration was signed, UN Security Council Resolution 1929 passed (with Turkey and Brazil opposed), levying heavy restrictions on commercial, financial, travel, and other activities relating to the Islamic Republic.

For the next three years, progress between the West and Iran was negligible. Accumulating sanctions, Ahmadinejad's destructive policies, Iran's growing nuclear capacity, the unfolding of the Arab Spring, and pressure from Washington's Saudi and Israeli allies combined to erode hopes for engagement.

During this period, two extraordinary sets of developments played out that underscored the stakes involved with Iran's nuclear program. One was the revelation in summer 2010 that Iran's nuclear facilities had come under a major cyberattack. The United States and Israel soon emerged as the likely architects – neither offered strenuous denials – because of the sophistication of the virus, known as Stuxnet [Document 57]. According to the *New York Times* and others, Bush-43 initiated the overarching program and Obama expanded it; suggesting their serious concerns over the possibility that diplomacy would fail and pressures (largely from Israel) would mount for military action against Tehran.[2] Also in 2010, three Iranian nuclear scientists were assassinated in separate incidents and another followed in 2012. Israel again topped the list of suspects. Iran reportedly reacted by launching modest attacks of its own. It remains a minor mystery how the leadership responded behind the scenes and whether these provocative events came up in subsequent nuclear talks with the P5+1.

In 2013, Iran's ever-unpredictable domestic political scene finally produced a major and, for a change, positive outcome. In June, a cleric named Hassan Rouhani became Iran's president. A fixture in the country's national security apparatus since the Iran–Iraq War, he was neither an extreme hardliner nor a true reformer. After the corruption and demagoguery of Ahmadinejad, who managed to alienate ordinary citizens and conservative power brokers alike, Rouhani was a relatively safe consensus choice. The new president had clear opinions on what the country needed to do to regroup economically and was able to obtain Khamenei's consent to pursue a nuclear deal in order to gain relief from oppressive sanctions. He also turned out to be skillful at promoting his case to both domestic and international audiences. In this he had skilled backing from his top advisors, chief among them Mohammad Javad Zarif, the disarming, American-educated diplomat who became foreign minister and would lead his country's negotiating team.

For once, the United States and Iran seemed to have all the necessary pieces in play at the same time: determined, pragmatic leaders backed by committed advisors (especially after John Kerry replaced Hillary Clinton as secretary of state); a common objective; an ability to empathize despite political, cultural, and linguistic divides; a reliable intermediary in Sultan Qaboos of Oman; and, not least, a shared sense of urgency. Also key to their success would be the ability to hold hardliners in check. Though Rouhani had all-important backing from the hyper-skeptical Khamenei, both governments agreed on the need to hold talks in secret – at least at first.

Through the good offices of the Sultan of Oman, small teams of negotiators met several times during 2013, somehow managing to avoid any leaks to the media. Even Washington's P5+1 partners were kept mostly in the dark until just a few weeks before an important, confidence-building interim agreement, the Joint Plan of Action (JPOA), was signed in late November. At that point, news of the back channel broke and the talks entered a public and frenetic twenty-month final round leading to the Joint Comprehensive Plan of Action (JCPOA) on July 14, 2015.

Although both countries had their critics who complained of the deal's dangerous defects [see the description for Document 61], the JCPOA was a landmark event considering what each side had to overcome. Among other factors, success depended on learning from the experiences – negative as well as positive – of their predecessors. Had Khatami and Clinton not shown that public outreach was politically tenable and had the strident approaches under Bush-43 and Ahmadinejad not fed desires for stability and moderation, the ground would not have been as well prepared.

And yet, the results were far from perfect. The JCPOA raised concerns from more than just political naysayers. Obama, who had grown accustomed to taking unilateral action to get around congressional obstructions, chose to make the deal an executive agreement rather than a formal treaty that would have required a huge Senate fight. (Earlier in the year, the Republican-controlled House had signaled their party's vigorous opposition by inviting Israeli Prime Minister Benjamin Netanyahu – without consulting the White House – to give a formal address to the Congress in which he deplored the deal.) The problem with Obama's approach was that it created an opening for a successor to rescind it. In the end, neither Obama nor Rouhani managed to fully dispel the distrust and animosity of prior decades and ensure that both governments would accept the agreement.

Document 50. State Department, Note, William J. Burns for the Secretary of State, "A New Strategy toward Iran," SECRET, January 24, 2009

Barack Obama comes into the presidency with an unusually clear goal in mind for Iran. "To the Muslim world," he intones at his inauguration on January 20, 2009, "we seek a new way forward based on mutual interest and mutual respect." Then, in an indirect call to the Islamic Republic, he adds: "To those who cling to power through corruption and deceit and the silencing of dissent, know that you are on the wrong side of history, but that we will extend a hand if you are willing to unclench your fist."

Days later, the new secretary of state, Hillary Clinton, receives this note from Under Secretary William Burns which puts forward a package of ideas that will come to animate the new administration's approach. Burns opens: "our basic goal should be to seek a long-term basis for coexisting with Iranian influence while limiting Iranian excesses, to change Iran's behavior but not its regime." This is a crucial divergence from previous administrations, which, while never adopting it as official policy, often threatened regime change. Burns reminds Clinton of some of the main threats, or opportunities, that will influence US policy: Iran's nuclear program, its support for terrorist groups, and its involvement in the politics of neighbors Iraq and Afghanistan.

Anticipating an arduous process, Burns recommends several specific steps, including participating in the P5+1 process on the nuclear issue, which Obama does several months later, and taking the "opportunity following the inauguration to set a new tone with Iran, and then ... carefully test the waters ... and set in motion preliminary contacts with authoritative Iranian representatives." Obama takes the first steps along this path two months later on the Iranian New Year.

....

Note for the Secretary

From: P – Bill Burns
Subject: A New Strategy Toward Iran

Madam Secretary,

It is natural, and sensible, for the new Administration to conduct a review of Iran policy over the next month or two, but as you requested here are some initial ideas on how you might think about Iran strategy and frame a plan of action:

Purpose

Recognizing that Iran is a significant regional player, our basic goal should be to seek a long-term basis for coexisting with Iranian influence while limiting Iranian excesses, to change Iran's behavior but not its regime. That means, among other things, preventing Iran from achieving nuclear weapons capability; channeling its behavior so that it does not threaten our core interests in a stable, unitary Iraq and an Afghanistan that is not a platform for the export of violent extremism; and gradually reducing Iran's capacity to threaten us and our friends through support for terrorist groups. We should also speak out consistently against human rights abuses in Iran.

Assumptions

1. Only a comprehensive diplomatic initiative, aimed ultimately at normalized relations, has any chance of success. As was the case with China in the early 1970s, we should employ careful and incremental tactics at the outset, but as part of a coherent long-term strategy. We should set an early tone of respect and commitment to direct engagement, however severe our differences.

2. Direct American engagement with Iran should be embedded in a wider international effort. That applies to the P5+1 process on the nuclear issue, and also to our approach to Afghanistan and Iraq, and potentially to Gulf security issues. Our engagement is not only an essential means of testing possibilities with Iran; it is also an investment in mobilizing broader international pressure against Iran, and of tapping into "Iranian popular interest in better relations with the U.S. and the outside world.

3. Dealing with Iran will require enormous patience, persistence and determination. Deeply conspiratorial and suspicious of American motives, and riven by factions – especially eager to undermine one another in the run-up to Iran's Presidential elections in June, the Iranian elite will be prone to false starts and deceit. Hostility toward America and its interests is a part of the Iranian regime's DNA; while regime survival is Tehran's most fundamental concern, it will be extremely hard to change its attitudes

and behavior toward us. While essential ground to be covered, direct engagement could turn out to be a deadend.

4. We should deal with the Iranian regime as a unitary actor, understanding that the Supreme Leader (not the President) is the highest authority. We have failed consistently in the past when we tried to play off one faction against another.

5. Iran is a formidable adversary – adept at employing asymmetric means against us, absolutely committed to developing nuclear enrichment and reprocessing capacity, and able to endure considerable outside pressures and hardships – but it is not ten feet tall. Its economy is badly mismanaged, with rising rates of unemployment and inflation. It is vulnerable to the ongoing sharp decline in oil prices, and to its dependence on imported refined petroleum products. It has no real friends in its neighborhood, distrusted by the Arabs and the Turks, patronized by the Russians, and suspicious of the Afghans.

6. We need to be always conscious of the anxieties of our friends, as well as key domestic constituencies, as we proceed with Iran. Our engagement with Iran will be portrayed by those trying to discredit Egypt and Saudi Arabia as tipping the balance in the Arab world away from our traditional moderate allies. Without careful consultation with our friends, any U.S. opening to Iran could be misread and abused. We will want to coordinate intensively with our P5+1 partners, other important international players, Israel and our Arab allies, and the Hill as we engage. And we must make sure that the Administration speaks with one voice, and avoids the divisions which beset the last Administration.

7. We should take immediate advantage of the window of opportunity following the Inauguration to set a new tone with Iran, and then use the next few months to carefully test the waters with Iran, maintain leverage through international coordination, and set in motion preliminary contacts with authoritative Iranian representatives. Following the Iranian elections in June, we might have an opportunity for a more durable high-level engagement across the range of issues which divide us.

Near-Term Plan of Action (January–June 2009)

We should pursue three parallel but interconnected tracks, aiming toward the possibility of more comprehensive, high-level engagement later in the year:

1. **Nuclear**: Begin with February 3–4 P5+1 Political Directors consultation in Germany. Use this to listen to views of partners, as we review our own approach. Consult also with key Arabs, Israelis and Hill. Complete our own assessment by early March, make choices on: whether we join P5+1 at Pol Dir level in future talks with Iranians (as we did last July in Geneva); whether basis for those talks is current "freeze for freeze" proposal (we hold off on new UNSC action, and perhaps on new unilateral measures, and Iranians don't add new centrifuges); whether time period for those talks should be current six week proposal or a longer period; whether suspension of enrichment should be condition for continuing talks or ultimate objective of negotiations; what we expect from partners on further sanctions if Iranians do not comply. Hold second P5+1 meeting in March to develop common approach. Present to Iranians.

2. **Bilateral**: In early February, after State of Union, have P or NEA phone Iranian Perm Rep Khazaee in New York and convey brief oral message from President Obama to Supreme Leader, emphasizing U.S. commitment to diplomatic resolution of serious issues of concern with Iran, in atmosphere of mutual respect and dignity. Confirm whether Iran is willing to open private channel between authorized representatives. In subsequent conversation, preview with Khazaee or authorized representative a proposal to send American diplomats to U.S. interests section in Tehran (under Swiss embassy), as well as interest in discussing an incidents at sea protocol to avoid friction in Persian Gulf. Continue private, direct talks on both through same channel if Iran is willing. President Obama issues Youtube message conveying best wishes to Iranian people for Iranian New Year in March. Secretary hosts Iranian cultural event at Department on same occasion. Make use of "track two" exchanges to reinforce messages to Iran.

3. **Regional**: Convey through NY channel, if opened, willingness to explore cooperation on Afghanistan issues (as we did in direct talks in 2001–03). Use opportunities to engage directly on margins of multilateral Afghan donors or "Friends of Afghanistan" groups. Express willingness to resume direct contacts in Baghdad, and to engage on margins of other "Neighbors of Iraq" meetings. Such contacts might provide basis for longer-term discussion of Gulf security issues, involving Iran and its neighbors. At same time, continue to bolster Iraqi government, work closely with Turks, encourage first-ever Ministerial meeting of "GCC Plus 3" with the Secretary in Baghdad in the spring. This grouping (GCC states plus Egypt, Jordan, Iraq and U.S.) sends strong signal of strength to discourage Iranian meddling. Also, reopen direct exchanges with Syria and return Ambassador, reinforcing to Iranians that even their erstwhile partners in Arab world may have higher priorities than ties with Iran.

All of this is obviously much easier said than done, but it offers a preliminary framework for thinking through a new approach. I am acutely aware of how fast the nuclear clock is ticking. We will need to move quickly to try to improve the overall atmosphere in relations with the Russians, who are critical to any serious multilateral effort to change the Iranian calculus.

> [*Source: "The Archive": Collection of documents released in tandem with William J. Burns,* The Back Channel: A Memoir of American Diplomacy and the Case for Its Renewal *(New York: Random House, paperback, 2020), Carnegie Endowment for International Peace, https://carnegieendowment.org/ publications/interactive/back-channel/.*]

Document 51. White House, Statement, President Obama, "Videotaped Remarks by the President in Celebration of Nowruz," UNCLASSIFIED, March 20, 2009

Recognizing the significance of the Nowruz holiday in Iran, Obama sees the same chance for conciliation Madeleine Albright expressed toward the end of

Bill Clinton's term in office. In what has become an annual spring event for American presidents, he releases remarks – but this time videotaped and notably steeped in respectful and targeted language. His goal is to eschew the years of tough talk and reassure the leaders of the Islamic Republic that he genuinely wants to pave the way to the negotiating table.

After a nod to Iran's "great and celebrated culture" whose "accomplishments have earned the respect of the United States and the world," Obama declares that his administration will not continue to make threats, but instead will seek open and honest engagement. At the same time, he challenges Iran to meet him halfway. Returning to the international fold "cannot be reached through terror or arms, but rather through peaceful actions that demonstrate the true greatness of the Iranian people and civilization."

Khamenei's response the next day [Document 52] is hardly warm but when Obama reaches out again a couple of months later, the Supreme Leader unexpectedly replies with a personal letter of his own. The negotiation table is being set.

....

THE PRESIDENT: Today I want to extend my very best wishes to all who are celebrating Nowruz around the world.

This holiday is both an ancient ritual and a moment of renewal, and I hope that you enjoy this special time of year with friends and family.

In particular, I would like to speak directly to the people and leaders of the Islamic Republic of Iran. Nowruz is just one part of your great and celebrated culture. Over many centuries your art, your music, literature and innovation have made the world a better and more beautiful place.

Here in the United States our own communities have been enhanced by the contributions of Iranian Americans. We know that you are a great civilization, and your accomplishments have earned the respect of the United States and the world.

For nearly three decades relations between our nations have been strained. But at this holiday we are reminded of the common humanity that binds us together. Indeed, you will be celebrating your New Year in much the same way that we Americans mark our holidays – by gathering with friends and family, exchanging gifts and stories, and looking to the future with a renewed sense of hope.

Within these celebrations lies the promise of a new day, the promise of opportunity for our children, security for our families, progress for our communities, and peace between nations. Those are shared hopes, those are common dreams.

So in this season of new beginnings I would like to speak clearly to Iran's leaders. We have serious differences that have grown over time. My administration is now committed to diplomacy that addresses the full range of issues before us, and to pursuing constructive ties among the United States, Iran and the international community. This process will not be advanced by threats. We seek instead engagement that is honest and grounded in mutual respect.

You, too, have a choice. The United States wants the Islamic Republic of Iran to take its rightful place in the community of nations. You have that right – but it comes with real responsibilities, and that place cannot be reached through terror or arms, but rather through peaceful actions that demonstrate the true greatness of the Iranian people and civilization. And the measure of that greatness is not the capacity to destroy, it is your demonstrated ability to build and create.

So on the occasion of your New Year, I want you, the people and leaders of Iran, to understand the future that we seek. It's a future with renewed exchanges among our people, and greater opportunities for partnership and commerce. It's a future where the old divisions are overcome, where you and all of your neighbors and the wider world can live in greater security and greater peace.

I know that this won't be reached easily. There are those who insist that we be defined by our differences. But let us remember the words that were written by the poet Saadi, so many years ago: "The children of Adam are limbs to each other, having been created of one essence."

With the coming of a new season, we're reminded of this precious humanity that we all share. And we can once again call upon this spirit as we seek the promise of a new beginning.

Thank you, and Eid-eh Shoma Mobarak.

[*Source: Barack Obama White House archived website, https://obamawhitehouse.archives.gov/the-press-office/videotaped-remarks-president-celebration-nowruz.*]

Document 52. Islamic Republic of Iran, Speech, Ayatollah Ali Khamenei, UNCLASSIFIED, March 21, 2009

Just a day after Obama's Nowruz speech, Ayatollah Khamenei delivers his own address that includes a message to "whoever is the decision-maker in the United States." The message is much more in line with the poor state of relations at this point. He tosses some of Obama's language back at him and reiterates the litany of Iran's grievances against the USA, but at the very end he breaks from the norm and leaves the window open a crack.

"Please pay attention," he says to the crowd, but may as well be addressing Obama personally, "If you go on with the slogan of discussion . . . saying you will negotiate with Iran, and at the same time impose pressure, threats, and changes, then our nation will not like such words." But: "We do not have any experience with the new US President and Government. We shall see and judge. You change, and we shall change as well."

....

Regarding the foreign affairs of our country, I would like to mention one point, and that is the issue between us and the United States. One of the main challenges for the Revolution, right from the beginning, was the same issue. Right from the first day of the Revolution's victory, a phase was opened for the Iranian nation, as a major test in its relations and interactions with the government of the United States of America. This major and important test continued for the past 30 years. The US Government faced this Revolution with an angry and frowning face, and opposed us from the beginning. Of course, they had the right to do so, considering their own calculations. Before the Revolution, Iran was in the hands of the United States, its vital resources were in the hands of the United States, its political decision-making centers were in the hands of the United States, decisions to appoint and depose its vital centers were in the hands of the United States, and it (Iran) was like a field for the United States, the US military, and others on which to graze. Well, this was taken away from them. They could have expressed their opposition in not such an aggressive manner. But from the beginning of the Revolution, both their

Republican presidents, and the Democrats, did not behave well toward the Islamic Republic. This is not secret from anyone.

(People chant: "Death to America")

[Several paragraphs describing actions of the United States over the years.]

This is how they treated the Iranian nation for 30 years, and now the new US Government says that they would like to negotiate with Iran, that we should forget the past. They say that they extended their arm towards Iran. What kind of a hand? If it is an iron hand covered with a velvet glove, then it will not make any good sense. They congratulate the Iranian nation on the occasion of the New Year (Iranian New Year started 20 March 2009), but in the same message call the Iranian nation supporters of terrorism, who seek nuclear weapons, and accuse it of such things.

I would like to say that I do not know who makes decisions for the United States, the President, the Congress, elements behind the scenes? But I would like to say that we have logic. Since the beginning, the Iranian nation moved with logic. Regarding our vital issues, we are not sentimental. We do not make decisions based on emotion. We make decisions through calculation. They tell us to negotiate, to start relations. They have the slogan of change. Where is the change? What has changed? Clarify this to us. What changed? Has your enmity toward the Iranian nation changed? What signs are there to support this? Have you released the possessions of the Iranian nation? Have you removed the cruel sanctions? Have you stopped the insults, accusations, and negative propaganda against this great nation and its officials? Have you stopped your unconditional support for the Zionist regime? What has changed? They talk of change, but there are no changes in actions. We have not seen any changes. Even the literature has not changed. The new US President, from the very moment of his official appointment as President, made a speech, and insulted Iran and the Islamic government. Why? If you tell the truth, and there are changes, where are these changes? Why can we see nothing? I would like to say this to everyone. US officials should also know that the Iranian nation cannot be fooled, or scared.

(People chant)

First of all. (Interrupted by chanting)

Changes in words are not adequate; although we have not seen much of a change there either. Change must be real. I would like to say this to US officials, that this change that you talk about is a real necessity; you have no other choice, you must change. If you do not change, then divine traditions will change you, the world will change you. You must change, but this change cannot be in words only. It should not come with unhealthy intentions. You may say that you want to change policies, but not your aims, that you will change tactics. This is not change. This is deceit. There can be true change, which should be seen in action.

I advise US officials, whoever is the decision-maker in the United States, whether the President, Congress, or others, that the US Government has not worked to the benefit of the American people. Today, you are hated in the world. You should know this, if you do not already. Nations set fire to your flag. Muslim nations across the world chant "Death to America."

(People chant: "Death to America")

What is the reason behind this hatred? Have you ever studied this? Analyzed it? Have you learnt from it? The reason is, that you treat the world like a pupil, you talk snobbishly, you want to impose your own will on the world, you interfere in the affairs of other countries, and you implement double-sided criteria. [...]

If the US Government continues its same behavior, method, course, policies against us, as in the past 30 years, we are the same people, the same nation that we were for the past 30 years.

(People chant)

Please pay attention. If you go on with the slogan of discussion and pressure, saying that you will negotiate with Iran, and at the same time impose pressure, threats, and changes, then our nation will not like such words. We do not have any experience with the new US President and Government. We shall see and judge. You change, and we shall change as well. If you do not change, our people became more and more experienced, stronger, and more patient in the past 30 years.

[*Source: Accessed from PBS Frontline website:* www.pbs.org/wgbh/pages/frontline/tehranbureau/2009/03/they-say-we-say.html.]

Document 53. Mir-Hossein Mousavi, Speech, "Fraud of the Government Necessitates Annulment of Election," UNCLASSIFIED, June 20, 2009

Election fraud is far from a new accusation in the Islamic Republic (or the Shah's regime, for that matter). But in 2009, when incumbent hardliner Mahmoud Ahmadinejad officially defeats Mir-Hossein Mousavi by a suspicious 2:1 margin, it leads to an unprecedented public outcry and the rise of the Green Movement.

Mousavi's leading role in the largest uprising in Iran since the revolution reflects some of the complexities of the country's political environment. Prime minister throughout the Iran–Iraq War, he is still a staunch revolutionary whose platform in 2009 is conservative enough to raise concerns from many in the reformist coalition. Some of his remarks in this address are almost a paean to the revolution and some of its guardians who have been responsible for so many excesses. The scene is not unlike 1979, when so much of society came together to oppose the Shah but had little else in common. Now, the main unifying element is an aversion to the political corruption behind the fraudulent elections. Mousavi himself questions how the votes for Ahmadinejad in some precincts can outnumber registered voters.

The Green Movement makes groundbreaking use of social media (which would feature prominently again during the Arab Spring), first to coordinate the protests and then to publicize their brutal suppression. The impact on Americans of witnessing scenes like the sniper shooting of an unarmed student, Neda Agha-Sultan, heightens the political stakes in the United States. Calls to support the protesters come from all sides and force Obama to make a tough choice between publicly backing the opposition or appearing to side implicitly with a ruthless regime. Eventually, he makes the divisive decision to keep open the possibility of negotiations down the line.

....

God commands you to return what you've been entrusted with to its owners, and to judge in justice when you judge among the people. [Koranic quote]

Honorable and intelligent people of Iran,

These days and nights a turning point is being forged in the history of our nation. People are asking each other and also me, when amongst them, what should be done and in which direction we should go. I consider myself responsible to share what I believe with you, to talk to you and learn from you. Let us hope that we will not forget our historical mission and will not shirk from the burden of duty put on our shoulders by the destiny of generations and ages.

Thirty years ago a revolution succeeded in our country in the name of Islam; a revolution for freedom, a revolution for the rekindling of the compassion of human beings, a revolution for truth and honesty. During this period, and especially during the life of our perspicacious Imam, vast investments of life, property, and honor were made to consolidate this blessed monument, and precious achievements were attained. An illumination, never experienced before, encompassed our society and people arrived at a new life that was sweet for them, in spite of most difficult hardships. I am confident that people who have seen those days will not consent to anything less.

Have we people become unworthy, resulting in our not experiencing that exhilarating atmosphere anymore? I had come to say that is not the case; it is not too late yet and our path is not far from that illuminated atmosphere. I had come to show that you can live spiritually within today's world. I had come to retell the warnings of our Imam about ossification. I had come to say that bypassing the law results in tyranny; to remind that attention to human beings' generosity does not weaken the foundations of the regime, but strengthens them. I had come to say that people expect truth and honesty from their servants [a government dedicated to serving the people] and a lot of our troubles have arisen from lies. I had come to say that backwardness, poverty, corruption, and injustice is not our destiny. I had come to invite to the Islamic Revolution as it was, and to the Islamic Republic as it should be.

I was not eloquent in this invitation, but the noble message of [original 1979] Revolution was so pleasant, even coming from my inadequate expressions, that it excited the younger generation, a generation that had not seen those times and felt a distance between themselves and this great inheritance, and reconstructed scenes only seen during in the times of the [Iranian revolution] movement and the Holy Defense [the Iran-Iraq War]. The spontaneous movement of the people chose the color green as its symbol. I confess that I followed them in this matter. And the generation that was accused of being far from religious roots, arrived at Takbir among its slogans and leaned against "Victory Comes from God and an Opening is Around", "O Husayn" and the name of Khomeini to prove that this fine tree brings similar fruit whenever it bears fruit. Nobody had taught them these slogans except the Innate Teacher [God]. So unfair are those whose little interests make them call this miracle of the Islamic Revolution fabricated by foreigners and a "velvet revolution".

But as you know, all of us were confronted with lies and fraud in the way of renewing the life of the nation and realizing the ideals that have roots in the heart and soul of our old and young, and our prediction of the consequences of lawlessness materialized in the most explicit shape possible and in the shortest time.

The great participation in this election was, in the first degree, indebted to the efforts for creating hope and trust among the people, to obtain a befitting response to the existing administrative crises and the widespread social dissatisfaction, whose accumulation can target the bedrock of the Revolution and the Regime. If this good faith and trust coming from the people is not answered by protecting their votes, or the people cannot react in a civil and peaceful way to defend their rights, there will be dangerous pathways ahead, responsibility for which lies with those who can't stand peaceful behaviors.

If the high volume of cheating and vote manipulation, that has put a fire to the foundations of people's trust, is itself introduced as the proof and evidence of the lack of fraud, the republicanism of the regime will be slaughtered and the idea of the incompatibility of Islam and republicanism would be practically proven. Such a fate will make two groups happy; one group being those who arrayed their troops against the Imam [Khomeini] from the beginning of the Revolution and assumed that the Islamic government is the same as the Tyranny of the Rightful and, in their false surmise, want to bring people to Heaven by force; and the other group being those who, by claiming to defend the rights of the people, basically consider religion and Islam to be blockers for the realization of republicanism. The wondrous craft of the Imam was rendering the witchcraft of these dualisms null and void. I had come to neutralize the efforts of the witches who have found a new life.

Now by endorsing what happened in the elections, the government officials have taken responsibility for it and have

set limits on the results of any further investigation and
auditing in such a way that such an investigation should not
annul the election or change its results, even while the number
of votes cast in 170 voting centers has exceeded the number of
people eligible to vote there. In this situation, we are being
told to follow up on our objection with the Guardian Council, but
this council has proven its lack of neutrality in its acts,
before, during, and after the election. But a prerequisite for
any fair arbitration is observing impartiality.

I still strongly believe that the request for annulment of this
election and a renewed election is a given right and it should be
investigated impartially by a board trusted nationally,
instead of rejecting the possibility of any positive results
from the investigation beforehand; or propose the possibility
of bloodshed in order to keep people from rallying and
demonstrating; or the National Security Council, instead of
answering the righteous question about the role of plainclothes
in attacking people and public property, and inflaming public
movements, resolves to [psychological projection] and blaming
others for the tragedies that have happened.

As I look at the scene, I see that it has been set to achieve more
than just forcing an unwanted government on the nation, it is set
to achieve a new type of political life in the country. As a
companion who has seen the beauty of your green wave of
participation, I will never allow anybody's life to be
endangered because of my actions. At the same time, I stand by my
firm belief of this election being null and void, and insist on
reclaiming people's rights, and in spite of the little power
I possess, I believe that your motivation and creativity can
still result in following up your legitimate rights in new and
civil guises. Be confident that I will stand by your side at all
times. What this brother of yours advises for finding these new
solutions, especially to the beloved youth, is: Don't let the
liars and fraudsters steal the flag of defending the Islamic
regime from you; Don't let the delinquents and the strangers
confiscate from you the precious heritage of the Islamic
Revolution, which is built from the blood of your honest
fathers. With trust in God and hope for the future and relying on
your capabilities, continue your social movements based on
freedoms explicitly stated in the constitution and stay away

from violence, as you have been doing. In this road, we are not up against the Basij members; Basiji's are our brothers. In this road, we are not up against the Revolutionary Guard members; they are protectors of our Revolution and regime. We are not up against the military; they are the protectors of our borders. We are not up against our sacred regime and its legal structures; this structure guards our Independence, Freedom, and Islamic Republic. We are up against deviations and deceptions and we want to reform them; a reformation that returns us to the pure principles of the Islamic Revolution.

We recommend those involved [the office-holders], in accordance with Article 27 of the constitution, to not only facilitate non-violent gatherings in order to achieve peace in the streets, but also encourage such gatherings and release radio and television from the shackle of ill-speaking and biased behavior. They should let the voices, before becoming cries, get corrected and balanced in this flowing media in the shape of good argumentation and disputation. They should let the press criticize, report the news as it is, and in short provide a free space for people to express their agreements and disagreements. Let us let those who like to say Takbir's say them, and let us not treat them as opposing us. It is perfectly clear that in this case there won't be a need for the presence of military and regulatory forces in the streets, and we won't come face to face with scenes that upon watching them or hearing about them bring pain to the hearts of everyone interested in the Revolution and the country.

Your brother and companion, Mir-Hossein Mousavi.

[*Source: Accessed from Iran Data Portal, Syracuse University, https://irandataportal.syr
.edu/fraud-of-the-government-necessitates-annulment-of-election-20-june-2009.*]

Document 54. Defense Department, Report to Congress, "Unclassified Report on Military Power of Iran," UNCLASSIFIED, April 2010

This Pentagon report on Iran's military power, required annually by Congress, reflects constant concern over the Islamic Republic's ability to menace American interests and those of its allies in the region. Detailing

Iran's means of projecting power, the report finds some "formidable" but others "relatively ineffective." Interestingly, the picture that emerges is not one of undiluted threat. Even though the authors point to an "aggressive foreign policy" that relies on terrorism and other tools, they regularly refer to the government's defensive motives. "Since the revolution, Iran's first priority has consistently remained the survival of the regime," reads the very first sentence on goals. Exporting its theocracy is the leadership's "ideological goal," yet ideology has "taken a back seat to pragmatic considerations" in recent times. And while the report singles out concerns with the nuclear portfolio and missile program, it repeatedly returns to concepts of deterrence and defense in Iranian strategy. Relatively minor shifts in emphasis and interpretation in cases like this can sometimes lead to significant differences in policy.

....

[. . .]

Goals of Iranian Strategy

Since the revolution, Iran's first priority has consistently remained the survival of the regime. Iran also seeks to become the strongest and most influential country in the Middle East and to influence world affairs. The theocratic leadership's ideological goal is to be able to export its theocratic form of government, its version of Shia Islam, and stand up for the "oppressed" according to their religious interpretations of the law. In recent years, Iran's ideological goals have taken a back seat to pragmatic considerations.

To ensure regime survival, Iran's security strategy is based first on deterring an attack. For years it has publicly discussed its "20-Million Man Army" and its asymmetric warfare doctrine as deterrents to any would-be invader. Iran has also extended its outreach and support to governments and dissident groups that oppose U.S. interests. Diplomacy, economic leverage, soft power, and active sponsorship of terrorist and paramilitary groups are tools Iran uses to drive its aggressive foreign policy. In particular, it uses terrorism to pressure or intimidate other countries and more broadly to leverage it as a strategic deterrent. The most notable example of this strategy includes Iran's support for Lebanese Hizballah as well as its influence over proxy groups in Iraq.

Iran's military strategy is designed to defend against external
or "hard" threats from the United States and Israel. Iran's
principles of military strategy include deterrence,
asymmetrical retaliation, and attrition warfare. Iran's nuclear
program and its willingness to keep open the possibility of
developing nuclear weapons is a central part of its deterrent
strategy. Iran can conduct limited offensive operations with its
strategic ballistic missile program and improved naval forces.
   [...]

Effectiveness of Iranian Conventional Forces

Iran maintains very sizeable military forces, but they would be
relatively ineffective against a direct assault by well
trained, sophisticated military such as that of the United
States or its allies. At present, Iran's forces are sufficient to
deter or defend against conventional threats from Iran's weaker
neighbors, such as post-war Iraq, the GCC, Azerbaijan and
Afghanistan, but lack the air power and logistical ability to
project power much beyond Iran's borders or to confront regional
powers such as Turkey or Israel.
   [...]

Special Forces and IRGC-Qods Force

Iran established the Islamic Revolutionary Guard Corps-Qods
Force (IRGC-QF) in 1990 as an elite unit within the IRGC.
Although its operations sometimes appear at odds with the public
voice of the Iranian regime, it is not a rogue outfit; it receives
direction from the highest levels of government, and its leaders
report directly, albeit informally, to Supreme Leader Ali
Khamenei, employing complementary diplomatic and
paramilitary strategies.

   The IRGC-QF stations operatives in foreign embassies,
charities, and religious/cultural institutions to foster
relationships with people, often building on existing socio-
economic ties with the well established Shia Diaspora. At the
same time, IRGC-QF engages in paramilitary operations to
support extremists and destabilize unfriendly regimes. IRGC
and IRGC-QF have been involved in or behind some of the deadliest

terrorist attacks of the past 2 decades, including the 1983 and 1984 bombings of the U.S. Embassy and annex in Beirut, the 1983 bombing of the Marine barracks in Beirut, the 1994 attack on the AMIA Jewish Community Center in Buenos Aires, the 1996 Khobar Towers bombing in Saudi Arabia, and many of the insurgent attacks on Coalition and Iraqi Security Forces in Iraq since 2003. It generally directs and supports the groups that actually execute the attacks, thereby maintaining plausible deniability within the international community.

Support for these extremists takes the form of providing arms, funding, and paramilitary training. In this, IRGC-QF is not constrained by ideology; many of the groups it supports do not share, and sometimes openly oppose, Iranian revolutionary principles, but Iran supports them because they share common interests or enemies.

IRGC-QF maintains operational capabilities around the world. It is well established in the Middle East and North Africa, and recent years have witnessed an increased presence in Latin America, particularly Venezuela. If U.S. involvement in conflicts in these regions deepens, contact with the IRGC-QF, directly or through extremist groups it supports, will be more frequent and consequential.

Each Provincial Corps in the IRGC-GRF [IRGC – Ground Resistance Forces] possesses a unit, called Saberin, which has limited special operations capabilities. These units rotate to the northwest to perform counter-insurgency against Kurdish PJAK. and to the southeast to operate against Jundallah.

[...]

Iranian Unconventional Capabilities

Iran's unconventional forces, to include its paramilitary forces that are trained according to its asymmetric warfare doctrine, would present a formidable force on Iranian territory. These forces would include commando and special forces units, smaller specially trained teams embedded within the conventional force units, selected Basij forces, and combat patrols of the Law Enforcement Forces. The combined numbers of personnel could exceed one million.

However, Iran has a limited capability to project force beyond its borders. Attacks on U.S. forces in other countries would likely be limited to surrogates or small numbers of trained personnel disguised as civilians.

[...]

Iranian Nuclear Weapons Capabilities and Developments

Iran is developing technological capabilities applicable to nuclear weapons and, at a minimum, is keeping open the option to develop nuclear weapons, if it chooses to do so. Iran continues its uranium enrichment and heavy water nuclear reactor activities in violation of multiple U.N. Security Council resolutions and also continues to develop ballistic missiles which could be adapted to deliver nuclear weapons.

Iran has installed over 8,000 centrifuges at Natanz and accumulated more than enough low enrich uranium for a nuclear weapon, if further enriched and processed. However, according to the IAEA, Iran also appears to be experiencing some problems at Natanz and is only operating about half of the installed centrifuges, which constrains its ability to produce larger quantities of low-enriched uranium.

For several years, Iran has been constructing an underground enrichment facility near Qom, and has stated it intends to begin enrichment operations there in 2011. Iran has been building this facility in contravention of U.N. resolutions and in violation of its international nuclear safeguards obligations.

Tehran has also refused to cooperate with the International Atomic Energy Agency's requests for access to facilities, documents, and personnel as part of its investigation of Iran's past nuclear weapons-related work. Iran's nuclear activities and related lack of openness with the international community pose a significant threat to the peace and stability of the Middle East.

Iran has gone to lengths to protect its nuclear infrastructure from physical destruction and has placed an emphasis on a number of factors to include locating facilities in buried, hardened facilities and is attempting to acquire sophisticated air defense systems, like the Russian S300, to be installed at nuclear installations.

[...]

Iranian Ballistic Missiles

With sufficient foreign assistance, Iran could probably develop and test an intercontinental ballistic missile (ICBM) capable of reaching the United States by 2015. Iran could also have an intermediate-range ballistic missile (IRBM) capable of threatening Europe. In late 2008 and early 2009, Iran launched the Safir, a multi-stage space launch vehicle, which indicates progress in some technologies relevant to ICBMs.

Over the past two decades, Iran has placed a significant emphasis on developing and fielding ballistic missiles to counter perceived threats from Israel and coalition forces in the Middle East and to project power in the region. Iran actively began acquisition and production programs in the 1980s during the Iran-Iraq war to address its inability to counter Iraqi missile attacks. In developing and expanding its missile program, Iran has received assistance from North Korea and China. At present, Iran is assessed to have the largest deployed ballistic missile force in the Middle East with approximately 1,000 missiles that range from 90 to 1,200 miles. To demonstrate its missile capabilities, Iran has conducted a total of four highly publicized exercises ("Noble Prophet"), since 2006.

Short-range ballistic missiles provide Tehran with an effective mobile capability to strike coalition forces in the region. Iran continues to improve the survivability of these systems through technological advances, such as solid-propellant and the use of antimissile defense tactics.

Iran has also developed medium-range ballistic missiles to target Israel and continues to increase the range, lethality, and accuracy of these systems. For example, the Shahab 3, based on the North Korean No Dong, can reach all of Israel. The Ashura or "Sejil" is an indigenous, two-stage missile that is in development. It uses solid-propellant technology, which reduces the launch preparation time and footprint.

Cruise Missiles

Coastal defense cruise missiles (CDCMs) are an important layer in Iran's defense of or denial of access to the Gulf and Strait of Hormuz. Iran can attack targeted ships with anti-ship cruise missiles (ASCMs) from its own shores, islands, and oil platforms using relatively small mobile launchers.

The C801/802 is Iran's primary CDCM, first imported from China in 1995. The C801/802 is capable of engaging targets at a range of six nautical miles, and has greater accuracy, a lower cruising altitude, and a faster set-up time than the Seersucker missile Iran used during the Iran–Iraq War. The C801/802 allows Iran to target any point within the Strait of Hormuz and much of the Persian Gulf and Gulf of Oman. Iran has also worked with China to develop shorter range missiles, including the C701, for deployment in narrow geographic environments.

Iran can readily deploy its mobile CDCM launchers anywhere along its coast. These systems have auto control and radar homing guidance systems, and some can target using a remote air link. Mobile CDCMs, combined with multiple rocket launchers (MRLs), coastal artillery, and ballistic missiles, Iran hopes to overwhelm enemy air defenses.

[...]

[*Source: US Department of Defense, Freedom of Information Act release.*]

Document 55. Islamic Republic of Iran, Speech, Ayatollah Ali Khamenei, [Message to Conference on Nuclear Disarmament], UNCLASSIFIED, April 17, 2010

The debate over Iranian attitudes toward nuclear weapons has been contentious among Western governments and analysts. When the Islamic Republic first came into being, Ayatollah Khomeini declared all forms of WMD tools of colonialism and contrary to Islam. He pointed to the United States as the foremost hypocrite on the nuclear question. Why then has Iran pushed so fervently for its own program?

Ayatollah Khamenei has reiterated the sentiments of Khomeini, calling nuclear weapons haram *– forbidden – as he does at the end of this speech. At the same time, he sometimes comes across as a major proponent of a nuclear program. Iranian officials – as the Shah did before them – say nuclear power addresses the country's long-term energy needs. Besides, they say, recalling the oil nationalization era, it is their sovereign right. Still, numerous*

Iranian public figures have argued that nuclear weapons can serve as a deterrent against military threats from the region – or calls for regime change by the United States.

The reality is that the above reasons taken together reflect the multifaceted nature of the issue. No one doubts the right of a nation to a peaceful nuclear program and while many outsiders dismiss the long-term energy claim, there are those who agree it could reduce Tehran's reliance on oil and natural gas, especially when sanctions are taking their toll on those revenue sources.

On the other hand, it has been public knowledge for years that the Iran–Iraq War drove the argument inside the regime in the late 1980s toward creating a future deterrent. And as one Iran policy analyst has noted: "No leadership that watches the international community bombard Libya will ever concede its nuclear advantage in exchange for rapprochement and trade ties."[3] Moreover, despite Iran's explicit renunciation of nuclear weapons in the JCPOA, most observers believe the evidence is clear that Iran has at least aspired toward an ability to build a bomb. As to fatwas and other religious injunctions, the debate continues as to how binding they may or may not be.[4]

....

In the Name of Allah, the Beneficent, the Merciful

I would like to welcome the honorable guests who have gathered here. It is a pleasure that the Islamic Republic of Iran is hosting the International Conference on Nuclear Disarmament today. [...]

Since the detonation of the early nuclear weapons by the US government in Hiroshima and Nagasaki created a human disaster of unprecedented proportions in history and exposed human security to a great threat, the global community has reached a unanimous agreement that it is necessary to completely destroy such weapons. The use of nuclear weapons resulted not only in large-scale killings and destruction, but also in indiscriminate massacre of people – military members and civilians, young and old, men and women. And its anti-human effects transcended political and geographic borders, even inflicting irreparable harm on future generations. Therefore, using or even threatening to use such weapons is a serious violation of the most basic humanitarian rules and is a clear manifestation of war crimes.

From a military and security perspective, after certain powers were armed with this anti-human weapon, there remained no doubt that victory in a nuclear war would be impossible and that engagement in such a war would be an unwise and anti-human act. However, despite these obvious ethical, intellectual, human, and even military realities, the strong and repeated urge by the global community to dispose of these weapons has been ignored by a small number of governments who have based their illusory security on global insecurity.

The insistence of these governments on the possession and proliferation of nuclear weapons as well as increasing their destructive power – which are useless except for intimidation and massacre and a false sense of security based on pre-emptive power resulting from guaranteed annihilation of everyone – has led to an enduring nuclear nightmare in the world. Innumerable human and economic resources have been used in this irrational competition to give the superpowers the imaginary power to annihilate more than a thousand times their rivals as well as other inhabitants of the world including themselves. And it is due to this reason that this strategy has been known as "Mutual Assured Destruction" or MAD.

In recent years, a number of governments who possess nuclear weapons have even gone beyond the pre-emptive strategy based on mutual annihilation in dealing with other nuclear powers to the extent that in their nuclear policies they insist on maintaining the nuclear option even if they are faced with conventional threats from countries violating the NPT. This is while the greatest violators of the NPT are the powers who have reneged on their obligation to dispose of nuclear weapons mentioned in Article 6 of the Non-Proliferation Treaty. These powers have even surpassed other countries with respect to promoting nuclear weapons in the world. By providing the Zionist regime with nuclear weapons and supporting its policies, these powers play a direct role in proliferating nuclear weapons which is against the obligations they have undertaken according to Article 1 of the NPT. These countries, headed by the bullying and aggressive US regime, have posed a serious threat to the Middle East region and the world.

It behooves the International Conference on Nuclear Disarmament to investigate the threats posed by the production and stockpiling of nuclear weapons in the world and propose realistic solutions to counter this threat to humanity. This will prepare the ground for taking steps towards safeguarding peace and stability.

We believe that besides nuclear weapons, other types of weapons of mass destruction such as chemical and biological weapons also pose a serious threat to humanity. The Iranian nation which is itself a victim of chemical weapons feels more than any other nation the danger that is caused by the production and stockpiling of such weapons and is prepared to make use of all its facilities to counter such threats.

We consider the use of such weapons as *haram* and believe that it is everyone's duty to make efforts to secure humanity against this great disaster.

[*Source: Official website of Ayatollah Ali Khamenei, https://english.khamenei.ir/news/ 1287/Leader-s-Message-to-International-Conference-on-Nuclear-Disarmament.*]

Document 56. White House, Letter, President Obama for President Luiz Inácio Lula da Silva, Classification Unknown, April 20, 2010

After Iran in late 2009 reneges on a potential nuclear fuel swap deal that would have seen its enriched uranium go to Russia in exchange for fuel from France to help run the Tehran Research Reactor (TRR), Obama begins to pursue the second element of his "dual-track" policy, falling back on increased sanctions while remaining open to further negotiations. Reflecting the intricacy of Iran's internal politics, Green Movement leaders actually opposed the deal because they did not want to see Ahmadinejad notch a political victory. Having lost his best option, the Iranian president now needs new international partners to strike a deal. Enter the leaders of Brazil and Turkey.

Hoping to capitalize on a brief window of opportunity after the collapse of the TRR deal, representatives of Lula da Silva of Brazil and Recep Erdogan of Turkey ask US officials if Washington would support them in talks with Iran. Tehran had signaled its interest as early as September 2009, before Under Secretary Burns' milestone one-on-one meeting with Saeed Jalili on October 1. Senior Americans like Secretary of State Hillary Clinton are not supportive; nevertheless, Lula, Erdogan, and Ahmadinejad begin negotiations and the following May sign the Tehran Declaration, which has similarities to the previous deal although with some notable exceptions, including that Iran's uranium would now go to Turkey instead of Russia.

But the deal does not sit well with the big powers. For one thing, the numbers have changed. The new agreement does not account for the growth in Iran's stockpile during the six months since the original proposal, and furthermore it looks like Tehran is hoping to accumulate additional fuel without actually reducing its existing store of enriched uranium. Moreover, Washington has already set off in a different direction – toward sanctions – and has invested capital in getting Russia to go along.[5]

In this letter to Lula, a month before the Declaration is signed, Obama, albeit in quite mild terms, cautions that Tehran is putting on an act and that he doubts its "good faith" toward Brazil. He says more plainly that Tehran's actions raise "real questions about Iran's nuclear intentions." Yet, he stops short of telling (or even asking) Lula not to proceed, which seems to go against the stance taken by some of his senior advisors. Eventually, everything falls apart for the troika of Brazil, Turkey, and Iran. The day after the Declaration is signed, the United States introduces a new draft for a UN Security Council resolution applying sanctions on Iran. Resolution 1929 passes on June 9 (opposed only by Brazil and Turkey) and becomes a watershed as a means of generating an effective multilateral response to Iranian behavior.

Dear Mr. President:

I want to thank you for our meeting with Turkish Prime Minister Erdogan during the Nuclear Security Summit. We spent some time focused on Iran, the issue of the provision of nuclear fuel for the Tehran Research Reactor (TRR), and the intent of Brazil and Turkey to work toward finding an acceptable solution. I promised to respond in detail to your ideas. I have carefully considered our discussion, and I would like to offer a detailed explanation of my perspective and suggest a way ahead.

I agree with you that the TRR is an opportunity to pave the way for a broader dialogue in dealing with the more fundamental concerns of the international community regarding Iran's overall nuclear program. From the beginning, I have viewed Iran's request as a clear and tangible opportunity to begin to build mutual trust and confidence, and thereby create time and space for a constructive diplomatic process. That is why the United States so strongly supported the proposal put forth by former International Atomic Energy Agency (IAEA) Director General ElBaradei.

The IAEA's proposal was crafted to be fair and balanced, and for both sides to gain trust and confidence. For us, Iran's agreement to transfer 1,200 kg of Iran's low enriched uranium (LEU) out of the country would build confidence and reduce regional tensions by substantially reducing Iran's LEU stockpile. I want to underscore that this element is of fundamental importance for the United States. For Iran, it would receive the nuclear fuel requested to ensure continued operation of the TRR to produce needed medical isotopes and, by using its own material, Iran would begin to demonstrate peaceful nuclear intent. Notwithstanding Iran's continuing defiance of five United Nations Security Council resolutions mandating that it cease its enrichment of uranium, we were prepared to support and facilitate action on a proposal that would provide Iran nuclear fuel using uranium enriched by Iran – a demonstration of our willingness to be creative in pursuing a way to build mutual confidence.

During the course of the consultations, we also recognized Iran's desire for assurances. As a result, my team focused on ensuring that the IAEA's proposal contained several built-in measures, including a U.S. national declaration of support, to send a clear signal from my government of our willingness to become a direct signatory and potentially even play a more direct role in the fuel production process, a central role for Russia, and the IAEA's assumption of full custody of the nuclear material throughout the fuel production process. In effect, the IAEA's proposal offered Iran significant and substantial assurances and commitments from the IAEA, the United States, and Russia. Dr. ElBaradei stated publicly last year that the United States would be assuming the vast majority of the risk in the IAEA's proposal.

As we discussed, Iran appears to be pursuing a strategy that is designed to create the impression of flexibility without agreeing to actions that can begin to build mutual trust and confidence. We have observed Iran convey hints of flexibility to you and others, but formally reiterate an unacceptable position through official channels to the IAEA. Iran has continued to reject the IAEA's proposal and insist that Iran retain its low-enriched uranium on its territory until delivery of nuclear fuel. This is the position that Iran formally conveyed to the IAEA in January 2010 and again in February.

We understand from you, Turkey and others that Iran continues to propose that Iran would retain its LEU on its territory until there is a simultaneous exchange of its LEU for nuclear fuel. As General Jones noted during our meeting, it will require one year for any amount of nuclear fuel to be produced. Thus, the confidence-building strength of the IAEA's proposal would be completely eliminated for the United States and several risks would emerge. First, Iran would be able to continue to stockpile LEU throughout this time, which would enable them to acquire an LEU stockpile equivalent to the amount needed for two or three nuclear weapons in a year's time. Second, there would be no guarantee that Iran would ultimately agree to the final exchange. Third, IAEA "custody" of Iran's LEU inside of Iran would provide us no measurable improvement over the current situation, and the IAEA cannot prevent Iran from re-assuming control of its uranium at any time.

There is a potentially important compromise that has already been offered. Last November, the IAEA conveyed to Iran our offer to allow Iran to ship its 1,200 kg of LEU to a third country – specifically Turkey – at the outset of the process to be held "in escrow" as a guarantee during the fuel production process that Iran would get back its uranium if we failed to deliver the fuel. Iran has never pursued the "escrow" compromise and has provided no credible explanation for its rejection. I believe that this raises real questions about Iran's nuclear intentions, if Iran is unwilling to accept an offer to demonstrate that its LEU is for peaceful, civilian purposes. I would urge Brazil to impress upon Iran the opportunity presented by this offer to "escrow" its uranium in Turkey while the nuclear fuel is being produced.

Throughout this process, instead of building confidence Iran has undermined confidence in the way it has approached this opportunity. That is why I question whether Iran is prepared to engage Brazil in good faith, and why I cautioned you during our meeting. To begin a constructive diplomatic process, Iran has to convey to the IAEA a constructive commitment to engagement through official channels – something it has failed to do.

Meanwhile, we will pursue sanctions on the timeline that I have outlined. I have also made clear that I will leave the door open to engagement with Iran. As you know, Iran has thus far failed to accept my offer of comprehensive and unconditional dialogue.

I look forward to the next opportunity to see you and discuss these issues as we consider the challenge of Iran's nuclear program to the security of the international community, including in the U.N. Security Council.

Sincerely,
Barack Obama

[Source: Politica Externa Brasileira, www.politicaexterna.com/archives/
11023#axzz0pGg7fCnS (no longer accessible).]

Document 57. Department of Homeland Security, PowerPoint, Bradford Willke, "Moving toward Cyber Resilience," UNCLASSIFIED, July 27, 2011

One of the least understood and most intriguing – not to mention potentially hazardous – arenas of the US–Iran conflict is the realm of cyberwarfare. The Bush-43 administration first turned its sights on Iran's nuclear infrastructure as a target in the mid-2000s, evidently with the idea that – as with traditional covert operations – the USA could achieve significant aims with low risk of being discovered as the source of the attacks. The code name of the operation was Olympic Games. Barack Obama has chosen to continue the program, seeing in it another major benefit – its potential to create serious disruptions of Iran's nuclear program that will allow Washington to deflect pressure from Israel and the GOP away from high-risk conventional military strikes.

In 2010, according to widespread reports that neither the USA nor Israel flatly denies, the two governments combined to create and implant the Stuxnet virus into the Natanz uranium enrichment facility, causing considerable damage to hundreds of delicate centrifuges. The problem is that the virus will eventually spread beyond Iran's secret facilities and be discovered and decoded by independent cybersecurity firms. Stuxnet's exposure immediately raises alarms that Iran – a significant cyber actor in its own right – might retaliate. Indeed, in the years since, an unknown number of attacks by the USA and Iran (sometimes by hackers whose ties to the regime are unclear) will be recorded as experts worry that the asymmetrical nature of cyberwarfare may offer Iran advantages in exploiting US vulnerabilities.

Stuxnet

"We have not seen this coordinated effort of information technology vulnerabilities, industrial control exploitations, completely wrapped up in one unique package. For us, to use a very overused term, it's a game changer. Stuxnet ... modifies the physical settings of a process control environment."
-- Seán P. McGurk

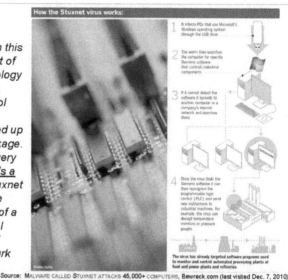

How the Stuxnet virus works:

Source: MALWARE CALLED STUXNET ATTACKS 45,000+ COMPUTERS, Bewreck.com (last visited Dec. 7, 2010)

Homeland Security

National Cyber Security Division

13

Stuxnet

"The world's first precision cybermunition" - Hunting an Industrial-Strength Computer Virus Around the Globe, PBS Newshour, Oct. 1, 2010.

Possible developers
▸ United States
▸ Israel
▸ United Kingdom
▸ Russia
▸ China
▸ France

Countries affected
▸ Iran
▸ Indonesia
▸ India
▸ Pakistan
▸ Germany
▸ China
▸ United States

Rootkit.Win32.Stuxnet geography

Homeland Security

National Cyber Security Division

14

Stuxnet

"Proliferation [of cyber weapons] is a real problem... We have about 90 days to fix this [new vulnerability] before some hacker begins using it." – Melissa Hathaway

▶ **Suspected target**
  – Iran's SCADA controlled nuclear facilities

▶ **Motive**
  – Not designed to steal information, but rather designed to disrupt control systems and disable operations

▶ **Effects**
  – Reports vary from several centrifuges shutting down for days in November, to several centrifuges blowing up

▶ **Possible consequences**
  – National Security concerns
  – A cyber arms race
  – Falling into "the wrong hands" and becoming more potent
  – Unknown and/or unintended secondary or tertiary effects

Source: PAUL K. KERR ET AL., THE STUXNET COMPUTER WORM: HARBINGER OF AN EMERGING WARFARE CAPABILITY (Congressional Research Service, Dec. 9, 2010).

Homeland Security   **National Cyber Security Division**

15

[*Source: Accessed from the Cyber Vault Library, The National Security Archive, https://nsarchive.gwu.edu/dc.html?doc=2700133-Document-52.*]

Document 58. Sultanate of Oman, Letter, Sultan Qaboos for Ayatollah Ali Khamenei, [as reproduced in memoirs of Ali Akbar Salehi], Classification Unknown, March 1, 2012

After the setbacks of 2009 – the crackdown on the Green Movement and Tehran's reneging on the Tehran Research Reactor deal – the Obama administration moves away from talks and toward bulked up sanctions. For the next three years, the US–Iran relationship regresses into yet another stalemate. But the White House has not abandoned engagement entirely and under the surface there is much more going on.

In July 2009, three American backpackers are apprehended by the Islamic Revolutionary Guard Corps near the Iran–Iraq border. Over the next two years, through the offices of the Sultan of Oman, who has built a

reputation as a conciliator in broader Arab–Iranian disputes, secret nego-
tiations take place for their release. The Omanis' success in September
2011 removes a source of tension between Washington and Tehran and,
importantly, boosts the Sultan's credibility as a trusted intermediary.
During the fall, the Americans and Iranians exchange signals that they
are again ready to talk, using the Omanis as mediators. None of this is
apparent to the outside world, where the usual litany of bad news – from an
alleged Iranian plot to assassinate the Saudi ambassador to Washington to
the downing of a CIA drone inside Iran – seems to represent a steady
downturn in relations.

This letter from Sultan Qaboos to Ayatollah Khamenei, according to Ali
Akbar Salehi, Iran's foreign minister at the time, is the first concrete sign for
Tehran that the Americans "really want to enter a serious dialogue." Salehi
receives the letter from a go-between sent by the Omanis, then forwards it to
the Supreme Leader's aide, former Foreign Minister Ali Akbar Velayati
(whom the German chancellor praised to President Bush two decades earlier
[Document 29]), who then delivers it to Khamenei. According to Salehi's
account, he is the one who provided the "Iranian points" to Oman. Salehi
writes later that Khamenei was skeptical, as always, about American inten-
tions, but willing to take a risk because Oman was involved. The letter
appears, with minor cosmetic edits, as reproduced in Salehi's memoir; its
authenticity is presumed to be likely though it has not been possible to confirm
it with US officials.

....

"In the name of God the most gracious and the most merciful"
Your Eminence, Ayatullah Sayyid Imam Ali Khamenei
The Supreme Leader of the Islamic Republic of Iran

May the Almighty's peace and blessings be upon you. We wish
to take this opportunity to express to your Eminence the
immense appreciation and sincere gratitude we hold towards
the Islamic Republic of Iran in its relationship with the
Sultanate of Oman and your Eminence's major role in further
strengthening the established historical relationship that
binds our two friendly nations. We pray to the Almighty from
the depths of our hearts to bestow lasting peace to the Islamic

Republic of Iran and bless it with more progress
and prosperity.

Within the framework of our well-intentioned efforts, we wish
to inform your Eminence that we have communicated with the
American President Barack Obama on the Iranian points presented
to us through an Iranian envoy to resolve the issue pertaining to
the Iranian nuclear program. The American president has
welcomed the initiative to resolve the issue through direct or
indirect negotiations.

From our earnest efforts and the Iranians' honest intentions,
we wish to assure your Eminence that we will directly supervise
and provide special attention to such process.

> May the Almighty grant your Eminence good
> health, long life and protect the Islamic
> Republic of Iran and save it from all evil.

The Sultan of Oman

3 rabii thani 1433: March 1, 2012

[*Source: Ali-Bakheshi, Hassan (editor)*, A Transition in History: The Memoirs of Dr. Ali
Akbar Salehi. *Tehran: Department of Oral History of the Ministry of Foreign Affairs of
the Islamic Republic of Iran, 2018.*]

**Document 59. White House, Letter, President Obama for Sultan
Qaboos, [as reproduced in memoirs of Ali Akbar Salehi], Classification
Unknown, October 11, 2012**

*Prior to the first high-ranking meetings in Muscat (a mid-level encounter has
already taken place in July 2010), the Obama administration apparently sends
this illuminating letter to Sultan Qaboos. (As with Document 58, it is reproduced in the memoirs of Ali Akbar Salehi; the letter's authenticity is presumed
to be likely though it has not been possible to confirm it with US officials.) The
American elections are on the horizon and the administration is focusing
most of its attention on domestic issues. Worried that the Iranians will be
disheartened by the rhetoric coming out of his opponent's camp, Obama
reassures them that he is still very much interested in holding negotiations –
after the elections.*

In early March 2013, secret, direct talks begin, at the deputy foreign minister level. Ahmadinejad is still president of Iran, however, and his representatives lack real autonomy to negotiate. Under Secretary William Burns is struck by the "powerful cognitive dissonance" in the room, reporting to Washington that the two sides are "miles apart on substance," but, as he writes later, "it was at least a start."[6]

The tide will not truly change until Iran holds its own presidential elections in June 2013 and the technocratic cleric Hassan Rouhani beats out more hardline opponents with a promise to restore a degree of stability and pragmatism to Iranian life and politics that has been absent under Ahmadinejad. Rouhani's foreign minister, Mohammad Javad Zarif, an experienced and engaging, Western-educated diplomat, soon becomes the face of Iran's new foreign policy. Secretary of State John Kerry, who has replaced the more skeptical Hillary Clinton, makes clear he sees talks with Iran as a high priority. With new players in position, the Oman talks pick up again in September, a month after Rouhani's inauguration, and the change in atmosphere is immediate, exemplified by a switch to English as the only language at the table. For the most part, the rest of the P5+1 are unaware of the secret channel, a bit of deception the Americans profess to be slightly abashed about but are convinced is absolutely critical to the success of the overall negotiations.[7]

The President wishes to extend his greetings to HM the Sultan of Oman and reiterates his deep commitment to the initiative of 2+1. He also wishes once again to confirm that the Sultanate of Oman is the only channel authorized for the initiative and remains positive that through this channel the parties will be able to amicably reach an agreement.

The United States wishes to convey its concurrence with the purpose and the proposed agenda of the meeting and its willingness to send a senior team to Muscat for an extended period of time to negotiate until all issues pertaining to the Iranian nuclear program are resolved satisfactorily.

The President requests his Majesty to convey to the Iranian team with all sincerity the limitation of time and resources during this period of elections. As stated by the President's non-paper of June 10, 2012, members of his senior team are individuals who are closest to him. Currently the team will be assisting the President with the remaining Presidential debates till the end of October 2012, leaving only two weeks before the election.

The President wishes to request HM the Sultan to use his office to convey to the Iranian government that Iran will be highly featured in the U.S. elections and it is anticipated that the Republican candidate will attack the President's policy towards Iran as being lenient and having failed to protect its traditional allies in the region. The President will have to defend against such accusations; once again, such statements should not be considered as a change of United States commitment towards the 2+1 initiative. The United States is committed to work through the Sultanate of Oman until all issues of dispute are resolved.

[*Source: Ali-Bakheshi, Hassan (editor)*, A Transition in History: The Memoirs of Dr. Ali Akbar Salehi. *Tehran: Department of Oral History of the Ministry of Foreign Affairs of the Islamic Republic of Iran, 2018.*]

Document 60. State Department, Email, Office of the Secretary of State for All Posts Collective, "Under Secretary of State Sherman's Briefing for the Diplomatic Corps on ISIL and Iran," SENSITIVE BUT UNCLASSIFIED, September 16, 2014

On November 24, 2013, the P5+1 and Iran sign an interim deal called the Joint Plan of Action (JPOA), seen by all sides as a critical confidence-building measure. The achievement does not mean the final stretch will not be arduous. Here, the lead US negotiator, Under Secretary of State Wendy R. Sherman, describes for a group of foreign diplomats some of the remaining bumps. Among them, she says, is simply getting Iran to see "the status quo is not acceptable" and that it still needs to "demonstrate with verifiable actions that its nuclear program is exclusively peaceful."

This cable also serves as a useful reminder to latter-day observers that crises constantly crowd the agendas of US policymakers. At this juncture, regional instability is in focus as the Syrian civil war, raging since 2011, has sparked the rise of a new militant group, known as ISIL (or ISIS[8]), whose members Iranians call Takfiri, *or "heretics." ISIL's terror tactics and exhibitions of violence on social media are spreading alarm across the region. But while the USA and Iran are both participating in the global fight against ISIL's Sunni extremists, they are on opposite sides of the civil war, with Iran standing by its longtime ally, President Bashar al-Assad.*

The Obama administration is as anxious to keep the nuclear talks isolated from disruptive world events as it is to separate them from competing problems in the bilateral relationship – for example, the cases of Americans "missing and detained in Iran," as the cable notes. For the administration, the nuclear issue is "the most combustible challenge on the international landscape" and a necessary first hurdle before tackling other problems with Tehran.[9] It is a tough sell to critics, however. Sherman later recalls how much time she spent building consensus among US allies, in the Congress, and even inside her own department. "Occasionally," she jokes, "I actually negotiated with Iran."[10]

....

[...]

ISIL

2. (SBU)[11] The Under Secretary explained our approach to degrading and destroying ISIL and emphasized the need for international unity (Ref A), which will be a major focus of the upcoming UN General Assembly. Many of the ambassadors present at the briefing asked about how their governments could assist our efforts against ISIL. They also tied the fight against ISIL to their own efforts to address terrorist organizations in their own regions such as Boko Haram and Al Qa'eda in the Islamic Maghreb (AQIM) or narco-traffickers in Latin America and the Caribbean, and sought greater cooperation with the United States.

3. (SBU) The Under Secretary emphasized that counterterrorism requires a worldwide effort as terrorism could affect all of us. Many of the threats are regional in nature, and require a coordinated approach amongst governments. She urged all states to think about what they could do to help counter ISIL. Each state has different capabilities, but there is much that all can do to improve security, share information, cut off financing, curb recruitment, furnish humanitarian aid to victims, and expose the lies that ISIL and other terrorists

spread to attract support for their evil cause. She also urged countries to be watchful as foreign fighters who have joined ISIL return home and noted the President's plan to chair a Security Council session on foreign fighters.

4. (SBU) Posts are encouraged to provide to country desks and the Coalition Support Working Group ideas on how their host country governments can contribute to efforts against ISIL as outlined in reftel.

Iran Nuclear Negotiations

5. (SBU) As we approach the UN General Assembly, we have stepped up our outreach to other countries on Iran's nuclear program. The Under Secretary noted that we are urging countries to convey messages urging Iran to seize this opportunity and to understand that it must reduce its current uranium enrichment activities if it wants to reach a deal and obtain sanctions relief.

6. (SBU) Enrichment remains one of the core issues on which the E3+3 and Iran are furthest apart. Iran would like the world to think that it should be able to maintain its current enrichment activities. Iran must understand that the status quo is not acceptable. As we approach the UN General Assembly, we are emphasizing that this negotiation offers Iran's leaders an opportunity to demonstrate with verifiable actions that its nuclear program is exclusively peaceful. Iran must understand that we will agree to suspend and then lift sanctions only if Iran is willing to reduce its enrichment activities and take verifiable steps to demonstrate convincingly that its nuclear program is and will remain wholly peaceful.

7. (SBU) We are also emphasizing that the E3+3 and the EU has remained united in its approach to Iran throughout the negotiations, in spite of our differences on other issues. The E3+3 has demonstrated creativity and flexibility in the negotiations, while also being fair and fully respectful of Iran's civilian nuclear needs and scientific knowhow. We have also offered Iran the promise of comprehensive nuclear-related sanctions relief, with all the benefits to Iran's

challenged economy that would result. Iran needs to demonstrate similar creativity and flexibility.

8. (SBU) A successful outcome to this negotiation would make a major contribution to Middle East security. If Iran were to acquire a nuclear weapon, it would be able to threaten others in the region, possibly spark a new and extremely dangerous arms race, and further exacerbate sectarian tensions. A peaceful resolution of the issue is greatly preferred because it would provide more assurance of long-term success and carry with it fewer unpredictable consequences and risks.

9. (SBU) We are also asking other countries to raise the issue of U.S. citizens missing and detained in Iran. Robert Levinson went missing in Iran more than seven years ago. Amir Hekmati has been in jail there for more than three years, wrongly accused of being a spy. Saeed Abedini has spent more than two years in prison simply for following his religious beliefs. And most recently, Iran detained Washington Post reporter Jason Rezaian.

10. (SBU) Please alert the Office of Iranian Affairs if you learn that host country officials may meet with Iranian officials at the UN General Assembly. Please email the Iran Office at [addresses redacted]

11. (U.S.) Minimize Considered

Kerry

[*Source: US Department of State, Freedom of Information Act release, Case No. F-2016-08328, Doc. No. C06096694.*]

Document 61. Joint Comprehensive Plan of Action, UNCLASSIFIED (Preamble and General Provisions only), July 14, 2015

After nearly 40 years of conflict, broken up by fleeting moments of cooperation, the United States and Iran finally strike a formal agreement on Iran's nuclear program. Though far from flawless and opposed by – or at least of deep concern to – many Americans (and Iranians), it is by far the most significant step towards reconciliation to date.

The Joint Comprehensive Plan of Action (JCPOA) outlines a means for Iran to maintain a peaceful nuclear program and puts concrete limits on its ability to develop nuclear weapons in the future. In exchange for a relaxation of sanctions and increased global investment, Iran agrees to reduce its number of centrifuges by two-thirds over a period of 10 years, cut its uranium stockpile by 97% over 15 years, and cap uranium enrichment to 3.67% while eschewing any new nuclear facilities. Iran must also consent to varying degrees of international monitoring. If it complies, the UN Security Council, the EU, and the United States will terminate all sanctions related to the country's nuclear program, paving the way for vital investment by foreign companies and Iran's future membership in the World Trade Organization.

The JCPOA contains various elements that raise concerns. First, many Americans still do not trust Iran to stick to its promises given its history of concealing aspects of its nuclear program. Second, they worry that the numerous sunset provisions will not restrain Iran's potential permanently. Third, even though the agreement has always been depicted as a first step, criticisms are raised that it does nothing to rein in Tehran's missile program or its support for regional extremists. Tellingly, there are also complaints from the Iranian side. Hardliners, ironically, mirror the same fears in the USA and Israel that they have been cheated. For their part, proponents worry that the sanctions relief and economic benefits that are so crucial to Rouhani's credibility will take too long to bear fruit. Fatefully, Obama opts to structure the deal as an executive agreement rather than a formal treaty that would require approval from the Republican-controlled Senate. He is taking a huge gamble, though, because this will make it much easier for future presidents to withdraw from it unilaterally.

For all of these concerns, the JCPOA proves that, despite the many barriers and years of effort, the United States and the Islamic Republic are capable of reaching a major agreement that leaders of both sides agree is in their respective interests.

....

Preamble and General Provisions

  i. The Islamic Republic of Iran and the E3/EU+3 (China, France, Germany, the Russian Federation, the United Kingdom and the United States, with the High Representative of the European Union for Foreign Affairs and Security Policy) have decided upon this long-term Joint Comprehensive Plan of Action (JCPOA). This JCPOA, reflecting a step-by-step approach, includes the reciprocal commitments as laid down in this document and the annexes hereto and is to be endorsed by the United Nations (UN) Security Council.

ii. The full implementation of this JCPOA will ensure the exclusively peaceful nature of Iran's nuclear programme.

iii. Iran reaffirms that under no circumstances will Iran ever seek, develop or acquire any nuclear weapons.

iv. Successful implementation of this JCPOA will enable Iran to fully enjoy its right to nuclear energy for peaceful purposes under the relevant articles of the nuclear Non-Proliferation Treaty (NPT) in line with its obligations therein, and the Iranian nuclear programme will be treated in the same manner as that of any other non-nuclear-weapon state party to the NPT.

v. This JCPOA will produce the comprehensive lifting of all UN Security Council sanctions as well as multilateral and national sanctions related to Iran's nuclear programme, including steps on access in areas of trade, technology, finance and energy.

vi. The E3/EU+3 and Iran reaffirm their commitment to the purposes and principles of the United Nations as set out in the UN Charter.

vii. The E3/EU+3 and Iran acknowledge that the NPT remains the cornerstone of the nuclear non-proliferation regime and the essential foundation for the pursuit of nuclear disarmament and for the peaceful uses of nuclear energy.

viii. The E3/EU+3 and Iran commit to implement this JCPOA in good faith and in a constructive atmosphere, based on mutual respect, and to refrain from any action inconsistent with the letter, spirit and intent of this JCPOA that would undermine its successful implementation. The E3/EU+3 will refrain from imposing discriminatory regulatory and procedural requirements in lieu of the sanctions and restrictive measures covered by this JCPOA. This JCPOA builds on the implementation of the Joint Plan of Action (JPOA) agreed in Geneva on 24 November 2013.

ix. A Joint Commission consisting of the E3/EU+3 and Iran will be established to monitor the implementation of this

JCPOA and will carry out the functions provided for in this JCPOA. This Joint Commission will address issues arising from the implementation of this JCPOA and will operate in accordance with the provisions as detailed in the relevant annex.

x. The International Atomic Energy Agency (IAEA) will be requested to monitor and verify the voluntary nuclear-related measures as detailed in this JCPOA. The IAEA will be requested to provide regular updates to the Board of Governors, and as provided for in this JCPOA, to the UN Security Council. All relevant rules and regulations of the IAEA with regard to the protection of information will be fully observed by all parties involved.

xi. All provisions and measures contained in this JCPOA are only for the purpose of its implementation between E3/EU+3 and Iran and should not be considered as setting precedents for any other state or for fundamental principles of international law and the rights and obligations under the NPT and other relevant instruments, as well as for internationally recognised principles and practices.

xii. Technical details of the implementation of this JCPOA are dealt with in the annexes to this document.

xiii. The EU and E3+3 countries and Iran, in the framework of the JCPOA, will cooperate, as appropriate, in the field of peaceful uses of nuclear energy and engage in mutually determined civil nuclear cooperation projects as detailed in Annex III, including through IAEA involvement.

xiv. The E3+3 will submit a draft resolution to the UN Security Council endorsing this JCPOA affirming that conclusion of this JCPOA marks a fundamental shift in its consideration of this issue and expressing its desire to build a new relationship with Iran. This UN Security Council resolution will also provide for the termination on Implementation Day of provisions imposed under previous resolutions; establishment of specific restrictions; and conclusion of consideration of the Iran nuclear issue by the UN Security Council 10 years after the Adoption Day.

xv. The provisions stipulated in this JCPOA will be implemented for their respective durations as set forth below and detailed in the annexes.

xvi. The E3/EU+3 and Iran will meet at the ministerial level every 2 years, or earlier if needed, in order to review and assess progress and to adopt appropriate decisions by consensus.

[*Source: US Department of State, https://2009-2017.state.gov/e/eb/tfs/spi/iran/jcpoa//index.htm*]

Questions for further discussion

- How did President Obama approach the idea of a dialogue with Iran? What signals did the United States send in his first term and how did Tehran's response compare with previous years?

- How did domestic politics in both countries play out in the wake of the 2009 Iranian elections and the crushing of the Green Movement?

- In what ways were the nuclear negotiations between the United States and Iran during this period either a continuation of or a departure from late Bush-43 administration policy?

- What was Stuxnet and how did its use – and disclosure – affect developments during this period?

- What lessons might be drawn from the JCPOA process for how to carry out sensitive negotiations – from the mediation of Oman, to each side's familiarity with the politics and culture of the other, to the commitment of both countries' leadership?

Notes

1. Barack Obama, "Inaugural Address," Washington, DC, January 21, 2009: https://obamawhitehouse.archives.gov/blog/2009/01/21/president-barack-obamas-inaugural-address.

2. David Sanger, *The Perfect Weapon: War, Sabotage, and Fear in the Cyber Age* (New York: Crown, 2018), pp. 45–46; Kim Zetter, *Countdown to Zero Day: Stuxnet and the Launch of the World's First Digital Weapon* (New York: Crown, 2014).

3. Suzanne Maloney, "Téhéran/Washington: Une relation immobile?" *Politique Étrangère* 2011/3, pp. 573–585.

4. See, for example, Michael Eisenstadt and Mehdi Khalaji, "Nuclear Fatwa: Religion and Politics in Iran's Proliferation Strategy," The Washington Institute for Near East Policy, Policy Focus #115, September 2011. Article ii of the JCPOA states: "Iran reaffirms that under no circumstances will Iran ever seek, develop or acquire any nuclear weapons."

5. It is also worth recalling that the Stuxnet computer virus was currently operational inside the Natanz nuclear facility at this time.

6. William J. Burns, *Back Channel: A Memoir of American Diplomacy and the Case for Its Renewal* (New York: Random House, paperback, 2020), pp. 366–367.

7. Wendy R. Sherman, *Not for the Faint of Heart: Lessons in Courage, Power & Persistence* (New York: Public Affairs, paperback, 2020), pp. 59–67.

8. The acronym spells out Islamic State in Iraq and the Levant (or Syria).

9. Burns, *Back Channel*, p. 383.

10. Sherman, *Not for the Faint of Heart*, p. 126.

11. Sensitive But Unclassified.

Epilogue: Back to Basics:
Déjà Vu after Four Decades, 2017–2018

Document 62. White House, Memorandum, President Trump for the Secretary of State *et al.*, "Ceasing Participation in the JCPOA and Taking Additional Action to Counter Iran's Malign Influence and Deny Iran All Paths to a Nuclear Weapon," UNCLASSIFIED, May 8, 2018

President Donald Trump has made no secret of his aversion for the Obama-backed JCPOA. Throughout his election campaign he called it "terrible" and "the worst deal ever." Yet, for various reasons he does not act immediately to abrogate it once in office. In fact, it takes him almost a year-and-a-half to do so, perhaps constrained in part by repeated reports from the IAEA that Iran has been abiding by its agreement. In the meantime, he signals that he is prepared to use his self-styled negotiating virtuosity to strike a better deal for the United States. Reflecting a 180-degree turn away from Obama's approach to the Islamic Republic and back to darker days of mutual antagonism, Trump revives the practice of relitigating decades-old grievances dating back to the 1979 revolution.

....

[...]

As President, my highest priority is to ensure the safety and security of the United States and the American people. Since its inception in 1979 as a revolutionary theocracy, the Islamic Republic of Iran has declared its hostility to the United States and its allies and partners. Iran remains the world's leading state sponsor of terrorism, and provides assistance to Hezbollah, Hamas, the Taliban, al-Qa'ida, and other terrorist networks. Iran also continues to fuel sectarian violence in Iraq, and support vicious civil wars in Yemen and Syria. It commits grievous human rights abuses, and arbitrarily detains foreigners, including United States citizens, on spurious charges without due process of law.

There is no doubt that Iran previously attempted to bolster its revolutionary aims through the pursuit of nuclear weapons and that Iran's uranium enrichment program continues to give it the capability to reconstitute its weapons-grade uranium program if it so chooses. As President, I have approved an integrated strategy for Iran that includes the strategic objective of denying Iran all paths to a nuclear weapon.

The preceding administration attempted to meet the threat of Iran's pursuit of nuclear capabilities through United States participation in the Joint Comprehensive Plan of Action (JCPOA) on Iran's nuclear program. The JCPOA lifted nuclear-related sanctions on Iran and provided it with other significant benefits in exchange for its temporary commitments to constrain its uranium enrichment program and to not conduct work related to nuclear fuel reprocessing, the two critical pathways to acquiring weapons-grade nuclear material. Some believed the JCPOA would moderate Iran's behavior. Since the JCPOA's inception, however, Iran has only escalated its destabilizing activities in the surrounding region. Iranian or Iran-backed forces have gone on the march in Syria, Iraq, and Yemen, and continue to control parts of Lebanon and Gaza. Meanwhile, Iran has publicly declared it would deny the International Atomic Energy Agency (IAEA) access to military sites in direct conflict with the Additional Protocol to its Comprehensive Safeguards Agreement with the IAEA. In 2016, Iran also twice violated the JCPOA's heavy water stockpile limits. This behavior is unacceptable, especially for a regime known to have pursued nuclear weapons in violation of its obligations under the Treaty on the Non-Proliferation of Nuclear Weapons.

Iran's behavior threatens the national interest of the United States. On October 13, 2017, consistent with certification procedures stipulated in the Iran Nuclear Agreement Review Act, I determined that I was unable to certify that the suspension of sanctions related to Iran pursuant to the JCPOA was appropriate and proportionate to the specific and verifiable measures taken by Iran with respect to terminating its illicit nuclear program. On January 12, 2018, I outlined two possible paths forward – the JCPOA's disastrous flaws would be fixed by May 12, 2018, or, failing that, the United States would cease participation in the agreement. I made clear that this was a last chance, and that absent an understanding to fix the JCPOA, the United States would not continue to implement it.

That understanding has not materialized, and I am today making good on my pledge to end the participation of the United States in the JCPOA. I do not believe that continuing to provide JCPOA-related sanctions relief to Iran is in the national interest of the United States, and I will not affirm what I know to be false. Further, I have determined that it is in the national interest of the United States to re-impose sanctions lifted or waived in connection with the JCPOA as expeditiously as possible.
   [...]

Donald J. Trump

Conclusion

US policy toward Iran since 1979 has represented an extraordinary and unwelcome challenge to seven presidential administrations – and an object lesson in managing adversarial relationships. The documents in this volume depict a confused, often ill-informed, angry, frustrated cluster of policy-makers, often unable to reach consensus and profoundly unenthusiastic about tackling the Iran problem.

The documents also indicate that the Islamic Republic has been impos-sible to pigeon-hole, which makes pat solutions unworkable. Others have commented that the IRI itself has never decided whether its *raison d'être* is to pursue a cause or develop as a country. It is too big a problem to ignore (or to crush militarily), but not a big enough direct threat to justify making it a top priority.

From the start of the revolution, American policymakers were caught unprepared by the hostility of its more hardline adherents who gradually took control of the new government. The Carter administration worked hard to create opportunities for a positive relationship but that was not to be. Even during the time of the Provisional Government, punctuated by the brief takeover of the US Embassy in February, the level of rancor was palpable and American diplomats had little success establishing ties to Islamists close to Ayatollah Khomeini.

For officials on the ground in Iran, the immediate reasons were apparent enough and they tried to convey them in cables to Washington reporting on their sporadic conversations with representatives of Iran's new rulers. But the true depths of Iranian resentment at years of backing for the Shah were harder to grasp. They finally became clear after months of rising tensions with the Khomeini camp culminated with the US decision to admit the Shah for medical treatment and the Students Following the Line of the Imam made the fateful decision to overrun the US Embassy in November. In the students' telling of it, the initial rationale was to fend off a rumored reprise of the US clandestine operation a generation earlier that restored the Shah to power.

If the coup of 1953 marked the historical starting point of the Khomeini regime's anger at the United States, the hostage crisis was the crucible that turned Americans against the Islamic Republic. For the next four decades, the image of blindfolded captives, displayed nightly on television screens for the duration of the crisis, indelibly colored US policy.

The decade of the 1980s intensified the hostility on both sides. The Islamic Republic's leaders were genuinely outraged by the silence of the international community after Saddam Hussein's forces invaded in October 1980 and by the favoritism most of the big powers lavished on Iraq over the next eight years, the United States included. Washington and Tehran were appalled at each other's actions – the USA by Iran's brutal battlefield tactics and refusal to talk peace, the Iranians by the US failure to speak out more forcefully against Iraq's use of chemical weapons and by the shooting down of a civilian airliner by an American warship. By war's end, the animosity was more pronounced than ever.

The 1990s, however, offered opportunities to reduce tensions as key Iranian leaders, following the death of Khomeini, sought to rebuild after the devastation of a decade of revolution and war. Unfortunately, the distraction of revolutionary events of a different kind in Eastern Europe as well as a new war in the Persian Gulf, signs of reconstituted Iranian terrorism (albeit temporarily directed at non-American targets), and the Bush administration's inability to read the complex political signals coming out of Tehran frustrated aspirations for improving the relationship.

Hopes brightened significantly in 1997 with the surprise election of a reform-oriented president in Iran. The Clinton administration reversed its earlier thinking and seemed ready to move beyond the bitter past, but this time misunderstandings on both sides about expectations and a hardline backlash against the reform movement in Iran once again scuttled well-intentioned efforts. The subsequent Bush-43 administration surprised reformists in Iran by dismissing any and all potential openings, a consequence of its innate distaste for the regime and of the impact of the September 11, 2001, terrorist strikes.

Although Bush would authorize direct nuclear talks with Iran during his second term, it would take several more years before new presidents in both countries would back serious negotiations. In a remarkable break from the hidebound practices of the past, presidents Barack Obama and Hassan Rouhani managed to shepherd through the Joint Comprehensive Plan of Action in 2015, which they counted on being a major boon to their respective countries. Yet, despite the euphoria in some quarters at a significant accomplishment, Obama's successor, Donald Trump, eventually made good on campaign promises and tore up what he called a "terrible" deal.

The consequences of Trump's decision continued to play out over the remainder of his term and beyond. Iran eventually declared it would be restarting aspects of its nuclear program suspended under the JCPOA. The rhetoric of both governments reached a shrillness not heard since the Bush-43/Ahmadinejad years. And episodes such as the killing of Qods Force leader Qasem Soleimani, Iranian retaliatory moves, and strikes against Gulf state oil facilities, as well as numerous reported cyberattacks by both the USA and Iran, resurrected earlier fears of direct military conflict. In short, the two adversaries had come full circle, raising questions as to why it happened and where things might go next.

The aim of this book is to allow an unfiltered look back at some of the available evidence to see what problems existed and whether any positives came out of the experience. What then are some of the takeaways from the documents? There are many of course, and, depending on their perspective, readers will undoubtedly come up with examples of their own. Here are a few broad points to consider for starters.

First of all, the US–Iran relationship is highly complex and nuanced and defies simple solutions. American officials have consistently lamented how hard it is to comprehend Iranian society, culture, and politics (one of the main arguments often advanced for reestablishing diplomatic ties). While critics have many compelling reasons to hold the US government to account for its shortcomings, an honest appraisal of the matter should make clear that most of the outside world has also been at sea in trying to grasp the intricacies of the Islamic Republic. It would hardly be surprising if Iranian officials did not quietly acknowledge the same difficulties on their side about the United States.

Secondly, belief systems – including the sense of "exceptionalism" that exists on both sides – are deeply entrenched and in Iran's case have been centuries in the making. The authors of the Islamic Republic's constitution went so far as to incorporate the mission to oppose global oppression and the specific role of the United States in catalyzing the "Muslim nation" into the document.

Thirdly, both governments, and societies to some extent, feel they are the ones who have been victimized over the years and that their adversary's conduct has been inexcusable, even irrational in its cruelty. There have been relatively few cases where one side has acknowledged that the other's concerns or responses may have some validity. (The Clinton administration's regrets about the 1953 coup were a rare example.)

Fourthly, the shallowness of each side's state of knowledge about the other has repeatedly caused problems that might have been avoided. These range from failing to recognize the important role religion and tradition have always played in Iranian history, the tenuousness of the Shah's hold on

power, the depth of collective resentment over perceived American miscon-
duct, the complexities of the decision-making process and the importance of
building internal consensus on major issues like US relations, and the lack of
control by Tehran over the likes of Hezbollah. These and other examples
have created exaggerated expectations, unrealistic demands, and misconcep-
tions that in turn have unnecessarily tainted American attitudes.

Each of the cases mentioned has in turn contributed to missed
opportunities that might have mitigated animosities and reduced tensions.
Some notable examples are: the decision to admit the Shah into the United
States in 1979; the failure to condemn Iraq for its 1980 invasion; giving the
cold shoulder to Rafsanjani's 1990s overtures; and dismissing the post-9/11
openings to cooperate on Afghanistan and other issues.

While all of the above points are expressed from the American perspective, much the same can of course be said about Iran's conduct. And it is
certainly the case, at least in the view of the authors, that it is very much in
both sides' best interests – and the world's – for these two antagonists to
find a way to begin to reduce tensions and lessen the risk of a wider,
unpredictable conflict.

The final takeaway we would note here is that despite the cumulative
effects of so grim a record of hostility, pain, embarrassment, and bad timing,
it is remarkable that US decision-makers – along with their Iranian counterparts – have consistently found opportunities to reach out in search of ways
to come to terms. They have learned, adapted, overcome domestic opposition, avoided war, and ultimately proven that reaching major agreement
is possible.

Each of these steps is critical in its own right but the path to a realistic and
enduring arrangement begins with understanding the history of how the two
sides arrived at this point.

Glossary – Names

Ahmadinejad, Mahmoud – President of Iran, 2005–2013

Alawi bin Abdullah, Yusuf bin – Foreign Minister of Oman, 1997–present

Albright, Madeleine K. – US Secretary of State, 1997–2001

Araghchi, Abbas – Iranian diplomat; nuclear negotiator, 2013–present

Armitage, Richard L. – Numerous policy positions in US government starting in 1981; US Deputy Secretary of State, 2001–2005

Baker, James A. – US Secretary of State, 1989–1993

Bakhtiar, Shapour – Prime Minister of Iran, 1979

Bani-Sadr, Abol Hasan – President of Iran, 1980–1981

Bazargan, Mehdi – Prime Minister of Iran, 1979

Beheshti, Mohammad – Senior cleric and a leading figure in the revolution; assassinated in June 1981

Brzezinski, Zbigniew K. – US National Security Advisor, 1977–1981

Buckley, William F. – CIA Station Chief, Beirut; hostage in Lebanon 1983–1985

Burns, R. Nicholas – Career foreign service officer; Under Secretary of State for Political Affairs, 2005–2008

Burns, William J. – Career foreign service officer; Assistant Secretary of State for Near Eastern Affairs, 2001–2005; US Deputy Secretary of State, 2011–2014; lead US negotiator with Iran

Bush, George H.W. – President of the United States, 1989–1993

Bush, George W. – President of the United States, 2001–2009

Carter, Ashton B. – US Secretary of Defense, 2015–2017

Carter, Jimmy – President of the United States, 1977–1981

Cave, George W. – Deputy CIA Station Chief, Tehran, mid-1970s; participant in arms-for-hostages talks with Iran, 1986

Cheney, Richard B. – US Secretary of Defense, 1989–1993; Vice President of the United States, 2001–2009

Christopher, Warren M. – US Deputy Secretary of State, 1977–1981; US Secretary of State, 1993–1997

Clark, William P. Jr. – US National Security Advisor, 1982–1983

Clinton, Hillary Rodham – US Secretary of State, 2009–2013

Clinton, William J. – President of the United States, 1993–2001

Crocker, Ryan C. – Career foreign service officer with various Middle East ambassador-rank postings, 1990–2012

Dobbins, James F. – Career foreign service officer; US Special Representative to Afghanistan & Pakistan, 2013–2014

Ebtekar, Massoumeh – Spokeswoman for embassy takeover during the hostage crisis, 1979–1981

ElBaradei, Mohamed M. – Director General of the IAEA, 1997–2009

Erdogan, Recep Tayyip – Prime Minister and President of Turkey, 2003–present

Ghotbzadeh, Sadegh – Foreign Minister of Iran, 1979–1980

Guldimann, Tim – Swiss Ambassador to Tehran, 1999–2004

Hadley, Stephen J. – US Deputy National Security Advisor, 2001–2005; US National Security Advisor, 2005–2009

Haig, Alexander M. – US Secretary of State, 1981–1982

Higgins, William R. – American hostage in Lebanon, 1988–1990

Hussein, Saddam – President of Iraq, 1979–2003

Huyser, Robert E. – USAF Deputy for European Command, 1979–1981; US envoy to Iranian military, January–February 1979

Indyk, Martin S. – Senior Director for Near East and South Asian Affairs on NSC staff during Clinton administration; US Assistant Secretary of State for Near Eastern Affairs, 1997–1999

Jalili, Saeed – Secretary of the Supreme National Security Council, 2007–2013

Karoubi, Mehdi – Speaker of the Parliament of Iran, 1989–1992 and 2000–2004; prominent figure in Green Movement starting in 2009

Kerry, John F. – US Secretary of State, 2013–2017

Khalilzad, Zalmay M. – Among other posts, US Ambassador to Afghanistan, 2004–2005; to Iraq, 2005–2007; to the United Nations, 2007–2009

Khamenei, Ali – President of the Islamic Republic of Iran, 1981–1989; Supreme Leader of Iran, 1989–present

Kharazzi, Kamal – Foreign Minister of Iran, 1997–2005

Kharazzi, Sadeqh – Deputy Foreign Minister of Iran; Iranian Ambassador to France, 2002–2006

Khatami, Mohammad – President of the Islamic Republic of Iran, 1997–2005

Khomeini, Ruhollah – Supreme Leader of Iran, 1979–1989

Laingen, L. Bruce – Career foreign service officer; Chargé d'Affaires of the USA in Tehran, 1979–1981

Lula da Silva, Luiz Inácio – President of Brazil, 2003–2010

McFarlane, Robert C. – US National Security Advisor, 1983–1985

Moghaddam, Nasser – Chief of SAVAK, 1978–1979

Moniz, Ernest J. – US Secretary of Energy, 2013–2017

Montazeri, Hossein Ali – Deputy Supreme Leader of Iran, 1985–1989

Mottaki, Manouchehr – Foreign Minister of Iran, 2005–2010

Mousavi, Mir-Hossein – Prime Minister of Iran, 1981–1989; presidential candidate in 2009; and prominent figure in the Green Movement

Mousavian, Hossein – Diplomat; nuclear negotiator, 2003–2005

Muskie, Edmund G. – US Secretary of State, 1980–1981

Naas, Charles W. – Director of Iranian Affairs, US State Department, 1974–1978; Deputy Chief of Mission, US Embassy in Tehran, 1978–1979

Netanyahu, Benjamin – Prime Minister of Israel, 1996–1999, 2009–present

North, Oliver L. – NSC staff member, 1981–1986

Obama, Barack H. – President of the United States, 2009–2017

Pahlavi, Ashraf – Princess of Iran, 1919–1979

Pahlavi, Farah – Empress Consort of Iran, 1961–1979

Pahlavi, Mohammed Reza – Shah of Iran, 1941–1979

Peres, Shimon – Prime Minister of Israel, 1977, 1984–1986, 1995–1996; President of Israel, 2007–2014

Pérez de Cuellar, Javier – Secretary General of the United Nations, 1982–1991

Picco, Giandomenico – Assistant Secretary General of the United Nations for Political Affairs, 1973–1992; helped negotiate an end to the Iran–Iraq War and for the release of Western hostages in Lebanon

Powell, Colin L. – Career military officer; peripherally involved in Iran-Contra affair; US Secretary of State, 2001–2005

Precht, Henry – Political-Military Officer, US Embassy in Tehran, 1972–1976; Country Director for Iran, US State Department, 1978–1980

Qaboos bin Said Al Said – Sultan of Oman, 1970–2020

Rafsanjani, Akbar Hashemi – Speaker of the Parliament of Iran, 1980–1989; President of Iran, 1989–1997; held numerous other high-ranking positions until his death in 2017

Reagan, Ronald W. – President of the United States, 1981–1989

Rezaie, Mohsen – Commander in Chief of the IRGC, 1981–1997

Rice, Condoleezza – US National Security Advisor, 2001–2005; US Secretary of State, 2005–2009

Riedel, Bruce O. – CIA analyst, 1977–2006; Special Assistant to the President and Senior Director for Near East and North African Affairs on the NSC, 1997–2002

Ross, Dennis B. – NSC staff; Director of Policy Planning for US State Department, 1989–1992

Rouhani, Hassan – President of Iran, 2013–present

Rumsfeld, Donald H. – US Secretary of Defense, 1975–1977, 2001–2006

Salehi, Ali Akbar – Head of the Atomic Energy Organization of Iran, 2013–present

Shariatmadari, Mohammad Kazem – Iranian Grand Ayatollah, 1961–1986

Sherman, Wendy R. – US Under Secretary of State, 2011–2015; lead US nuclear negotiator with Iran

Shultz, George P. – US Secretary of State, 1982–1989

Sick, Gary G. – Member of the NSC staff, 1976–1981

Soleimani, Qasem – Commander of the Iranian Quds Force, 1998–2020

Soltanieh, Ali Asghar – Iran's representative to IAEA, 1982–1987 and 2006–2013; nuclear negotiator

Sullivan, Jake J. – National Security Advisor to Vice President, 2013–2014

Sullivan, William H. – US Ambassador to Iran, 1977–1979

Takht-Ravanchi, Majid – Iranian Ambassador to UN, 2019–present

Talwar, Puneet – Chief Middle East, North Africa, and South Asia Advisor, US Senate Committee on Foreign Relations, 1995–1999, 2001–2008; NSC staff, 2009–2014

Timbie, James P. – Senior Advisor at US State Department, 1983–2016

Trump, Donald J. – President of the United States, 2017–2021

Vance, Cyrus R. – US Secretary of State, 1977–1980

Velayati, Ali Akbar – Foreign Minister of Iran, 1981–1997

Yazdi, Ibrahim – Deputy Prime Minister of Iran, 1979

Zarif, Mohammad Javad – Foreign Minister of Iran, 2013–present

Zimmermann, Warren – US Political Counselor in Paris, 1977–1980; met with Ibrahim Yazdi to open a channel to Khomeini

Glossary – Organizations

Assembly of Experts – Committee of eighty-six elected members, tasked with choosing and dismissing Iran's Supreme Leader, as necessary.

Basij – A volunteer force constituted in 1979 to enforce internal security and morality laws; they are nominally under the direction of the IRGC.

Bonyads – Iranian state-owned charitable trusts, typically run by the office of the Supreme Leader, that control a large percentage of Iran's aboveground economy.

Central Intelligence Agency (CIA) – Civilian foreign intelligence agency of the United States, tasked with both intelligence gathering and conducting clandestine operations.

Council of Guardians – A twelve-member judicial body tasked with vetting candidates for election to political office and checking legislation for compliance with the constitution.

European Union – Political and economic organization representing most of the nations of Europe; a participant in nuclear negotiations with Iran leading to the JCPOA.

Expediency Council – A mediating body appointed by the Supreme Leader that adjudicates disputes between the Majlis (Iranian parliament) and the Council of Guardians.

Gulf Cooperation Council (GCC) – An intergovernmental organization including all Arab countries along the Persian Gulf.

Hezbollah – A Shia political party and militia; the most widely known branch is based in southern Lebanon and is backed by Iran; responsible for numerous terrorist attacks on Western targets.

International Atomic Energy Agency (IAEA) – A global body tasked with promoting peaceful nuclear research and stopping the proliferation of nuclear weapons.

International Court of Justice (ICJ) – The highest court for adjudicating disputes between UN member states; site of numerous cases involving the USA and the Islamic Republic.

Islamic Republic of Iran Army (IRIA) – Together with the IRGC, the Army (known as "Artesh") is one of the conventional forces comprising the Iranian military.

Islamic Revolutionary Guard Corps (IRGC) – A branch of Iran's armed forces established by Ayatollah Khomeini in April 1979 to defend the gains of the Iranian revolution; the IRGC has also become a major political and economic force controlling much of the Iranian economy.

Majlis – The parliament of Iran.

Ministry of Foreign Affairs (MFA) – Executive branch agency responsible for carrying out Iran's foreign policy.

Ministry of Intelligence and Security (MOIS) – A key component of Iran's security forces; tasked with foreign and domestic intelligence, including clandestine operations, and reporting directly to the Supreme Leader.

National Security Agency (NSA) – Intelligence agency of the Department of Defense, under the authority of the director of National Intelligence; responsible for conducting electronic surveillance abroad and code breaking, among other tasks.

National Security Council (NSC) – Principal forum for the president of the United States to consider national security and foreign policy matters.

National Security Planning Group – A top-level advisory body established under the Reagan administration and consisting of the president, vice president, secretary of defense, secretary of state, assistant for national security affairs, and the director of the CIA.

Northern Alliance – An Afghan military coalition, mostly consisting of non-Pashtuns, opposed to the Taliban and allied with the Islamic Republic.

Nuclear Energy Agency – A group of OECD countries formed to advance peaceful nuclear technology.

Organization of the Islamic Conference (OIC) – Formed in 1969 and now known as the Organization of Islamic Cooperation; an international body of fifty-seven Muslim-majority states aimed at advancing interests and goals of the Muslim world.

Qods Force – A branch of the IRGC specializing in unconventional warfare and military intelligence operations outside of Iran.

Six-plus-Two Group – Coalition formed under UN auspices in 1997 consisting of the six countries bordering Afghanistan plus the USA and Russia, with the aim of finding a peaceful settlement in Afghanistan; disbanded after the 2001 US invasion of the country.

State Department – Lead executive branch agency responsible for determining and implementing US foreign policy.

Supreme Council for the Islamic Revolution in Iraq (SCIRI) – Iraqi Shia political party with ties to Iran; founded in 1982 with the aim of assisting Iran in its war with Baghdad and later of overthrowing Saddam Hussein.

Supreme National Security Council – Key coordinating body responsible for formulating Iran's national security strategy; formed in 1989 and operates under the authority of the Supreme Leader.

United Nations Security Council (UNSC) – A UN body tasked with identifying threats to international peace or major acts of aggression (such as Saddam Hussein's invasion of Iran in 1980) and authorizing measures to restore the peace; permanent members are the US, UK, France, Russia, and China.

United Nations secretary general (UNSYG) – The "chief administrative officer" of the UN who also has a broad mandate to uphold the UN's values and moral authority; the Islamic Republic has tended to turn to the UNSYG rather than the UNSC, for example during the Iran–Iraq War.

World Trade Organization (WTO) – An international body that aims to promote rules-based trade between countries.

Select Bibliography

This list has been culled from thousands of useful sources that exist on this subject. It includes some important Iranian materials but does not pretend to be comprehensive. The list also omits entire subsets of sources for space reasons, chief among them: memoirs of American presidents and policymakers (some Iranian memoirs are included); official government statements; congressional hearings and reports; Congressional Research Service reports; scholarly and media articles (including, notably, statements and interviews by important figures that often are published in the Iranian media).

Document Collections

National Security Archive, *Iran: The Making of U.S. Policy, 1977–1980*, edited by Eric Hooglund (ProQuest, 1990)

National Security Archive, *The Iran-Contra Affair: The Making of a Scandal, 1983–1988*, edited by Peter Kornbluh and Malcolm Byrne (ProQuest, 1990)

National Security Archive, *U.S. Policy toward Iran: From the Revolution to the Nuclear Accord, 1978-2015*, edited by Malcolm Byrne (ProQuest, 2020)

Woodrow Wilson International Center for Scholars, Digital Archive, *The Iran–Iraq War* (https://digitalarchive.wilsoncenter.org/collection/48/iran-iraq-war)

Woodrow Wilson International Center for Scholars, Digital Archive, *Iran's Tudeh Party* (https://digitalarchive.wilsoncenter.org/collection/627/iran-s-tudeh-party)

Woodrow Wilson International Center for Scholars, Digital Archive, *Iran–Soviet Relations* (https://digitalarchive.wilsoncenter.org/collection/199/iran-soviet-relations)

Government Online Document Databases

US and Western

UK, The National Archives (www.nationalarchives.gov.uk/)

US Central Intelligence Agency, Freedom of Information Act Electronic Reading Room (https://www.cia.gov/library/readingroom/)

US Department of State, *Foreign Relations of the United States* series (https://history.state.gov/historicaldocuments)

US Department of State, Freedom of Information Act Virtual Reading Room (https://foia.state.gov/Search/Search.aspx)
US National Archives and Records Administration, Access to Archival Database (AAD) (https://aad.archives.gov/aad/)

Iranian

Ali Khamenei, official website, *Khamenei.ir* (https://english.khamenei.ir)
Ruhollah Mousavi Khomeini, official website, *Imam Khomeini* (http://en.imam-khomeini.ir/)
Akbar Hashemi Rafsanjani, official website (www.rafsanjani.ir/)

Oral Histories

Foundation for Iranian Studies (www.fis-iran.org/en/oralhistory)
Frontline Diplomacy: The Foreign Affairs Oral History Collection of the Association for Diplomatic Studies and Training (www.loc.gov/collections/foreign-affairs-oral-history/)
Harvard University, Iranian Oral History Project (https://curiosity.lib.harvard.edu/iranian-oral-history-project?utm_source=library.harvard)

Books

US and Western

Alexander, Yonah, and Nanes, Alan. *The United States and Iran: A Documentary History*. Santa Barbara: Praeger Publishing, 1980.
Amanat, Abbas. *Iran: A Modern History*. New Haven: Yale University Press, 2017.
Ansari, Ali M. *Iran, Islam and Democracy: The Politics of Managing Change*. London: Gingko Publishing, 2019.
Ansari, Ali M. *Modern Iran since 1797: Reform and Revolution*. Oxford: Routledge, 2019.
Arjomand, Said Amir. *The Turban for the Crown: The Islamic Revolution in Iran*. Oxford: Oxford University Press, 1988.
Axworthy, Michael. *A History of Iran: Empire of the Mind*. New York: Basic Books, 2008.
Axworthy, Michael. *Revolutionary Iran: A History of the Islamic Republic*. Oxford: Oxford University Press, 2016.
Bakhash, Shaul. *The Reign of the Ayatollahs: Iran and the Islamic Revolution*. London: I.B. Tauris, 1985.
Bill, James. *The Eagle and the Lion: The Tragedy of American–Iranian Relations*. New Haven: Yale University Press, 1989.

Blight, James G. *et al. Becoming Enemies: U.S.–Iran Relations and the Iran–Iraq War, 1979–1988.* Lanham, MD: Rowman & Littlefield, 2012.

Bowden, Mark. *Guests of the Ayatollah: The Iran Hostage Crisis.* New York: Grove Press, 2006.

Brumberg, Daniel, and Farideh, Farhi. *Power and Change in Iran: Politics of Contention and Conciliation.* Bloomington: Indiana University Press, 2016.

Burns, William J. *The Back Channel: A Memoir of American Diplomacy and the Case for Its Renewal.* New York: Penguin Books, 2019.

Byrne, Malcolm. *Iran-Contra: Reagan's Scandal and the Unchecked Abuse of Presidential Power.* Lawrence: University Press of Kansas, 2014.

Council on Foreign Relations. *American Hostages in Iran: The Conduct of a Crisis.* New Haven and London: Yale University Press, 1985.

Crist, David. *Twilight War: The Secret History of America's Thirty-Year War with Iran.* New York: Penguin Books, 2012.

Dobbins, James. *After the Taliban: Nation Building in Afghanistan.* Washington, DC: Potomac Books, 2008.

Ebtekar, Massoumeh. *Takeover in Tehran: The Inside Story of the 1979 U.S. Embassy Capture.* Vancouver: Talonbooks, 2000.

Elbaradei, Mohamed. *The Age of Deception: Nuclear Diplomacy in Treacherous Times.* New York: Metropolitan Books, 2012.

Emery, Christian. *US Foreign Policy and the Iranian Revolution: The Cold War Dynamics of Engagement and Strategic Alliance.* London: Palgrave Macmillan, 2013.

Gasiorowski, Mark, and Byrne, Malcolm (eds.) *Mohammed Mosaddeq and the 1953 Coup in Iran.* Syracuse, NY: Syracuse University Press, 2004.

Indyk, Martin. *Innocent Abroad: An Intimate Account of American Peace Diplomacy in the Middle East.* New York: Simon & Schuster, 2009.

Keddie, Nikki. *Modern Iran: Roots and Results of Revolution.* New Haven: Yale University Press, 2006.

Khomeini, Ruhollah. *Imam Khomeini, Islam and Revolution: The Writings and Declarations of Imam Khomeini as Translated by Hamid Algar.* London: KeganPaul, 2002.

Kornbluh, Peter, and Malcolm Byrne. *The Iran-Contra Scandal: The Declassified History.* New York: The New Press, 1994.

Limbert, John. *Negotiating with Iran: Wrestling the Ghosts of History.* Washington, DC: United States Institute of Peace Press, 2009.

Maloney, Suzanne (ed.) *The Iranian Revolution at Forty.* Washington, DC: Brookings Institution Press, 2020.

Milani, Mohsen. *The Making of Iran's Islamic Revolution: From Monarchy to Islamic Republic.* Oxford: Routledge, 2018.

Moslem, Mehdi. *Factional Politics in Post-Khomeini Iran.* Syracuse, NY: Syracuse University Press, 2002.

Mottahedeh, Roy. *The Mantle of the Prophet: Religion and Politics in Iran*. London: Oneworld Publications, 1985.

Mousavian, Hossein. *Iran and United States: An Insider's View on the Failed Past and the Road to Peace*. New York and London: Bloomsbury Academic, 2014.

Mousavian, Hossein. *The Iranian Nuclear Crisis: A Memoir*. Washington, DC: Brookings Institution Press, 2012.

Murray, Donette. *US Foreign Policy and Iran: American–Iranian Relations since the Islamic Revolution*. Oxford: Routledge, 2009.

Nafisi, Azar. *Reading Lolita in Tehran: A Memoir in Books*. New York: Penguin Random House, 2003.

Parsi, Trita. *Losing an Enemy: Obama, Iran, and the Triumph of Diplomacy*. New Haven: Yale University Press, 2017.

Parsi, Trita. *A Single Roll of the Dice: Obama's Diplomacy with Iran*. New Haven: Yale University Press, 2012.

Parsi, Trita. *Treacherous Alliance: The Secret Dealings of Israel, Iran and the U.S.* New Haven: Yale University Press, 2007.

Peterson, Scott. *Let the Swords Encircle Me: Iran – A Journey behind the Headlines*. New York: Simon & Schuster, 2010.

Picco, Giandomenico. *Man without a Gun: One Diplomat's Secret Struggle to Free the Hostages, Fight Terrorism, and End a War*. New York: Times Books, 1999.

Polk, William R. *Understanding Iran: Everything You Need to Know, from Persia to the Islamic Republic, from Cyrus to Ahmadinejad*. New York: Palgrave Macmillan, 2009.

Pollack, Kenneth. *The Persian Puzzle: The Conflict between Iran and America*. New York: Random House, 2004.

Randjbar-Daemi, Siavush. *The Quest for Authority: A History of the Presidency from Revolution to Rouhani*. London: I.B. Tauris, 2018.

Sherman, Wendy. *Not for the Faint of Heart: Lessons in Courage, Power, and Persistence*. New York: PublicAffairs, 2018.

Siavoshi, Sussan. *Montazeri: The Life and Thought of Iran's Revolutionary Ayatollah*. Cambridge: Cambridge University Press, 2017.

Sick, Gary. *All Fall Down: America's Tragic Encounter with Iran*. New York: Random House, 1985.

Slavin, Barbara. *Bitter Friends, Bosom Enemies: Iran, the U.S., and the Bitter Path to Confrontation*. New York: St. Martin's Press, 2007.

Sullivan, William H. *Mission to Iran*. New York: W.W. Norton, Inc., 1981.

Takeyh, Ray. *Guardians of the Revolution: Iran and the World in the Age of the Ayatollahs*. Oxford: Oxford University Press, 2011.

Wright, Robin. *In the Name of God: The Khomeini Decade*. New York: Pocket Books, 1990.

Wright, Robin (ed.) *The Iran Primer: Power, Politics, and US Policy*. www.iranprimer.com/

Zelikow, Philip, and Zoellick, Robert (eds.) *America and the Muslim Middle East: Memos to a President.* Washington, DC: Brookings Institution Press, 1998.

Zetter, Kim. *Countdown to Zero Day: Stuxnet and the Launch of the World's First Digital Weapon.* New York: Crown Publishers, 2014.

Published in Iran

Ali-Bakheshi, Hassan (ed.). *A Transition in History: The Memoirs of Dr. Ali Akbar Salehi.* Tehran: Department of Oral History of the Ministry of Foreign Affairs of the Islamic Republic of Iran, 2018.

Hashemi-Rafsanjani, Ali Akbar. *Karnameh va Khaterat* [*Report and Memoir*]; 1360–1363 (1981–1985) (4 vols.) and 1367 (1988–1989) (published Tehran 1999–2011).

Montazeri, Hossein Ali. *Khaterat-e Ayatollah Montazeri* [*Memoir of Ayatollah Montazeri*]. Sweden, France, and Germany 2001.

Raji, M. Mehdi. *Aghaye Safir: Goftogoo ba Mohammad Javad Zarif* [*Mr. Ambassador: A Conversation with Mohammad Javad Zarif*]. Tehran: Nashr-e Ney, 2013.

Index

CPSIA information can be obtained
at www.ICGtesting.com
Printed in the USA
LVHW040053280821
696290LV00015B/1472

9 781108 971546